HOW TO BUY A COMPUTER

2nd Edition

OTHER BOOKS BY MYLES WHITE

How to Buy a Computer (1995)
How to Avoid Buying a New Computer (1997)

How to Buy a Computer

And a monitor, a printer,
a sound card, a scanner, etc . . .

2nd Edition

Myles White

M&S

Canadian Cataloguing in Publication Data

White, Myles, 1948-
    How to buy a computer, and a monitor, a printer, a sound card, a scanner, etc.

2nd ed.
Previously published under title: How to buy a computer, or upgrade what you have.
Includes index.
ISBN 0-7710-8831-0

1. Microcomputers – Purchasing.   2. Computers – Purchasing.   I. Title.
II. Title: How to buy a computer, or upgrade what you have.

QA76.5 W49   1998   004.16'029'7   C98-931779-X

We acknowledge the financial support of the Government of Canada through the Book Publishing Industry Development Program for our publishing activities. We further acknowledge the support of the Canada Council for the Arts and the Ontario Arts Council for our publishing program.

Typeset in Times by M&S, Toronto
Printed and bound in Canada

McClelland & Stewart Inc.
The Canadian Publishers
481 University Avenue
Toronto, Ontario
M5G 2E9

Myles White can be reached by e-mail (myles@idirect.com) or through his Web site (http://web.idirect.com/~myles).

CONTENTS

Acknowledgements   vii
Introduction   1

Part 1. Shopping Strategies

1   Making a Plan   7
2   Jargon   12
3   Basic Shopping Tips   20

Part 2. Into the Field

4   Nailing Down Some Basic Questions   33
5   Reading Computer Ads   38
6   Processors   56
7   Motherboards and Chipsets   72
8   Memory   88
9   Notebooks and Other Small Computers   97
10 Storage Devices   119
11 Multimedia and Telecommunications   140
12 Printers   182
13 Graphics   226
14 Things That Click When They Move, Bop
    When They Stop, and Whirr When
    They Stand Still   254

Part 3

15 Nailing Down Your Decision   273

    Specialty Index   289
    General Index   291

Once again, to my folks,
Phyllis and John Andrews.
Ready to go through it again?

ACKNOWLEDGEMENTS

No man is an island, and no book ever gets written without myriad varieties of help.

You can take as a given that almost every manufacturer of computer and peripheral equipment has – at one time or another – provided me with machines to review. Some, such as Xerox, have been slow to demand the return of their products. Epson, Hewlett-Packard, Toshiba, and IBM have all graciously gone through periods of finger-drumming and wondering when Myles was going to let go of their goods. I've also sometimes placed undue strain on public relations folk, such as (in no particular order) Kerry Moppett at Goodman Communications, Andrew Berthoff and David Morelli at Environics, Julie Rusciolelli at Cohn and Wolfe, Mary Sturgeon at Benchmark, John Swinimer at Hill and Knowlton, and the gang at Novus. I'd be remiss if I didn't also thank Doug Cooper of Intel Canada for hours of conversation.

In the first edition of *How to Buy a Computer*, I also singled out Walter Gollick, my colleague and friend of over twenty years, for his invaluable insights into the hardware side of the computer market. We continue to learn together.

Last, but by no means least, there are the editors and colleagues in my life who continue to both curb my excesses and set challenges that help me grow in new directions. They include Rob Wright, editor of the *Toronto Star*'s Fast Forward section, Eric McMillan, publisher and managing editor of *We Compute*, Murray Soupcoff, *We Compute*'s senior editor, and Craig Colby, producer, and Paul Kaliciak, host of Discovery Canada's short-lived EXN.TV. I also want to thank Steve Dotto, host of radio's Dotto on Data, and my colleague at the *Computer Paper*, Graeme Bennet, for so many Sunday afternoons answering listeners' questions.

You've all contributed to this book and I thank you.

INTRODUCTION

Since the first edition of *How to Buy a Computer* was published in the fall of 1995, there have been a great many changes in the computer industry. But this should come as no surprise. The computer industry is dynamic; the pace of change is fast and furious. What's more, the pace shows no sign of slowing in the near future.

This makes it rosy for those of us who write about computers, but it creates a quagmire for consumers. As soon as you've done the homework and have decided what to buy, the rules change; the products change, and it seems as if you'll have to start all over again.

Today, computers are common. Even the most conservative analysts suggest that over 40 per cent of Canadian homes have one, and that the figure rises dramatically to well over 60 per cent in urban centres, particularly in homes when there are school-aged children or adults with professional or managerial jobs.

Nevertheless, I'm still approached at seminars with the plaintive cry, "I'm so confused. How do I sort out the choices among computers? Where do I start?"

Buying a computer can be a daunting task, particularly if you're new to the hi-tech marketplace. You will be spending anywhere from one to several thousand dollars on the computer equipment alone, so you'll need to do homework first – and lots of it. According to one old IBM ad, the average person spends fifteen weeks, five days, twenty-three hours, and fifty-eight minutes searching for a new computer. I doubt if that figure has changed much since it was first published in early 1995. If you're like most consumers, you'll spend that time checking with a number of sources for the information you need to make decisions.

There's a wealth of information available to you when you're ready to dive into it. In fact there's too much to absorb in a short period. That's why I've shifted my approach in this edition. I'll still get into details about what's what in hardware, but this time I'm going to come at the problem from a slightly different direction.

The second edition of *How to Buy a Computer* is divided into three sections. We'll start by outlining the research process – setting you up so you can bring a systematic approach to doing your homework. This section contains many of the shopping strategies found in the first edition, as well as few new suggestions.

Section Two focuses on the homework itself, providing distinctions among the basic hardware options that should help you make some fundamental choices.

Section Three is the home stretch, where we'll discuss what's involved in nailing your decision down as well as pointing out some of the traps and tricks you might run into at the point of closing the sale.

Also new in the second edition of *How to Buy a Computer* are tables – lots of tables – comparing the leading products in many of the categories discussed. Information in the tables comes from a variety of sources, and they are as up to date as the deadlines in book publishing allow. At the very least, you'll discover toll-free phone numbers where you can get more information from the manufacturers and World Wide Web addresses so you can do some of your research on the Internet, if you have access.

Those of you who are especially sharp-eyed will also notice that the title of the second edition has changed. The first edition's title was *How to Buy a Computer or upgrade the one you already have*. We've dropped the reference to upgrading because there is much more about upgrading and trouble-shooting in my second book, *How to Avoid Buying a New Computer*. These two books are always going to leapfrog each other in time, and both, by necessity, will contain information on individual components. It's one way to try to keep both as current as possible, given the ever-changing nature of the market. *How to Avoid . . .* is the book you want if you plan to grab a screwdriver and get personal with your PC.

How to Buy . . . is your best bet for coping with the hundreds of retailers, each shouting that they have the best and fastest systems with the cheapest deals going. This is where I try to help you separate the good stuff from the junk, to cut through the hype and bafflegab, to alert you to new trends, and to put all of this into some kind of useful context.

You're probably thinking that anyone who would write a book titled *How to Buy a Computer* has to be some type of computer nerd (thick glasses, furtive expression, doesn't get out much). If you've seen me playing with the Weekly Webster on Discovery Canada's EXN.TV, you'll know that description doesn't fit me (well, at least I do get out some). I am fascinated by computers and their related products, but I only use them so I can have more time to play with my girlfriend, walk my dog, wrestle with my son (or one or the other with one or the other). In other words, I want my time with technology to be brief, efficient, satisfying, and fun. And I want it to serve me, not the other way around.

In this book I'm assuming that you and I are pretty much alike. You want a computer to make part of your life better – whether it's to make your work more efficient, to help your children with their homework, or just to have a new toy to play with – and you'll shop till you drop to find something that works properly, fits your budget, and meets your expectations.

There are as many books about computers and their software programs boasting that they're written for idiots and dummies as there were when we published the first edition of *How to Buy*. I'm assuming that you're neither an idiot nor a dummy. Instead, you're an intelligent person who wants sensible advice and is just a little curious about what computers are and how they do what they do. In this book, I'll tell you. If, in fact, you don't really what to know how, say, the central processing chip (the vital organ of your computer) does what it does, skip ahead in that chapter. I won't mind. But if you're just a bit curious, you'll learn not just how the chip (or adapter or printer or what have you) works but also the real differences among the myriad options that face you in the computer marketplace.

There's one thing I need to share with you first, and that's the bias I bring with me. If a particular bit of technology will make your life more efficient and enjoyable – particularly if the vendor recognizes that your time and enjoyment are valuable – I'll say nice things about it. However, if a product doesn't work as promised, doesn't install easily, or fights with other components, if it acts cranky and makes you crazy, if related software is poorly written or the manufacturers have forgotten that real people use their merchandise, then I'll let you know.

The computer market is full of traps – sinkholes full of alphabet soup, flashy numbers, and chameleon chips – and you almost have to learn a new language – compubabble – to understand what everyone is talking about. This book will, I hope, guide you through the major pitfalls. My recommendations, based partly on experience and partly on what my contacts in the industry tell me, are likely to annoy the odd advertiser and salesperson. *C'est la vie!*

You'll find that every item you want to purchase has its own terminology. Use a term incorrectly, or fail to understand what it means, and everyone from the computer zealot at your next dinner party to the nice salesperson in the computer store will pounce on you. There's no avoiding these terms, and so I've tried to explain them where they crop up in this book. However, because the jargon is always growing and changing, I invite you to visit my Web site, the White Pages (http://web.idirect.com/~myles), to get access to *White's Compubabble Dictionary*, a searchable glossary of computer terms that just may be one of the largest on the World Wide Web. You'll also be able to find up-to-date articles from the various publications to which I contribute.

I hope the second edition of *How to Buy a Computer* will be the "friend in the business" that will give you the guidance you'll need to buy your computer.

One last thing: the prices I cite in the book are only approximate, don't include taxes, and are in Canadian dollars unless otherwise noted. If you are in the United States, you'll find prices somewhere between 30 per cent less and the same, depending on the item and the vendor.

Part 1

Shopping Strategies

Making a Plan

1

According to International Data Corp. (IDC) Canada, there were nearly 900,000 computers sold in Canada in the first six months of 1998. And it is projected that over 2 million will be sold by the end of the year. If you're about to join the shopping throng, you'll have company. However, shopping for a personal computer (PC) isn't quite like shopping for any other appliance. These are complex systems and no two are alike. There are about twenty mainstream companies with name brands you may recognize, but by the time you add local retailers who assemble their own systems (just under 50 per cent of the consumer market, says IDC), the number of choices rises out of sight.

If you take nothing else away from reading this book, you'll have made a great leap forward by understanding that no one makes a whole computer. This is the single most important principle for you to understand. A computer system is an assemblage of individual components designed to work together, each of which can be bought separately, and no two components from two different manufacturers are identical. Each component has a manufacturer, a brand name, a model number, and characteristics you can check. Your biggest problem is going to be in sorting out the good products from the not-so-great while keeping your costs reasonable.

This is why we need to talk first about basic shopping strategies. Trying to buy your first computer without help can make you crazy, and even if you've been through the process before, it won't help – everything you learned three or more years ago is out of date.

Before you go shopping you'll have to learn computer jargon – the names and abbreviations of the thousands of gizmos and ways of doing things that make up a computer system – in order to hold informed conversations with other computer users and with sales-people. You'll also have to learn the differences among the flavours of gizmos, so you're not paralysed by the normal and healthy fear of paying too much and receiving too little. You won't find more untrust-worthy people in the computer industry than in any other retail trade, but you won't find fewer, either. So I'll also warn you about common sales practices that both reputable retailers and I abhor.

It doesn't matter when you buy your computer; within a few weeks, in some publication or other, you'll read that a recent round of price cuts has brought even more powerful systems within your reach. This has always been true in the computer marketplace. Prices for existing systems *always* go down. Newer, fancier, and faster systems appear at the old top price point, and there is always something newer and faster "just around the corner." There's no point in waiting. The time to buy a computer is when you need one. It will open up new worlds for you and your family. Make it fun.

Step 1 – the Plan

Your first step along the way to purchase your computer is to do your homework – homework, homework, and more homework until you're sick of it. PCs can perform more tricks than ever before, so buying one keeps getting more, not less, complicated.

If you look around at today's PC market, you quickly discover that the choice of processor alone is daunting. At any given time, there are over ten different processors available from five different companies, and each of the processors has several distinct models running at different speeds. Does the market change quickly? You betcha! In the five weeks between the first and second draft of this book, for example, seven new processors either arrived on the market or were announced as imminent. And that's just the central processor.

By the time you add the motherboard, logic chipset, memory, hard drive, video graphics and audio controllers, monitor, CD- or DVD-ROM drive, keyboard, mouse, not to mention a printer, scanner, modem, speakers and so on, it's easy to see why first-time buyers so often have glazed eyes and haunted expressions.

Finding answers

This book can help you narrow down exactly what you want in your computer system, but it can't make your decision for you. Nor can it tell you where to buy, because there are thousands upon thousands of retailers across the continent. You'll need to supplement what you learn here. The best source of supplementary information will come from someone who already has a computer. The people closest to you will share advice on what (or what not) to buy and where (or where not) to buy it.

If you're striking out on your own, however, the next most likely place to get information to supplement this book is through computer-related publications. Your local daily newspaper may have a computer section (for example, the Fast Forward section in the *Toronto Star* each Thursday). There are also monthly computer newspapers. In Canada, there are a number of free Canadian publications such as the *Computer Paper*, *Our Computer Player* (Vancouver), *Toronto Computes!*, *Ottawa Monitor*, *Winnipeg Computer Post*, *Québec Micro!* (Montreal), and *We Compute* (where I'm associate editor). In most major cities in the United States, you'll find *Computer Currents* as well as local publications. Although the articles in these specialty papers can get technical, they're primarily written for new computer users and prospective purchasers, providing reviews and shopping guides to complete systems and components.

There are the glossy magazines, too, most of them American. Some of the less technical include *PC Magazine*, *PC Computing*, *PC World*, *Computer Shopper*, and *Windows Magazine*.

If you have access to the Internet, all these publications can be found on the Web. The Internet also has various newsgroups that specialize in the subject (from whole systems to groups dedicated to individual components). There are also a variety of independent sites on the Web hosted by individuals with a mission to provide analysis (such as System Optimization at http://www.sysopt.com, Motherboard World at http://www.motherboards.org, and Tom's Hardware at http://www.tomshardware.com).

Four times a year in the Toronto area, you can also visit Computer Fest. I'll be there along with others delivering free seminars on buying computers, and there's a free advice table. The show is an excellent place to start to pick up information, then to shop for deals after you've done your homework.

There are also computer user groups, which are composed of people who have little else in common except a desire to get the most out of their computers. There are PC groups, Mac groups, and groups dedicated to specific kinds of software or activities. You don't have to own a computer to attend a meeting, and there's ample opportunity to talk to folks during the breaks. A few casual queries at computer stores where you live and/or perusal of a local computer monthly will soon reveal how to get in touch with a user group in your area.

Finally, we come to salespeople. In a very unscientific survey at a recent computer show in Kitchener, I asked retailers what was the most common mistake first-time computer buyers made and what their hardest job was. Almost unanimously, they said the biggest mistake buyers made was to assume that all PCs and all the components in them were the same. Their hardest job, they said, was to educate consumers about the differences among brands and components. Oddly enough, this intention doesn't seem to translate into reality.

Every year, IDC Canada, in conjunction with Service Dimensions, does a "secret shopper" survey of computer retailers. During a recent survey, the companies discovered that salespeople rarely listened to the surveyor's cover story. Instead of recommending a computer suitable for the customer's needs, the sales staff tended to promote and sell what they had – the same system to everyone who asked, regardless of what they wanted to do with it. Worse, anyone who walked into a store without a specific brand name in mind had the store's own brand pushed on them instead.

In short, the last place to go for advice is to a store. Salespeople are a good source of information on price, but not necessarily on whether brand A is better than brand B.

Developing a plan of attack

Your needs and expectations set the software required to accomplish your tasks. That software sets the hardware and level of performance required to run it. But no matter how convinced you are that your needs are modest ("I just want to do some word processing and/or get on the Internet"), you'll see more possibilities once you start using your computer. You don't want to cramp your ability to do more with the computer than you thought possible.

Start a binder so you can keep notes and estimates together. See the checklist on page 288. You have my permission to photocopy it. Use the copies to help you organize your research. For instance, fax the checklist to various vendors to get quotes.

When setting your budget, don't forget to add taxes, plus something extra for a printer and any software you need that doesn't come with the computer.

Look at prices from department stores; from computer, general electronics, furniture and appliance stores; from office supply super-stores, from warehouse outlets, and from corner stores specializing in computers. You may even consider buying through mail order or over the Internet (very, very cautiously).

But first read the rest of this book. Then you'll know what to look for and what to avoid. You'll be able to decipher compubabble, and you'll be wise to all the tricks of the trade.

2

Jargon

Remember, no one makes a whole computer. What we think of as a computer is an assemblage of discrete parts, each of which is manufactured by a different company. The theory is that the parts will work together and do interesting things. The purpose of this chapter is to introduce you to some of the basic terms applied to these components. But a word before we start. When you see the letter "x," as in Windows 3.1x, the "x" stands for all the versions of, for example, Windows 3.1 (e.g., 3.10 and 3.11). Where appropriate, "Windows 9x" means both Windows 95 and Windows 98. That said, an "X" in reference to the speed of a CD-ROM drive simply means "times as fast" (as the original drives). Also, when I mention a company and its product, the product is named in parentheses.

Computer: An assemblage of parts designed to do many marvellous things much faster than most people can comprehend. Microcomputers for consumers come in three broadly defined classes:

1. Desktop/tower – big, uses a lot of space, but holds lots of components.
2. Notebook – also known as a laptop. They have an average width and length of a letter-sized piece of paper, but may be slightly larger or smaller.

3. Palmtop – the term used to describe electronic organizers and very small hand-held computers known as H/PCs (they have a keyboard) and Palm PCs (they don't).

Hardware: A collective term used to describe the physical components in the computer and the computer itself. You can pick hardware up, and you generally need to feed it electrical power for it to operate. It often lights up and says, "beep."

Software: A collective term used to describe the instructions given to the hardware to make it do something. Specific collections of these instructions are called programs or applications (and if they are very small applications, they may be called applets). Software is written to run on specific CPUs (see below) and operating systems, which simply means that if a software program is written to run on a PowerMac (see below), the same set of instructions won't work on a PC (see below).

A special type of software application, known as an operating system, is required before a computer can employ the applications that allow you to do things such as write letters, store and retrieve information, or get on the Internet. Examples of operating systems include MS-DOS (Microsoft Disk Operating System), Microsoft Windows (3.1x, 9x, or NT 4.0, 5.0), UNIX, Linux, FreeBSD, IBM OS/2, the Apple "Mac OS," and Rhapsody, or Be Systems' BeOS. Operating systems are designed to work with specific classes of hardware (except for the BeOS, which can work on both Mac and PC).

Data: The words, numbers, graphics, and so on that you create on your computer and store in files on the hard disk (see below). Program files are also data files.

Hardware Basics

A computer comprises several basic components:

Chip is a general term used to describe collections of very tiny transistors etched on a wafer of silicon. Depending on what device the chip is on and what the device is intended to do, the chip can have a relatively simple or quite complex job.

The **central processing unit** (or CPU, or simply "processor") is the computer inside the computer. All instructions received by the system – or sent from it – are manipulated by the CPU. Although it's a very complex device containing millions of transistors, the processor's sole job is to accept instructions, add fast, then send the results in the form of more instructions to all other components in or attached to the system.

PC is short for personal computer. It is a collective term for computers with a CPU made by Intel Corporation or by National Semiconductor (Cyrix), IBM, Advanced Micro Devices (AMD), and a relatively new player, Centaur/IDT (Integrated Device Technology). PCs used to be called "IBM compatibles" because IBM was the first to use an Intel processor in a microcomputer. However, IBM is no longer the dominant player in the PC industry, so the name has become much more generic. PCs need software written to run specifically for them.

PowerPC/PowerMac is the term used to describe computers based on the MPC600 series CPUs jointly developed by Motorola with the help of IBM and Apple. PowerPC/PowerMacs need software written to run specifically for them unless they have expensive additional circuit boards and/or special emulation software that allows them to run PC software (slowly).

The **motherboard** is the main system board to which all other components are attached in one way or another – plugged into slots, into sockets, or connected by cable to connectors hardwired to the board. You may also see the motherboard called the main board or main system board by people who wish to be politically correct.

Two components on the motherboard determine what it can do. The **BIOS** (basic in/out system) acts like a combination map and traffic manager, providing information to the CPU about devices in the system and assisting in routing information to them so that each receives the appropriate instructions. Although it's usually classed as hardware, the BIOS is actually software embedded in ROM chips (see below). Some large, name-brand companies may write their own BIOS software, but the majority of systems use BIOS software developed by Phoenix Technologies, Award Software, or American Megatrends International (AMI).

The **logic chipset** (or simply "chipset") usually comprises two chips (or as many as nine in some high-end systems). The chipset provides the connection between the CPU and everything else in the system. The chipset determines what types and speeds of main system memory (RAM) and cache memory (see below) can be used and how it is used. It determines how various expansion slots communicate with the CPU, the type of video graphics controller you may have, the types of external connectors you can use, and how quickly hard drives and CD-ROM drives can pass data to the system.

Although the BIOS was once *the* determinant of computer compatibility (i.e., how well it would run software and cope with various pieces of hardware), in today's PC the chipset is much more important in determining how up to date a system is and how well it will perform.

About 75 per cent of the motherboards on today's market have chipsets designed by Intel. Chipsets that are nearly as desirable come from VIA, AMD (which uses VIA chipsets), and Acer Labs (Ali). Others include SiS, OPTi, HiNT, Neptune and roughly a dozen more. The least desirable products are the VXpro, HXpro, and TXpro by PC Chips. (See the chipset table on pages 86-87.)

Memory: While the CPU is adding, the instructions it receives and the results it gets have to be parked somewhere. Three forms of memory are commonly found in computers:

ROM (read only memory) is where instructions that do not change are stored. Your new computer will have ROM chips on various devices, and generally you don't need to worry about how many chips there are or how much memory you'll get. The amount of ROM you get is significant only in Palmtops, H/PCs, and Palm PCs, where it is an indicator of how much software the unit is capable of running right out of the box. (Unlike larger computers, in these units the operating system and most applications you'll use are stored in ROM, not on a hard drive.)

RAM (random access memory) is where the CPU gets instructions that do change; it is also where the CPU parks the results of interim calculations while processing more. RAM sits in slots on the motherboard. The amount of RAM you have in your computer will vary among vendors, and you can generally add more. To run

Windows 9x you'll need 16 megabytes (MB) of RAM as a bare minimum; 32 MB is recommended; 64 MB is lavish, but may be required by some graphics-intensive applications. It is possible to have too much or at least to have more than you can use productively, but the general rule is the more RAM you have (up to 64 MB), the more applications can run in electronic memory and the faster your system will be overall. I'll expand on these points in subsequent chapters.

Other forms of RAM may be found on a graphics controller and on a wave-table sound controller. I'll talk about these matters in the appropriate chapters.

Cache RAM (also called external cache, level 2 cache, or L2 cache memory) is a super-fast type of RAM memory used as a temporary holding facility to bridge the difference in speed between the very fast CPU and slightly slower main system RAM. Having zero L2 cache is the equivalent of dropping the CPU a speed level (or cutting about 20 per cent from its performance). The minimum you'll want is 128 kilobytes (KB) of cache RAM, and 512 KB is becoming more common.

Cache memory may be found on the motherboard, in the processor (level 1 cache) or closely associated with it (Pentium II, Xeon, and newer Celeron processors), on a hard drive controller, and on some high-end hard drives themselves. Again, I'll talk about the specifics where appropriate.

Hard disk drive: Also known as a hard file if you work for IBM, or a fixed disk, this is a mass storage device for information. It is where software programs are stored and where you keep documents or other things you produce with your computer. Hard drive capacity (the amount of information it will hold) has nothing to do with the amount of memory in the computer, and the two shouldn't be confused.

In today's market, hard drive capacity is measured in billions of bytes, or gigabytes (GB). Small is 3.2 GB; large is 16 GB. Typical in a mid-range system circa mid-1998 is 4.5 to 6.3 GB.

Hard drives come in two basic flavours. The most commonly found is known as an enhanced integrated drive electronics (EIDE) or AT attachment-3 (ATA-3) drive. ("AT" as used here and when referring to the now-obsolete "AT-286" computers stands for Advanced Technology.) You may also find Ultra DMA (or UDMA) drives, which are similar, but can pass more data to the CPU over a shorter period. (DMA? It depends on who you ask and when. It first meant Dynamic Memory Allocation. Today it's more commonly defined as Direct Memory Access.) The main control circuitry for this type of drive is usually hardwired to the motherboard.

Other EIDE devices include CD-ROM drives (compact disc, read only memory), CD-R (recordable) and CD-RW (rewritable) drives, DVD-ROM (digital video disc or digital Versatile Disc) drives, and a variety of removable storage devices. I'll go into detail in Chapter 10.

The second type of hard drive is known as a small computer systems interface (SCSI, pronounced "scuzzy") drive. SCSI drives can be very fast and have very high capacities (faster and hold more data than even Ultra DMA drives). Other SCSI devices include scanners, printers, CD-ROM drives, tape drives, and a variety of other external mass storage devices. SCSI drives require a special controller that may be a separate circuit board or integrated into high-end motherboards. Both the controllers and devices tend to be more expensive than EIDE equivalents, but because of greater efficiency and flexibility they are coveted by high-end users (SCSI devices can be outside or inside the computer case while EIDE is an internal-only specification).

Floppy drive: So called because, once upon a time, the diskettes used in the drives could bend. Today's standard, 3.5-inch stiff plastic case, able to hold (usually) 1.44 MB of data, doesn't bend, but the little disk inside will if you ever pry one open (you'll kill it in the process – so don't, unless you're sure you'll never, *ever* want to use it again). Various companies are trying to replace the floppy with devices that will hold more information, but none has emerged as the "floppy killer" yet. We'll talk more about removable storage/floppy alternative devices in Chapter 10.

CD-ROM drive: Uses CDs that are able to hold 650 MB to 720 MB of information. They are slower to deliver data than either a floppy or hard drive. Today, most software comes on CD, which is why it's a good idea to include a CD-ROM in your new system (in fact, finding a new computer *without* one today is difficult). See Chapter 10 for a discussion of CD-R and CD-RW alternatives.

DVD drive: May eventually replace CD-ROM drives, but not immediately. DVD is an evolving standard, and there are already three types on the market (see Chapter 5 on reading computer ads). It's becoming more common to find DVD drives in high-end systems, but the version may be only vaguely described in promotional material. See Chapter 10 for a discussion of the incompatible DVD recordable options.

Monitor: The big glass eye that sits on your desk and shows anyone looking over your shoulder exactly what you're doing.

Video graphics controller: This may be on a separate circuit board plugged into the motherboard or may be integrated into the motherboard or CPU. This is the device that translates instructions from the CPU into the pictures you see on the computer's monitor.

Audio controller: Like the video graphics controller, this may be on a separate board or integrated into the motherboard or CPU. Although once an optional add-on, sound in a PC is another feature that today you'll have to struggle to avoid. The controller translates instructions from the CPU into music, voices, sound effects – and complaints from the neighbours if you crank the speakers up too high.

Modem: Short form for MOdulator/DEModulator, this is the device that translates digital signals from the computer into the analog signals required by telephone systems (and vice versa) so you can communicate with other computers over a telephone line. It's required if you wish to get on the Internet. It may be a circuit board inside the computer, a chip integrated into the motherboard, or an external device attached to the outside of the computer (see Chapter 11 on telecommunications.)

Keyboard: The device you use to type letters to your relatives or otherwise issue instructions to the computer. We'll discuss continuous speech dictation and command recognition software later in Chapter 11.

Mouse: A pointing device used to single out images or words on the computer screen. Clicking one of its buttons makes the computer respond. Today, the mouse is one of several pointing devices which include trackballs (sort of a stationary, upside-down mouse), touchpads (stationary pads sensitive to finger motions), and digitizing tablets (which use a pen-like device instead of your finger).

Port: A yummy after-dinner wine. In a computer, however, ports are the points where external devices are attached to the computer. All ports originate on the motherboard or on circuit boards plugged into the motherboard. Typical external ports include the following:

• Keyboard (may soon disappear in favour of USB, see below)
• Monitor (may also disappear because of USB)
• Parallel (for printers and a growing number of other devices)
• Serial (for external modems and certain pointing devices)
• Universal Serial Bus (USB – for keyboard, mouse, printer, monitor, game controllers, scanners, and more)
• PS/2 (an alternative place to attach keyboard and mouse which may ultimately disappear in favour of USB)
• Game (for attaching game controllers, also known as joysticks. Ditto on disappearing)
• Audio (configurations differ, but generally include speaker out, line out, line in, microphone in).
• Optional ports may include network connections, SCSI connections, MIDI (musical instrument digital interface) connections, IEEE 1394 (FireWire) connections, and various television signal input and output connections.

Last, but not least, is the computer's **case**, which may lie flat on a desktop or stand on one end in a "tower" configuration. Today's cases may be designer shaped and coloured, but that can make adding components to the system later a headache. Terms applied to tower cases in particular, such as full-sized, mid-tower, or mini-tower, do not refer to any standardized system of measurement – their relative sizes are strictly in the eye of the beholder. Cases may have digital read-outs on the front which appear to report the computer's speed, but these numbers are set manually and are not speedometers. (Gotcha!) More important is finding out how many bays, or places for various drives, a case has; what size devices the bays will accept; and how many open to the front.

3

Basic Shopping Tips

Before we start to nail down details about the various components of a computer, there are some general points you should note.

The best source of information on buying a computer is someone you know who already owns one. If you're buying one for your kids without asking them what their friends are using, you're likely to land in deep soup. Unless you're already skilled enough to teach your children how to use the system, their friends are going to be doing that job. Salespeople are the last people you should consult on what to buy.

Knowing what your friends have will help you decide between a PC and a Mac. If you already own an older system and you're shopping for the next evolution in hardware, only extraordinary circumstances would prompt you to switch from a PC to a Mac or vice versa. Stick with what you know, warts and all. For a new purchaser, however, the choices are confusing.

Your friends will tell you where they bought their computer and if you should shop there, too. They can teach you how to use your system or at least tell you about the software they use and why, as well as giving you tips on what to do when you're stumped.

One evening when you've just done something unfortunate on your PC (such as wiping out all your programs by typing "format" and "C:" in the same sentence at the DOS prompt), your friends are the ones who are most likely to be available to help you out or share your misery. The local store where you bought the machine won't be open then (unless you bought it from a manufacturer with a twenty-four-hour hotline and paid big bucks for the service).

Think about work, too. If your office has nothing but PCs and you plan to bring work home, using a Mac will only exasperate you while you try to figure out how to move your data painlessly between the two platforms (there are ways, but few of them are simple).

If you plan to get a computer in order to retrain yourself, either to get back into the workforce or to improve your skills in it, a few calls to training schools or temporary help agencies will show you very quickly that most businesses use PCs and their software. Macs are a small (less than 5 per cent) share of the Canadian market.

What your clients and outside support companies use will play a role in your decision, too. For example, if you'll be using the computer to prepare advertising or other graphic and design material, you'll find most of the service bureaus (printers and film houses) you'll be working with have Macs. This is the case even though virtually all of the artistic design and desktop publishing programs, which used to be the exclusive preserve of the Mac, now have versions for the PC, running under Windows. Also take into consideration that many companies, banks, and government-reporting agencies now make it possible (and in some cases mandatory) to exchange data via computer.

Finally, ask your friends and acquaintances about their mistakes as well as their triumphs. Ask them where they bought their system. If they weren't treated well, don't go there!

You can't get quality for $1.98. If a deal sounds too good to be true or a price is dramatically lower than the competition's, something is wrong. If you focus simply on the lowest price to the exclusion of all other concerns, eventually you'll have to pay extra.

It *is* possible to find a specific component or a whole computer that is less expensive than other competing products, but all components are not the same. In order to offer a low price, the retailer has made some compromises. If you check the advertisements carefully, you'll notice that some of them are vague about the brand names of the components that form the system. Someone offering a nameless hard drive isn't telling you anything about its quality. In order to sell cheap, the retailer has bought components with price, not quality, in mind. Ads mentioning name-brand components tend to have slightly higher prices.

No one likes to spend more than they must, and with the fierce competition and brutally low markups in today's computer market, retailers don't have a lot of room to manoeuvre. But if a deal is remarkably lower than the general competition while appearing to offer the same thing, start wondering why. If the retailer is slashing prices to the bone and hoping to survive through volume sales, the company may not stay in business long enough to honour the warranty, or it may not have enough staff to spend time on the telephone with you when your machine acts funny. As well, without sufficient cash reserves to maintain a solid reputation with suppliers, the retailer may be forced to use low-quality parts in order to keep its prices down. The average length of time a computer retailer remains in business, according to the Canadian Computer Retailers' Association, is just under two years.

Some generic terms in advertisements such as EIDE (a style of hard drive), SVGA (used to describe both video cards and monitors), a description of a processor without the manufacturer's name, "tower or mini-tower" (a style of case), and "MS-compatible" mouse are so broad that they are virtually meaningless. A brand name on a video card or a mouse doesn't necessarily guarantee better quality, but it does give you a basis for comparison, and it also allows you to find out if your software is going to work with it.

If it doesn't walk like a duck, talk like a duck, or look like a duck, it isn't a duck. If everything you know about the performance, characteristics, and compatibility of a processor or a chipset comes from what you've read and heard about an Intel version of the product, keep in mind that when you pay less for a non-Intel "equivalent," less is what you're likely to get.

This doesn't mean I'm waving a flag for Intel or that in specific instances I don't think there are viable alternatives. I will be providing tables on and discussing the differences between Intel and non-Intel processors and chipsets in Chapter 6, but new products will arrive after this book goes to press. To help you find out just how "equivalent" these forthcoming products are, I'll explain where to look for the information.

This issue of hardware equivalency and compatibility will come back to haunt us. The simplest rule of thumb is that you won't be disappointed with a less expensive "compatible" product, so long as you don't expect it to behave exactly the way the (almost invariably) more expensive original does.

What you want to do with your computer determines the software programs you need. In turn, these programs determine what type of computer you need and what mix of components is required to do the task. Coming at this from any other direction will simply get you in trouble. When you start shopping, however, particularly if you have software in mind, you must discuss with the vendor exactly what you want to do with the computer. As noted in Chapter 1, many salespeople may not hear you. Their "Oh, sure; it will do that" may be merely a conditioned response. *If the verbal assurances you receive aren't also written on the sales agreement, they don't exist.*

First determine which operating system (see Chapter 2) you must use to run the software you need. If the software requires the MacOS or the BeOS, you need a PowerMac (a PC won't run them – although Be Inc. has now adapted its Be Operating System to the PC platform). If the software requires any flavour of Windows, you might be able to run it on a PowerMac with special hardware and/or software emulators (more slowly than on a PC), but you're better off running it on a PC. To run software that requires OS/2, UNIX, or any of its variants, such as Linux or FreeBSD, you'll also want a PC – although only aficionados of these operating systems will want to run them at all.

There is no such thing as a computer that is too powerful for you, particularly if the point of the exercise is to finish what you have to do so you can go and play golf. However, there may be one that's too expensive. The point of your homework is to find the correct balance between power and cost.

No one has a bottomless bank account, and some systems may be too expensive for you to purchase now, but regardless of whether this new computer is simply to do word processing or to run the odd game for the kids, the point of having a computer is to get it to do things for you as efficiently as possible.

You won't stop where you think you will. Once you discover how relatively easy it is to do the task you're buying the computer for in the first place, you'll find more things to do with your system. Count on it. The more you ask it to do, the more you'll appreciate the power it can give you.

If your budget is limited (whose isn't?), here is roughly the order I'd recommend for spending your limited resources:

- processor (as fast as you can find),
- memory (as much as you can afford),
- hard drive capacity (as big as possible, then start saving for another drive),
- video acceleration and monitor size (see Chapter 13),
- multimedia components (CD- or DVD-ROM drive, sound controller), and
- modem.

If you have any money left after you find an affordable printer, then start pricing backup systems (tape backup and power), case design, and software.

The time to buy a computer is when you need one. You can't get the fastest computer there is. The industry changes so quickly that it isn't here yet; it's on a truck somewhere between the factory and the store. If you wait for it to arrive, an even faster system will be on the next truck and you'll never buy a computer.

Think I'm kidding? As I write this, the fastest Pentium II processor runs at 450 MHz on a 100 MHz motherboard (take a deep breath – you'll understand exactly what this sentence means before we're

Price Grid	
Price Range	**Buys you**
$5,000 (± $1,500)	Leading technological edge with greater or lesser mixture of components, warranty provisions, and external devices. Includes monitor.
$3,500 (± $1,200)	One step back. Not the most recent processor or motherboard technology, but the one released last time. Includes monitor.
$2,500 (± $750)	Two steps back. Last year's leading edge from Intel or newer processors from AMD, Cyrix/IBM. Includes monitor.
$1,500 (± $500)	"Basic PC" system with Celeron or non-Intel processor. Modest components, may not include monitor.
$1,000 (± $200)	Trailing-edge technology at all levels, low-cost (and perhaps low-quality) components, processors, and chipsets from people you've never heard of or Intel products long since considered obsolete.

done). By the time this book gets onto store shelves, two new processors, "Katmai" and "Tanner," will have arrived and 500 MHz processors will be just around the corner. As noted earlier, between my first and second draft, seven new processors were either released or announced. There will be newer and faster Celeron processors (see Chapter 6), as well as newer and faster Xeon processors (ditto). In early 2000, the 64-bit processor currently code-named "Merced" will hit the streets. It simply never stops.

Everything you want today will be less expensive in six months. The price for existing technology *always* goes down. New technology comes in at the top price. This, too, is a never-ending cycle.

All other things being equal – without the addition of specialty items, but with enough memory, hard drive capacity, and a suitable graphics system for the software you'll want – the leading-edge PC system is always around $5,000. Complete systems that are one, two, and three steps back from the leading edge usually start at around $3,500, $2,000, and $1,500 respectively. One thing that has changed since the first edition of *How to Buy a Computer* is the arrival of "entry level" systems at the lower end of the price scale other than the technology's trailing edge (more detail in Chapter 6).

Keep in mind that you can play games with these numbers. Adding better graphics, a bigger monitor, more memory, different or higher-quality multimedia components, and a larger hard drive will push the numbers up. Cut back on some or all of them and you can push the price down.

Computers get old in a hurry. To prevent your new system from becoming inadequate ten seconds after you take it out of the box, buy as close to the technology's leading edge as budget and good sense will allow (see the discussion of price versus performance in Chapter 6). The further off the pace you go, the sooner your system will become unable to handle new software.

Plan your upgrade strategy before you buy. Ask pointed questions about which parts of the system can be upgraded and what the choices you make today will prevent you from getting in a year or two. Ask whether you can use industry standard parts to upgrade. One of the advantages of the "open architecture" of the majority of the PC market is that there are hundreds of suppliers making parts for computers which are all interchangeable. But a few name-brand systems have a unique design or proprietary engineering that may require you to get all future upgrades from the company that built the system in the first place. Most often this means you will have to spend more to upgrade than if you purchase a system that uses standard parts.

You're going to want another one. Advances in hardware and software, and your own sense of anticipation, will make today's fast computer appear old and tired long before you wanted.

Hardware will come along that you will talk yourself into needing, and it won't work with your existing system. People who purchased a PC manufactured before the advent of the peripheral component interconnect (PCI) type of expansion slot on the motherboard have already experienced this. They cannot use the fastest video graphics controllers currently available or the latest audio controllers, for example. In a few years, components that do fit their older industry standard architecture (ISA) or VESA local bus (VLB) slots will disappear, imposing further limits.

In 1998, we were hit with a flood of devices, particularly advanced game controllers, using the Universal Serial Bus (USB). Systems without USB ports are being left behind. Although your current system, if it isn't a Pentium II, won't have an accelerated graphics port

(AGP), your next system will – and it will need it. In mid-1998 the fastest graphics controllers used AGP. If your system doesn't have an AGP slot or a chipset that supports AGP, you can't get one of these new controllers unless you replace the entire motherboard.

Sooner or later software will arrive that either won't work to its full potential, won't work fast enough to be satisfying, or won't work at all on your present computer. Systems without MMX instructions (MultiMedia eXtensions) in the processor (for example, classic Pentium, Pentium Pro, Cyrix 6x86, and AMD K5) can't get the best out of software written for MMX. When AGP software arrives, only those systems with AGP slots on the motherboard and the graphics card to fit them will be able to use it effectively. Anyone trying to run Windows 95 on a 486 has too much time on their hands. Win95 won't run on a 386 or less at all, Win98 won't install on anything less than a 486DX2/66, and only Bill Gates knows what Windows 2000 – the next revision of the company's consumer version destined to be built on the Windows NT kernel – will use; and no current version of Windows will run on an old XT, period.

Last, but not least – and this is the big killer – your own sense of anticipation will do you in. Your ability to anticipate what the computer does next will always outstrip its ability to deliver. When you first get your system it will appear blindingly fast, with information whipping across the screen faster than you can absorb it. If you try to keep up, you run the risk of issuing commands before you understand what your choices are.

After the fortieth time you do the same thing, you know exactly how the computer responds. And, particularly if the task you want is several stages down the road, there you'll be, drumming your fingers on the desk, muttering, "C'mon, c'mon, damn you! Work!" It won't be too long after that you'll begin reading computer magazines again and haunting bookstores, wondering if Myles has done another new edition of *How to Buy a Computer*.

Hint: To put this day as far off into the future as possible, never, ever spend time on someone else's faster computer. When you get back to yours, you'll think it's useless. Don't believe me? Talk to me again in a couple of years – or less.

The only valid reason to upgrade software or hardware is to solve a problem you can't fix any other way. If you jump on the newest thing simply because it is the newest thing, then sooner, not later, the computer gods will getcha! Sometimes the leading edge is the bleeding edge, and the newest, greatest, most expensive thing this month vanishes without a trace the next. Remember the advice about not buying a car in its first model year because it takes a while to work out the bugs of any new design? Assume the same thing in spades for computer components.

What do you do? None of the above means you should go back to bed and pull the covers over your head. Rapid processor obsolescence does not mean you should wait for the next model you've heard is hovering over the horizon. If the object is to get a system that will run not only today's software, but also the applications coming next year and the year after that, simply buy the fastest system you can afford, use it to your heart's content, and start saving for your next one. By the time you're ready to upgrade, the system you wanted but couldn't afford will be available in quantity, will have had any instabilities worked out, and will be less expensive.

If you're still afraid of being ripped off, you haven't done enough homework. Do the homework until you're sick to death of it. There is a point at which you're ready to buy, and White's Computer Consumer's Bill of Rights will help. Remember:

- You have a right to ask questions.
- You have a right to expect complete and truthful answers
- You have a right to have all assurances written on the sales agreement *and honoured to the letter.*

Everyone else knows better. Even if you do everything you're supposed to do, I'll make you a tiny wager. Within two to three weeks of unpacking your shiny new system, one or more of the following things will happen. Despite all your hard work and research, total strangers or your smart-aleck, twelve-year-old niece will tell you where you could have bought more power for less money. You'll pick up a copy of one of the local computer newspapers and find ads for a fancier model at the price you just paid, or a lower price for the one you bought.

Ignore them all; it's simply part of the game. Hunker down and enjoy the heck out of your choice until you're ready to upgrade.

Part 2

Into the Field

4

Nailing Down Some
Basic Questions

Before we go much farther, we need to nail down a few basic issues, such as whether to buy a PC or a Mac, a name brand or a clone, and whether to shop at a store (and what kind), by mail order, or over the Internet.

Mac or PC?

When the first edition of *How to Buy a Computer* was published, Mac sales were just under 10 per cent of the North American market and Mac clones were just beginning to appear. By 1998, Apple's market share had dropped to around 4 per cent or less and the clone market had come and – after Apple co-founder Steve Jobs regained control of the company – disappeared again.

Both PCs and PowerMacs can do word processing, number crunching, data manipulation, desktop publishing, music, and everything associated with the Internet. The difference is that a top-of-the-line PowerMac G3 with all the bells and whistles will set you back nearly $10,000 (Cdn) while a similarly equipped PC will top out at just over half that amount.

In the past, you looked at what your friends already had, and if all your friends had Macs, you bought one too. Today, I no longer consider the Mac to be a consumer – as opposed to a commercial or business – computer. It has become a niche product serving a narrow market. Advertising agencies, professional designers, and publishers make up the dog that is being wagged by the tail: a printing industry that has invested heavily in Mac hardware and doesn't want to change. Another way of putting this is that nearly 97 per cent of people buying a computer today will purchase a PC.

I can hear (and have heard) the howls of rage coming from Mac fans. Every time I point out these facts in one of my columns, my e-mail basket overflows with irate tirades. I think they are reacting from the justifiable fear that their favourite hardware – and the support that goes with it – will vanish.

Name brand or clone?

If you've decided on a Mac, you no longer have the option of buying a clone. Only Apple makes Macs. But if you've decided on a PC, you have the choice between a nationally advertised name brand and a locally assembled clone. I suggest you delay making this decision until you know what you want in your system. Then you can shop for the best mix of performance and price.

Frankly, I don't like the term "clone." It was coined during the era when people first made illegal and unstable copies of name-brand products. Ironically, given Apple's historic antipathy to them, the first "clones" were of the old Apple II. In the PC industry, however, "clones" or "IBM compatibles" were never illegal. The first PCs, running Microsoft's Disk Operating System (DOS) and featuring Intel microprocessors, could be, and were, assembled by all kinds of people. However, IBM was the first to put its name on the box, so "IBM compatible" became the buzzword for all the others.

Today, IBM is just another PC manufacturer in a list of name-brand manufacturers that includes Compaq, Dell, Hewlett-Packard, Apple, and a host of others. Together, these five nationally advertised systems account for over 62 per cent of the total Canadian market – leaving the remainder of the "name" brands and local systems to fight over the remainder.

The choice between name brand and local assembly used to be simple. If you were new to computing, and particularly if you knew you wouldn't be able to detect whether it was hardware, software, or your own error that was making the computer misbehave, then a name brand with twenty-four-hour, seven-day, toll-free help was what you wanted.

Alas, those days have gone forever. No computer manufacturer offers unlimited software support any more. You'll be lucky to get 90 days on software pre-loaded onto the system, and if the problem is with software you've added later, you're out of luck. You can blame Microsoft for this one. The cost of supporting Windows 95 was simply too much for the industry to stand.

All that remains is hardware support. Remember my warning that all parts aren't the same and that no one builds a whole computer? This works to your advantage when it comes to buying locally assembled systems. Local retailers can and do get their components from the same companies that supply them to the nationals.

Local assembly also allows for greater customization. As one Compaq Canada staffer told me, "We can't afford to customize. We run a volume business and we have to crank 'em off the line."

'Tis to shudder.

With a local system, on the other hand, you can do the research to find the best components in every category and have the resulting hotrod assembled for you.

There's also no difference in the rate at which the systems will break down or the length of time that they will last. The industry average for computers coming out of the box with loose, damaged, or brain-dead components is the same, no matter where you shop (somewhere between 10 and 30 per cent, depending on who is providing the quote). Both are subject to what is unfortunately called electronic crib-death – where a component mysteriously gives up the ghost within the first month (something that can affect all electronic goods, not just computers).

Where the difference lies is in how the computer gets fixed during the warranty period. The approach you prefer will probably be determined by how you handle adversity. When something goes wrong, you may prefer to pick up the phone and either get a diagnosis on the spot or a technician who comes to your system to check it over with a part (or whole system) replacement arriving within a day or two. You'll pay extra for this service.

The alternative is to pile the computer back into the car, drive to where you bought it, and stand firmly but politely on the counter until the vendor fixes it.

Who gives the most reliable service? There is no nationally advertised brand-name manufacturer about which I've received no complaints (or to put it another way, I've received multiple complaints about every nationally advertised brand-name manufacturer, with no exceptions). However, in surveys conducted over a number of years by several glossy American magazines, Dell, Hewlett-Packard, and IBM are consistently given high ratings. Packard Bell/NEC is consistently given low ratings. The others generally land somewhere in between. Talking to your friends and to local user groups about local retailers will give you good feedback on their reputations.

Where to shop

During the IDC/Service Dimensions "secret shopper" survey noted in Chapter 1, the researchers checked electronics, appliance, computer, and office supply superstores, department stores, warehouse outlets, and corner computer stores. They rated the shopping experience based on how comfortable it was, on the quality of the information received, on the techniques used to close a sale, and on the price of the product.

Warehouse outlets scored lowest in all categories, although their prices were, indeed, often slightly lower. Department stores scored high in providing a comfortable shopping environment, but much lower in all other categories. Corner computer stores scored low in shopping comfort, but about average in price and quality of information. The result that surprised me the most (violating my bias in favour of the corner computer store) was that the superstores offered the best combination of shopping environment, quality of information, and price.

The survey did not examine mail-order and Internet shopping, but I've got some concerns of my own over both forms of marketing. For example, how does a company outside Canada honour its warranty when part of what you're paying for is on-site warranty protection?

I'm not too concerned about someone hacking into a Web site and ripping off my credit card over the Net (although I've never given it out this way). VISA reported in the spring of 1998 that it has no record of Internet credit card theft. However, there have been enough reports of other funny business practices from sleazy operators in both mail-order and Internet transactions to make me edgy.

For example, a "full money back guarantee" may not really be full. "Money back" may not include shipping in either direction, a "restocking fee," or – in one reported case – the full retail value of all software on the system.

Both Canadian and American residents can be hurt by these practices, but Canadian buyers also have to pay the GST and brokerage fees that likely will be charged as the system crosses the border.

That said, I do want to note that there are some reliable mail-order suppliers. One of the best known direct-marketers of computer systems in Canada (and the United States for that matter) is Dell Computer Corp. In the States there are other well-known alternatives such as Gateway 2000 and Micron, but only Dell among this group has Canadian assembly plants and offices across Canada. Other brand-name hardware manufactures have (albeit reluctantly) joined the "Buy Direct" club, including IBM.

Still, it doesn't hurt – and it may do you some good – to query each company's return policies, the precise nature of the warranty options it offers, and what you and the computer have to do in order to qualify. In fact, this is something you should do no matter how you purchase your system or from whom you buy it.

5

Reading Computer Ads

Ad primer

Unless you learn the meaning of the terms used in the newspaper ads and the brochures handed out at consumer shows, some salespeople will rub their hands together when they see you coming and think, "Victim!"

Because each component in the computer has a manufacturer's name (which is often different from the name on the case), a model name or number, and a set of characteristics and specifications that you can check, you have to know not only what the bits and pieces inside it are called, but also why some are better than others. If you go into a store without either a brand-name system or brand-name components in mind, the store will generally sell you what it has without getting into the fine points of the component mix.

A computer is composed essentially of a main circuit board (normally called the motherboard or the main system board). Attached to it are a number of devices, including a central processing unit (CPU), a logic support chipset, electronic random access memory (RAM), level 2 (or "external") cache memory, a basic in/out system (BIOS), "expansion" slots of various kinds, a floppy and hard drive controller, and various other widgets that make the computer work.

The expansion slots hold other circuit boards that have specialized functions, such as video graphics adapter (also called a graphics card or graphics controller), modem, audio card (sound controller), SCSI adapter, network interface, and more. To complicate things, the graphics, sound, SCSI, and network controllers – even the modem – may instead be integrated into the motherboard itself.

The motherboard, together with the circuit boards slotted into it, fits into the computer's case along with the hard disk drive(s), the floppy disk drive(s), and CD- or DVD-ROM drive. You may want to add additional drives, such as a tape or removable cartridge drive, later. All of these boards and drives get electricity from a power supply that comes with the case.

Once you plug a monitor, a keyboard, and other devices such as a mouse and printer into the appropriate places at the back of the case (called ports), you're ready to go computing. All of which sounds really simple. *Not!*

If you've never shopped for computer hardware before, the following composite set of specifications, with abbreviations culled from advertisements in various publications, may as well be written in Sanskrit. We're going to get through a composite ad to make sure you understand the jargon and the pitfalls.

Keep in mind that ads which are vague on component details (brand name, model designation) don't tell you anything you can use to make a valid price comparison. In the following discussion, I've refrained from reminding you to ask for the brand and model designation for each component. Take the question as given. Also, remember that x or xxx stands for any number. In the processor category below, for example, xxx could be 166 or 500, or anything in between.

xxx MHz MMX processor

This line tells you about the central processor that will power the system. If it doesn't specifically mention the name Intel (or the trademarked names, Pentium or Pentium II or Celeron or Xeon), it could be for a product by AMD, Cyrix, or Centaur/IDT (or IBM – which manufactures all Cyrix parts, then puts its name on some of them). You may have to ask to find out what's really being offered. There's

nothing wrong with buying a non-Intel processor, as long as you understand that there's a reason why it costs less. While this may change in the future, current non-Intel processors tend to match the Intel version in running business applications, but lag behind, sometimes a long way behind, when it comes to multimedia and floating point operations, which you need for certain applications, especially 3-D accelerated games.

There's more detail on this in Chapter 6, along with a table containing details of the processors available in 1998. By early 2000, you'll see ads for Intel's new 64-bit processors, currently code-named Merced, and even faster processors from everyone else.

Watch out for the term "Triton" in a computer advertisement. It is either inaccurate or something else is wrong. Once upon a time, "Triton" was an Intel product name – right up until the company abandoned it in mid-1995. Since then there have been no Triton chipsets of any kind. If you visited Intel's Web site in 1998 and did a search on the term "Triton," you got a page of references headed "Triton . . . is not an Intel product name."

So why do some retailers insist on using the term in their advertisements? Darned if I know. They either suspect you're too ignorant to know the difference and are hoping to confuse you, or they haven't kept up with industry developments. All of which are good reasons not to shop there.

Intel chipsets for classic Pentium systems are the 430FX, 430VX, and 430HX "PCIset." For Pentium MMX systems, chipsets include the 430VX, 430HX, or 430TX PCIset. For Pentium II systems, chipsets include the 440FX PCIset or 440LX, 440BX, and (for Celeron-based systems) 440EX "AGPset." For Xeon-based systems, the chipsets are the 450GX, 450NX Basic (up to two processors), and 450NX (up to four processors). Any other name given to an Intel motherboard chipset should be viewed with suspicion because you cannot be sure what you're being offered. (More on the individual chipsets in Chapter 7.) Get a friend to take you to Intel's Web site (www.intel.com) any time you wish to get an up-to-date list of its products.

There are chipsets comparable (but *not* identical) to the Intel versions, such as those from VIA (the Apollo line), AMD (re-named

VIA sets), and ALI (Acer Labs Inc.). There are also other chipset manufacturers.

Also watch out for ads for a Pentium or Pentium MMX system offering a "VX, HX, or TX motherboard." Not only are these motherboards old (and quickly moving out of the market now), the chipset may or may not be made by Intel. In mid-1997, ads began to appear for Pentium and Pentium MMX systems offering incredibly low prices on the systems themselves and the motherboards if purchased separately. They used a much slower and less reliable series of chipsets, called the VXpro, HXpro, and TXpro, produced by a company called PC Chips. Based on a discontinued VIA chipset (VIA launched a lawsuit about it), these chipsets are not equivalent to the Intel series, despite the deliberate similarity in name.

If the PC Chips parts were functionally identical to their Intel counterparts, we wouldn't have an issue here. But they're not. Although the motherboard manufacturers using the VXpro and HXpro (Sybercom, Precision America Inc., PAI, Amptron, PC Chips, New Generation, Alton, Houston Technologies, PC Ware, and Hsing Tech – and there may be others) claim the chipsets are as good as Intel's, independent tests aren't so cheery. Miami-based Carl Industries reports that using the industry standard ZD Winbench 97 test, the CPUs were at least 10 per cent slower, the hard drives 16 per cent slower, and the CD-ROM drives 23 per cent slower compared to Intel 430VX chipset boards. The company also reports unacceptably high return rates. On Internet computer newsgroups, you'll find numerous reports of failures and other stability problems.

This may be an apt place to repeat that if a deal sounds too good to be true, it's time to put your hand on your wallet to see if it's still there.

Phoenix (or Award or AMI) BIOS

The basic in/out system, or BIOS, chip acts in your system like both a traffic map and a traffic manager (in conjunction with the chipset). At one time we cared a lot about it because, in the pre-Pentium era, the skill of the BIOS programmers determined how "compatible" a system was (whether it could run all software and use all hardware designed for that class of computer).

It's still possible to get a poor BIOS, but writing the software is largely a mature art. You're more likely to get one that works well for whatever is available today, but it may fall short in running services and devices designed after the BIOS was written. This is why having the BIOS on what is technically known as an EPROM (erasable programmable read only memory) chip is a good idea. Popularly, a BIOS on an EPROM is known as a "flash" BIOS, and it can be updated using software. Once you get your new system it is a good idea to check the manufacturer's Web site periodically to see if there are any updates for your computer. You may discover you need a BIOS update to run certain hardware or software, to take advantage of certain services (such as Windows 9x's Advanced Power Management), or to make your system Year 2000 compliant. You may also get surprises, such as new services.

Many brand-name hardware manufacturers program their own BIOS software, but the three main third-party BIOS developers are Phoenix Technologies, Award Software, and American Megatrends International (AMI).

512 K PCI motherboard, 8 slots

The reference in this line of the ad to 512 K is to the amount of level 2 cache memory external to the processor, measured in kilobytes (KB). It may also say L2 cache or external cache. You'll want 128 KB as a minimum, but 512 KB should be enough. Without L2 cache memory there will be a performance drop equivalent to getting a processor one speed level lower than the one you just bought. It is not uncommon for some of the larger name-brand manufacturers to ship what they bill as low-cost systems without any cache memory at all. After you bought the computer is not the time to find out you don't have any or that you can't add any later even if you want to do so.

Note that the statement that the motherboard can accept up to 512 KB of cache memory doesn't mean it has that much on it. (Gotcha!)

Pentium II processors come in a cartridge that includes a cache memory module of either 256 KB or 512 KB. Some clever folks may be vague about exactly where the cache they're advertising is located.

Early Celeron systems at 266 and 300 MHz had no L2 cache attached to the processor and often had none on the motherboard, either. Designed to compete with products from AMD and Cyrix, these Celeron systems often performed poorly compared to the non-Intel alternatives as a result. Later Celerons, the 300A and 333 MHz renditions, had 128 KB of cache in the processor and produced performance exceeding Pentium II processors at the same speed.

If it isn't clear – particularly if you're being offered a 300 MHz Celeron – ask if it is the 300 without cache or the 300A with cache.

PCI (peripheral component interconnect) in the same line of the ad refers to the type of expansion slots on the motherboard. PCI slots generally are white (non-PCI are black), but simply because the ad says the board has them (there are no Pentium, Pentium II, or Celeron systems that don't), it doesn't mean that all the slots are PCI slots or that all are usable. Some slots may already be occupied by video and audio controllers. Some slots may be for AT-style industry standard architecture (ISA) boards. Almost certainly, one PCI slot will be so close to an ISA slot that you can use one or the other, but not both. Known as a "shared" slot, this is allowed in PCI specifications and in our example ad; what it really means is that although there may be eight slots, only seven will be usable at one time. Although Intel, Microsoft, and Compaq have published a set of guidelines known as the PC98 standards calling for the end of the shared slot, I expect the design to last well into 1999 and beyond, so long as there are people trading up from older computers who want to keep their old ISA adapters and peripherals to save a bit of money.

In systems with a small footprint case (see more on cases below), don't be surprised to see more than one pair of shared slots.

xx MB RAM

This line tells you the amount of memory installed on the motherboard. It should also tell you the type. Look for SDRAM (synchronous dynamic random access memory) or, at worst, the slightly slower

EDO RAM (extended data out memory) manufactured by a company with a name you recognize. Many of the better-known companies also manufacture memory, including, but not restricted to, NEC, Hitachi, Fujitsu, and Toshiba.

If SDRAM or EDO aren't specified, the memory may be the older and slower fast page mode (FPM) DRAM instead. Note that if the chipset was specified as 430TX, 440LX, 440BX, or 440EX, and the type of RAM isn't mentioned, something is odd. All support SDRAM. If the chipset isn't specified, it may be an older version that doesn't support SDRAM.

For Windows 9x, you'll want at least 32 MB of memory to be comfortable, but 64 MB will make you happier – particularly if you're planning to run graphics-intensive applications for photo retouching and the like. For Windows NT, start with 64 MB and buy more when you can.

Can you have too much memory in your new system? Yes, you can. If you have the 430TX or 430VX chipset, neither provides caching for memory over 64 MB. If you do add more, you can use it, but the result is that the system always runs at the speed of the slowest memory available, so the whole thing slows down, by as much as 20 per cent according to some published reports. This limitation does not occur with the 430HX chipset, the VIA Apollo VP2 or VP3, or with any of the Pentium II, Celeron, or Xeon chipsets. If, for some obscure reason, you decide to run the older Windows 3.1x and accompanying DOS 6.2x on your new computer, having more than 64 MB is simply a waste of money – neither will recognize more than 64 MB of RAM.

If you're running Windows 9x, however, the upper memory limit is more than most people you and I know will ever reach. In theory, Windows 9x can address up to 4 GB of RAM. In reality, it stops working if there is more than 2 GB in a system and may have problems in some brands of computer if there is more than 768 MB (just thought you'd like to know).

3.2 GB Ultra HDD

This line in our ad appears to indicate an EIDE (enhanced integrated drive electronics – aka ATA-3) type hard disk drive, with 3.2 gigabyte (GB) capacity, using the Ultra DMA scheme that allows it to transfer data to and from the system at a rate of up to 33 megabytes per second. (Note that some vendors, most notably Toshiba Canada, sometimes quote drive capacities in billions of bytes instead of gigabytes. Because of the vagaries of binary math and what happens when you convert from bytes to kilobytes to megabytes and gigabytes, this "billion byte" figure will be higher.)

If the ad doesn't also specify Intel 430TX, 440LX, 440BX, or 440EX, VIA Apollo VP2, VPX, or VP3, or ALI chipsets, the system does not support Ultra DMA.

If the motherboard does support Ultra DMA, and what you buy is supposed to be an Ultra DMA drive, does this mean you'll get 33 MB/sec throughput? Not necessarily. That's the current *upper* limit of the Ultra DMA "standard." It does not mean that either the controller on the motherboard or the specific model of hard drive will actually work that fast. (Gotcha!)

You'll need to ask for the drive's specifications. You'll be interested in knowing its **average access speed** (a combination of how long it takes to find a piece of data on the surface, plus the time it takes to read it), measured in milliseconds (ms). Twelve milliseconds or greater is slow. Ten milliseconds is average. Eight milliseconds or less is very, very fast. You can't feel a millisecond (at least I can't), but you can tell the difference between a slow and a fast drive.

You'll also want to hear about the drive's actual **transfer** or **throughput rate**, measured in megabytes per second (MB/sec) – how quickly the data, once found and read, gets moved. Note that some drive manufacturers (and some vendors) will quote the burst transfer rate instead of the sustained transfer rate you'll get most of the time. You'll want both.

1.44 FDD

This line in the ad describes a single, 3.5-inch floppy disk drive, which takes diskettes with the capacity to store up to 1.44 MB of data. This drive is a standard component and one is the normal number.

SVGA monitor 17" NI .28

Literally, this line says you'll get a Super Video Graphics Array-compatible monitor that is non-interlaced and has either a dot or a stripe pitch of .28 millimetres (mm). It doesn't say what range of resolutions it will support, what the viewable size actually is, what its vertical refresh rate is, or whether it's an aperture grille or shadow mask model. Baffled? Bear with me.

The term "resolution" refers to how many pixels are displayed on the screen. "Pixel" is short for picture element and represents the smallest area on the screen that the computer can change. Standard VGA resolution is 640 pixels per line across the screen and 480 lines (640 by 480). Other common resolutions include 800 by 600, 1024 by 768, 1152 by 920, 1200 by 1024, and 1600 by 1200. The cost of the monitor will rise depending on the upper resolution it can reproduce. See Chapter 13 for more detail and some hints about why screen size matters.

Today, you can forget about the difference between interlaced and non-interlaced monitors unless you're looking at a used system. Interlaced monitors have disappeared from the market for new systems. They flicker. Interlaced: not good.

All new monitors sold today are non-interlaced, but whether they flicker or not is determined by another factor: vertical refresh rate. You'll want to know how quickly the monitor refreshes its picture each second (expressed in Hertz, or Hz). The number you'll want to hear is 75 Hz or higher *at the resolution you wish to use* in order to avoid flicker. Non-interlaced: good.

Legislation requires the advertised diagonal size of a television set to be what you actually get. No so with computer monitors. Here, the screen size doesn't take into account the plastic mask around the screen. A 17-inch monitor usually provides a viewable diagonal size of about 15.6 inches. This actual viewable size will vary from brand to brand and from model to model within brands.

What we used to call the Trinitron tube now has a generic name because Sony lost the patent on its design. Although Sony still has the exclusive right to the name Trinitron, several companies manufacture monitors with Trinitron's rectangular grid. Generically, these monitors are now called aperture grille models. The alternative is a monitor that uses a mask filled with round dots, called a shadow mask.

The picture you see is composed of glowing dots (or stripes) and the spaces between them, and it's the size of the space that is measured in the dot pitch (shadow mask) or stripe pitch (aperture grille) figure. The distance measured is the distance between two dots or stripes of the same colour expressed in hundredths of a millimetre. The smaller the number, the smaller the space and the sharper the picture. A shadow mask monitor with a dot pitch of 0.28 mm is about average. One with 0.26 mm will produce an exceptionally sharp image (and is the closest to a stripe pitch of 0.25 mm). If the dot or stripe pitch number isn't included, you may be looking at a low-end monitor with a grainy image (0.39 or 0.43 mm) that you won't like.

By the way, if the system price is very low, look for "monitor not included" in the fine print.

2 MB DRAM, 64-bit (or 128-bit) SVGA video MPEG

This line suggests you're getting an SVGA-compatible video graphics controller with 2 MB of memory. It implies that this controller is a 64-bit piece of hardware and that it includes Motion Picture Experts Group (MPEG) decoding for motion video. It does not say whether the controller is on a separate graphics card using ISA (industry standard architecture), PCI (peripheral component interconnect), or AGP (accelerated graphics port). It doesn't mention whether it is integrated into the motherboard or provided through a special CPU–companion chip combination such as the Cyrix MediaGX (more about this in Chapter 7). It doesn't say whether you can add memory to the controller and, although in this case it specifies DRAM, the ad may be vague about the type of memory included (and it does matter).

What you want to know about the video controller is how quickly it moves information around on the screen, how many colours it provides and at what range of resolutions, how quickly it accelerates motion, and whether it provides 3-D rendering for games.

The speed of a video graphics controller is partially determined by the accelerator chipset it uses and by the type of memory is has, neither of which are specified in the ad. "SVGA" refers to a standard of sorts, but not one that anyone has taken seriously for many years. The amount of memory on the card (1 MB, 2 MB, 4 MB, 8 MB) merely tells us how many colours we can see at increasingly high resolutions. With 2 MB, you'll be able to see 65,535 colours at 1024 by 768. To see 16.7 million colours (needed only by people heavily into image retouching or artwork), you need to either use a lower resolution (800 by 600) or have more than 2 MB of memory on the card.

If the controller does have 3-D rendering and acceleration features, additional memory (8 MB was hot in early 1998) will help.

Most video controllers use slower DRAM. Some use EDO RAM. Others use faster SGRAM (synchronous graphics RAM), VRAM, or WRAM. At least this ad is up-front about the quality of this one (not great). There will be more about these memory types in Chapter 8.

Sixty-four-bit and 128-bit video cards send data internally among their own components 64 or 128 bits at a time. This has nothing to do with the number of colours you can see (it's a speed factor). It also has nothing to do with how many bits of data are exchanged between the graphics card and the CPU in any one cycle. The PCI slot architecture for PCs running Pentium, Pentium II, Celeron, Xeon, or equivalent processors is 32-bit. Period.

MPEG (motion picture experts group) is a method used to compress (encode) and decompress (decode) motion video you'll find on the Internet, in games, and especially on digital video/versatile disc movies. It works best if it's done through special circuitry on the video controller or through a separate circuit board. But just because you see it mentioned in an ad doesn't mean that's what happens. MPEG decoding can also occur through software emulation, which puts a heavy load on the central processor, resulting in jerky pictures and poor quality if videos are viewed full-screen instead of in a tiny window. MPEG also comes in two standards, MPEG-1 and a newer version, MPEG-2. (If you have MPEG-2, you can view MPEG-1 and -2 files; if you only have MPEG-1, you cannot view MPEG-2 files.) This ad doesn't tell us how it's done or to which standard.

24X (to 40X) CD-ROM

In this line, the "X" doesn't refer to a number, but means "times as fast" as the very first CD-ROM drives on the market. Although this CD-ROM drive says it is 24X, it delivers average performance equivalent to 12X (but it sounds good). I'll explain this in more detail for the curious in Chapter 10.

DVD-ROM drive

DVD-ROM originally meant digital video disc-read only memory, but you will occasionally see marketing material that calls them digital versatile disc drives. These are playback units; they don't record. You know you're getting an up-to-date DVD-ROM drive if all of the following are true:

- It says 2X (or greater) *and* it has a data transfer rate of 2760 KB/sec or higher.
- It says the drive will accept double-sided, dual-layer discs with a capacity of 17 GB. There were no DVD discs with this capacity in late 1998, but you'd like to be able to read them if there ever are any.
- It says "multi-read" or explicitly states that the drive will read CD-R (recordable) and CD-RW (rewritable) discs.
- It says the drive supports MPEG and digital Dolby (formerly AC-3) decoding in hardware.
- CD-ROM playback speed is 20X or higher.

Otherwise, you may have discovered why the system includes a DVD-ROM drive at such a low, low price.

There's more on DVD and the issue of CD-R and CD-RW discs, as well as a discussion of the state of recordable DVD, in Chapter 10.

16-bit Sound Blaster compatible

This refers to the system's audio controller, which, like video, can be on its own circuit board, wired to the motherboard, or come as part of a MediaGX processor/support chip combo. "Compatible" here – and elsewhere – means it works just like the real thing, sort of, some of the time, mostly. If you want the quality and compatibility across a wide range of software products provided by one of Creative Labs' Sound Blaster products, you won't get it from a cheaper "Sound Blaster compatible" knockoff. This doesn't mean that there aren't competing audio controller products that can provide good service. You'll find all sorts of competing products in Chapter 11.

Eight-bit sound cards have disappeared from the market and I doubt you could find one even if you looked. "Sound Blaster compatible" means it uses FM synthesis to extrapolate sounds purely from numbers. A sound controller that explicitly says wave table synthesis extrapolates sounds from samples of actual sound stored in its memory. The resulting quality is better (see Chapter 11 for an explanation of the difference between FM synthesis and wave table synthesis).

Other audio controller compatibility buzzwords include "business audio" (Microsoft Sound System compatible and not good for DOS games).

56K modem

This line says there's going to be a modem in the system. It also implies that it will run at 56 kilobits per second (Kbps). It doesn't say which standard it uses to achieve "56K" or reveal anything else about it. While you will want to know the brand of the modem, the more important issue, at least until early 1999 when the problem should be resolved, is the identity of the "56K" standard.

When "56K" modems first appeared on the scene there were two incompatible "standards" developed by USRobotics (now owned by 3Com – the X2 standard) and Rockwell Industries in conjunction with Lucent Technologies (the K56*flex* standard). Because each scheme required a special modem to be at the sending end in order to function at anything higher than 33.6 Kbps, whichever standard was employed had to be explicitly supported by your Internet Service Provider.

At the beginning of 1998, the battle between the two camps came to an end. The International Telecommunications Union (ITU) came up with a compromise, dubbed V.90, that allowed both camps to save face. The result was supposed (at least in theory) to allow users to upgrade whichever type of modem they had to the new scheme.

In the summer of 1998, it was possible for a consumer to purchase a brand-name "56K" modem using X2, K56*flex*, or V.90. Unfortunately, it was also possible to purchase an off-brand "56K" modem using either X2 or K56*flex* that couldn't be upgraded.

Look for a modem that has some specific characteristics. It should be from a mainstream company, it should be advertised as a V.90 modem, and it should have a flash BIOS (which can be upgraded by software). You also need to check with your Internet Service Provider (ISP) to ensure that your choice is a standard it supports.

We'll have a fuller discussion of the alternatives (standard modems, ISDN, ADSL, cable, satellite, and so on) in Chapter 11, but for now, there's one last point. The X2, K56*flex*, and V.90 standards are "asymmetric." In other words, the speed you get is different, depending on the direction the data is travelling. The data you send (upload) goes out at 33.6 Kbps. Only the data coming back to you (download) arrives at the faster speed, and only then if the location sending it has a special modem that's set up to do so. Transmissions between you and your buddy will be at the slower speed in both directions.

To make it even more fun, *no one* I know who tests these things (including me) has ever managed to receive data at 56 Kbps outside a lab (or unless they lived right next door to their ISP). Still, even at 44, 46, or 48 Kbps, these modems are slightly faster than the old V.34bis standard speed of 33.6 Kbps.

If your ISP still hasn't upgraded its equipment to V.90 and you have to choose blind, as a guideline, it helps to know that the majority of ISPs have X2 setups, while the majority of modem hardware manufacturers prefer K56*flex*. Various independent tests have determined that X2 modems consistently connect at a higher speed than K56*flex* models *unless* you live in an area with really bad-quality phone lines, where K56*flex* models appear to do better.

Free mouse

Sure, tell me another one. If it's cheap enough to be given away, expect to be buying a better one in a month or so. A line such as this, or one that says "free software," is hoping you were born yesterday.

104 keyboard or Win95 (Win98) keyboard

All standard PC keyboards have 104 keys. "Win95" or "Win98" key-boards have an extra key on both sides of the spacebar. They're used to call up the Start Menu as well as providing some other nifty short-cuts. (For example, hold down the WinKey – don't say it too fast – and hit M. All open windows on your desktop will minimize to the taskbar. Hold down the WinKey and Shift, then hit M to restore them.)

A "Windows 95 (98) keyboard" does *not* necessarily mean it's a Microsoft Natural Keyboard. By the way, there are at least two or three inexpensive boards on the market that *look* like the Natural board, but they don't tilt down and away from you – the factor about it that most relieves wrist stress.

2s/1p/1g

This line tells you about the external ports, indicating two serial ports, one parallel (printer) port, and one game port. A surprising number of ads are leaving this line out on the assumption that "everyone knows" that's what you get. No, they don't. To save a few cents, the motherboard connector for a second serial port may exist, but the external port connector and tiny cable used to wire it to the mother-board may have gone AWOL – or the second serial connector may be gone entirely.

More important is whether the model has Universal Serial Bus (USB) ports (having two of them is about right). If it doesn't, the ad will be silent. If it does, there'll be a mention – count on it. ***Do not buy a computer that doesn't have USB ports.***

Also talk to the vendor about adding a second parallel port. Although the parallel ports were once exclusively used by printers, today everyone and her maiden aunt is providing devices that use it, including external CD-ROM (as well as CD-R and CD-RW) drives, Zip drives and other removable storage devices, low-cost scanners, and so on. The recent pressure on the parallel port may be relieved by widespread use of USB, but I suspect these parallel port products will be around for some time to come until USB gains wide acceptance and a broad, installed base of systems with USB ports.

You may also wish to consider a second port because not all of these devices work and play well with others. Some printers don't understand parallel port sharing, and virtually every device I've tested has warned in the documentation not to put anything else except a printer on the same port.

Mini-tower case, 5 drive bays, 250W power supply

Whether a case is a desktop case (which lies flat) or a tower case (which stands on its short edge) has no effect on system performance. Whether the tower case is mini-, mid-, or full-sized is determined by the eye of the beholder. There is no recognized standard of measurement that determines which is which.

If you're purchasing the case separately, however, keep in mind that all cases are not interchangeable. If you plan to use an AT-style "Socket 7" motherboard typical to Pentium, Pentium MMX, AMD, Centaur/IDT, or Cyrix/IBM-based systems, that's one case configuration. If you're planning to install a Pentium II or Celeron-based motherboard, it will use the "ATX" form factor and needs a specially designed case to do the job. If you're purchasing a complete system, this won't be an issue, *unless* you're planning to upgrade later. Is there a brand of case that will accommodate both types of board? If there is, no one I know who builds systems for a living is willing to tell me about it. If you find one, let me know.

You should care about the number of available drive bays to aid in future expansion and upgrade. You should care even more about how many are free for you to use. But you'll care a lot more about how many bays open to the front of the case (you need this for adding drives, such as a DVD drive, with removable media). You'll also like to have an idea of how wide they are (CD-ROM and DVD drives require 5.25-inch openings; hard drives, floppy drives, most tape drives, and many other removable storage devices use 3.5-inch openings).

Of course, not all cases or power supplies are the same (just like the other components in the system). The power supply is usually sold as part of the case, and a low-quality (low-price) case may have one that lasts to the end of its warranty if you're lucky (and perhaps it won't fry your motherboard or drives when it dies if you're even luckier). Figuring out how many watts you need from the power supply is a black art. See Chapter 14 for more details.

Software included

If you don't get the shrink-wrapped software manuals with appropriate authentication stickers and registration cards, the retailer may have installed illegal copies of the software, which means you can't get help from the software developer when it starts acting weirdly. You should also get original disks or CDs or at least instructions detailing how to make backup copies of the software if you should ever need to reinstall it after something goes wrong.

Even in systems where the software is legitimate (as you would expect it to be from a nationally advertised brand name and most local retailers), you may not be getting what you think you're getting. Check to see how many of the offered titles are "lite" or "special edition" (SE) or "demonstration" versions that either don't have as many features as the real thing or quit working after a limited number of times they're used. Quite often, "free software" is merely a marketing gimmick to get you to buy the full version.

6

Processors

The problem I face in writing this chapter is the long lead-time in book publishing. Given the speed with which the computer industry changes, by the time you get this book, there will be new or improved components on the market.

Part of the solution to this dilemma is to share some observations I've made over the years that I'm sure will continue to be valid far into the future. I've already noted that the price of existing technology *always* goes down. New products arrive at the old top price and push everything older one notch down the list. Intel also has a habit of reducing prices on selected processors every three months or so, and the rest of the processor industry follows suit. So, no matter what is the leading processor of the day, it will be less expensive as soon as a newer model arrives.

It's also true that you will pay a premium for whatever is at the leading edge, simply because it *is* the leading edge. However, you may not get enough of an improvement in performance to justify the added cost. That's why virtually every computer pundit I know advises that one to two steps back from the top is where you get the most performance for the cash outlay (also known as "the sweet spot").

CPUs

Regardless of the type of computer you have, there is a chip at its heart that turns what would otherwise be a useless set of electronic components into an amazing machine capable of performing complex tasks. The chip is called the central processing unit (CPU), or the microprocessor, or simply the processor – and whether you buy a PC or a PowerMac, you'll get one.

Mainframes and early minicomputers contained circuit boards full of integrated circuits that made up the central processing unit. Single-chip central processing units are called microprocessors, and they made personal computers and workstations possible. The first microprocessor was developed in 1971 by a California company named Intel.

Examples of single-chip CPUs are the Motorola 68000, 68020, 68030, 68040, MPC601, MPC603, MPC603e, MPC604, and MPC604e chips. The 68000 series is what you'll find in Macs. The MPC60x series shows up in PowerPCs and PowerMacs. Despite some attempts to develop competing products in the mid-1990s, Motorola remains the sole supplier of CPUs for these types of computer.

The sole supplier of CPUs for the PC crowd used to be Intel. Its 8080, 8088, 8086, 80286, 80386, 80486, Pentium, Pentium MMX, Pentium Pro, Pentium II, Celeron, and Xeon processors are still inside about 85 per cent of all microcomputers on the planet. Unlike Motorola, Intel does have some serious competition (see below under "Intel wannabes").

David went with Dell?

What do CPUs do?

Reading this and the next few sections will help you to understand some of what goes on inside your computer, but when you come right down to it, you don't have to understand this stuff in order to use your system. If you want to skip ahead to the section below on current trends (which may help you to decide which CPU to buy in a new PC), go ahead.

At the simplest level, all a CPU does is add fast, but it also has the ability to fetch, decode, and execute instructions. The CPU can

What Does the CPU Do?

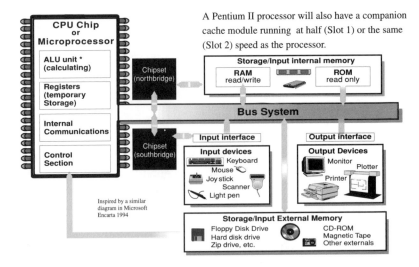

also transfer information to and from other resources over the computer's main data-transfer path, or bus. It is the chip that functions as the "brain" of a computer.

Everything that a CPU does is based on one operation: the ability to determine if a tiny transistor switch, or "gate," is open or closed. The CPU can recognize only two states in any of its microscopic circuits: on or off, high voltage or low voltage, represented by the binary numbers 1 and 0.

The speed at which the computer performs this simple act, however, is what makes it a marvel of modern technology. In essence, it sits there, ticking like a clock. On each "tick" something can happen. The speed at which the CPU ticks is often called the "clock speed" because of this similarity. It is measured in megahertz (MHz), or millions of cycles per second.

MHz isn't everything

How fast the CPU "ticks" is not the only way of determining how powerful it is or how a given computer system with a particular CPU will perform. CPU power is also determined by the amount of data it can handle during each "tick." If a computer checks only one switch at a time, that switch can represent only two commands – ON (or 1) to execute one operation or number, and OFF (or 0). By checking groups of switches linked as a unit, however, the computer increases the number of operations it can execute at each cycle.

Early microprocessors were generally able to check eight switches at a time. That is, they could check eight binary digits, or "bits," of data, during each tick or cycle. A group of eight bits is called a byte, and each byte contains 256 possible patterns of 1s and 0s.

The subsequent development of processors that can handle 16, 32, and 64 bits of data at a time has increased the overall speed of computers. The complete collection of recognizable patterns, the total list of operations of which a computer is capable, is called its instruction set. All factors – number of bits at a time, size of instruction sets, and the speed of the clock cycle – affect how much power is available from any given CPU.

Maybe this example will help you to visualize why the factors are related. Imagine a single-lane highway full of commuters in rush hour. The speed limit (the clock cycle) is the same for all vehicles on the road. However, some vehicles are carrying eight passengers (bits), while others are carrying 16, 32, or 64. All the vehicles would travel from one point to another at the same speed, but the larger vehicles (the instruction set) would deliver more people to their destination in the same amount of time.

So, a 16-bit CPU, such as the Intel AT-80286 or Motorola 68020, will have a slower processing rate than a 32-bit CPU, such as the 80386 and 80486 or the Motorola 68030 and 68040, even though they're all running at the same speed.

Now imagine that our single-lane highway becomes a freeway. Instead of having one lane, it has two in each direction. Congratulations; you've just figured out a fundamental difference between the Pentium-class processors and their predecessors. (They can process two 32-bit instructions at the same time.)

Apparent overall system speed is another issue. Two apparently identical computers running side by side can appear to perform quite differently. The video controller, disk controller, the disk drives themselves,

RAM chip speed, whether the CPU and/or system itself has a memory cache, the base speed of the motherboard, and the timing speed of the memory – these all make a difference.

Some examples? Add 256 KB of external (level 2 or L2) cache memory to a system without any cache and performance will increase 26 to 31 per cent. Get rid of that video graphics card in its old ISA slot running on the slow (8 MHz) ISA bus and replace it with an accelerated SVGA card running in a PCI slot on the faster (33 MHz) PCI bus and watch overall system performance appear to jump about 43 per cent. Take a hard drive with 15 milliseconds (ms) average access time and a built-in 64 KB cache buffer, then replace it with a hard drive with 8 ms average access, 10,000 rpm spin rate, and a 256 KB cache buffer, and your system performance will increase by about 20 per cent or more.

Current trends

The North American computer press was underwhelmed in mid-1998 by the performance differences between the 266 MHz Pentium II and its 300 and 333 MHz successors. When Intel introduced the 300 MHz Pentium II, various industry sources performing independent benchmark tests reported just a 3 to 5 per cent performance improvement over the older 266 MHz version. Likewise, the 266 MHz Pentium MMX desktop and "Tillamook" mobile versions of the processor showed a similar small increase. In the past, when the MHz numbers got bigger, they usually translated directly into performance improvements that were more or less in line with the increase. So what happened?

The remainder of this explanation will, of necessity, contain some numbers. Sorry about that.

If we look back to the 486 and early Pentium eras, new processors generally meant large increases in overall system performance. But that was before Intel started ramping up the internal speed of the processors while leaving the system's motherboard base speed the same.

PC processors and the motherboards to which they were attached once ran at the same speed. Data exchanged between the processor and RAM, as well as data transferred among various internal parts of the processor, travelled at the same rate.

Remember our freeway? In this case, it's the motherboard. Imagine that it ends in an office block full of elevators (the CPU). Regardless of the number of bits (er, passengers) arriving on the freeway at any one time, everybody gets to the office block at the same rate. Once they arrive, they also move up the building's elevators at the same speed. Are you with me so far?

When Intel introduced first the 486DX2, then 486DX4, processors, it introduced the idea of increasing the internal speed of the processor (the elevators), but not of the motherboard (the freeway). To be more accurate, they didn't change the speed of the main pathway on the motherboard that connected the processor to memory and other components, known as the system bus.

If we stick with our freeway/elevator scenario, passengers (er, data) arrived at the same old rate, but once they reached the building they were able to whip around inside it more quickly (and presumably get to spend time at more water coolers as a result).

At that point the wheels fell off most average users' understanding of exactly what went on inside their computer and how processor speed and performance were related. The first "clock-doubled" processor, the 486DX2, ran at 66 MHz *but only inside the processor.* The base speed of the motherboard's system bus remained at 33 MHz. This did produce better overall performance, but not as much as if both had been given a speed increase.

For those of you who want all the details, the 486DX4 was actually a clock-*tripled* processor, despite the use of "4" in the name, but that's a story for another campfire.

Now we come to the Pentium and all its children. The original Pentium processor came in two flavours, designed to run on either a 60 or 66 MHz main system bus. It came as a 60 or 66 MHz chip, so once again, everybody got a whopping speed increase. The Pentium system bus speed hasn't increased since, although as we'll see that's not entirely true of newer Pentium II systems (keep reading).

Up to the 333 MHz Pentium II and including the Basic PC Celeron processor family, the motherboard base speed stayed the same so that all Pentium, Pentium MMX, Celeron, and Pentium II processor internal speeds were multiples of 60 or 66 MHz. You're beginning, I hope, to get a glimmer of why recent overall performance increases haven't been huge. A 266 MHz processor runs internally at four times the 66 MHz system bus speed. A 300 MHz processor is only four and a half times the same speed, while a 333 MHz processor is just five times faster. To go from 300 to 333 MHz is about a 10 per cent increase in terms of raw numbers, but that increase isn't reflected in overall performance and will vary slightly depending on the brand and design of the motherboard.

PC performance is partially a product of the processor, but there are a number of other factors that affect it. Motherboard system bus speed is a biggie. Memory speed is also a factor, and memory timing is yet another. The expansion slot pathway to the processor as well as the pathway used by the peripheral component interconnect (PCI) bus is another. Size and speed of external cache memory are others – and so it goes.

Beginning April 15, 1998, it was possible to get a motherboard running at 100 MHz with Intel's 440BX AGPset. Along with the new motherboard chipset, Intel released two Pentium II processors at 350 and 400 MHz that would only run on a 100 MHz system bus. In this case, although these chips use 3.5x and 4x internal multipliers, the difference in performance between the 333 MHz Pentium II on a 66 MHz system bus and the 350 MHz Pentium II on a 100 MHz system bus is closer to 30 per cent.

In the summer of 1998, Intel raised the bar again, adding a 450 MHz Pentium II. If we don't see 500 MHz and more in 1999, I'll be very surprised. Even faster processors, both in the Pentium II and other categories, are sure to follow, but now we come full circle to where we started. Don't expect each new revision to give the same large performance improvement we got from 486 to Pentium and from 66 MHz motherboards to 100 MHz boards. Your homework assignment is to keep an eye on the processor market.

Traditionally, Intel announces price reductions on its processors every quarter (toward the end of January, April, July, and October), and system price reductions rapidly follow. Your best bet for performance versus price will still be one or two steps back from *whatever* is the leading edge of the day.

You'll also want to keep your eye on the trailing edge of the market so you don't get caught there. Processor families generally have a life span of about five years, during which their internal speed goes up and some tweaking gets done. Just before a processor falls off the market and drops out of sight, it's often given a push by the introduction of a completely new family. Processors at the trailing edge can usually, albeit with a struggle and not too quickly, run whatever is the operating system of the day. Within a very short period of time, however, the software "improves" to the point where it will not run on a trailing-edge system quickly enough to be satisfying (if it runs at all). Saving money by buying at the trailing edge may be a necessity, but it will not provide much longevity – and with the introduction of Intel's Celeron, AMD's K6-2, and the Cyrix/IBM M II, there are better alternatives.

During the Intel era, we've seen its numbering scheme for processors (286, 386, and 486) give way to names. What we know today as the Pentium would have been the 586. During the Pentium's lifetime, Intel added 57 new instructions to it, covering what the company called "natural data types" – sound, video animation, and telecommunications – otherwise known as MultiMedia eXtensions, or MMX. Think of the Pentium MMX as the 586a. By the way, it might be appropriate to have a moment of silence to mark the passing of the Pentium MMX. By fall 1998, Intel had stopped producing new Pentium MMX wafers and announced it would sell no more past the end of the year. The MMX joins the Pentium, the 486, 386, 286, and XT on a shelf somewhere in the Smithsonian. It's dead, Jim.

When what might have been called the 686 arrived on the market, Intel said it had too much product identification tied to the name Pentium to change it. The "686" became the Pentium Pro. When it, too, received the MMX package, the Pentium Pro became the Pentium II.

Permit a small digression, because it will come in handy in a moment. Physically, the Pentium, Pentium MMX, AMD K6 and K6-2, Cyrix 6x86 and M II (formerly 6x86MX) connect to a motherboard through a socket called Socket 7. I won't bore you with the technical details, except to say that it's a variation of the traditional chip-plugs-into-socket format for PC processors since their inception. The Pentium II, however, isn't visible to you. It comes in a cartridge with an edge connector similar to that found on circuit boards (known as the SECC – single-edged cartridge connector). It also doesn't fit the traditional socket. Instead, it slides into a newer architectural design, known as Slot 1. It's one of the primary reasons you cannot upgrade a Pentium or Pentium MMX system to Pentium II, unless you replace the entire motherboard and case. Now, back to our story.

More recently, Intel decided to reverse its marketing strategy and rely on the "Intel Inside" logo as its primary product identifier. The company announced that it would produce processors for four levels of computer user. Celeron, a Pentium II introduced initially without a companion cache module (although it still has its internal 16 KB data and instruction caches), would be the family for the "basic PC." Aimed at systems selling for under $1,500 Cdn (under $1,000 US), the Celeron family is designed for people on a budget and people for whom its performance is "good enough" to run basic software. When it was first released, however, the cacheless 266 and 300 MHz Celeron weren't good enough for most consumers. Products from both AMD and Cyrix handily out-performed them. At press time, Intel revised its strategy, introducing the 300 and 333 MHz Celeron "A" with 128 KB internal cache. The slower model was dubbed the 300A to distinguish it from the original, cacheless 300.

Interestingly, the cache in these new Celerons runs at the same speed as the processor. The cache in a Pentium II, however, runs at half the speed of the processor (different design). The result was a surprise to most analysts. The 300A and 333 MHz Celerons outperform Pentium II processors at the same speed (and at about two-thirds of the cost) even though the Celeron's 128 KB of cache memory is less than the Pentium II's.

You're most likely to base part of your choice on performance reports of whatever the current Celerons are, compared to similarly priced parts from AMD or others. However, there are other concerns to think about.

The first Celeron processors also fit Slot 1. However, the attachment mechanism that holds them in place, the so-called goalposts, is physically different from the mechanism for the Pentium II. As a result, you cannot upgrade a Celeron-based system to a full-blown Pentium II, again, unless you replace the entire motherboard. (Gotcha!) Then, in October 1998, Intel announced that it was taking the Celeron out of Slot 1 and that by the end of the year it would introduce a new socket-based version, also with cache, running at the same speed as earlier models. However, there will still be no upgrade path from Celeron to anything else without a motherboard transplant. (Gotcha again!)

At the other end of the Intel spectrum comes the Xeon family, with faster Pentium II processors on motherboards with chipsets capable of supporting multiple processors. Xeon systems will use Slot 2 (which is physically slightly longer than Slot 1, so once again, you cannot upgrade from Pentium II to Xeon). Xeon processors will have more cache memory in their cartridges, and it will run at the same speed as the processor. Intel says these systems will be designed for the corporate server market (and are priced appropriately).

In the middle are two more categories with somewhat vaguer descriptions. The Performance PC is designed and priced to be attractive to corporate and small business users as low-maintenance workstations. The Enthusiast PC will be designed for the arch-gamers and power users in the crowd. Processors for both of these system categories will retain the Pentium II name, but will be distinguished by more or less cache memory and differences in component mix. Performance PCs may come with integrated networking built in as well as remote diagnostic features, but lack sophisticated sound features. Enthusiast PCs are likely to contain the latest in multimedia gadgetry, including Pentium II and Xeon processors with enhanced multimedia instructions.

Two new Intel CPUs will be released in early 1999. Katmai is a Slot 1, Pentium II processor, with 70 new multimedia instructions. Dubbed Katmai new instructions, or KNI, they may also be called the MMX-2.

Tanner is a new Xeon processor (Slot 2) with the same new instructions as the Katmai and the ability, with proper chipset and motherboard, to use up to 2 MB of L2 cache memory in a four-processor system.

Initial speed of both Katmai and Tanner will be 450 MHz, and both will use 100 MHz motherboards.

Intel wannabes

While you research processors, you're bound to consider the non-Intel alternatives from Advanced Micro Devices (AMD), National Semiconductor (Cyrix), Centaur/IDT (WinChip), and anyone else who jumps on this train as time passes. There are more fundamental choices to make today (see Chapter 7 on motherboards), but there will be Intel competitors for the foreseeable future – and that's good. I have no particular fondness for Intel. Without competitors, Intel would have no real reason to innovate or to keep its prices down. Nevertheless, AMD and Cyrix have histories worth noting, and I am concerned that you get what you think you're paying for.

AMD

Advanced Micro Devices (AMD) has been a thorn in Intel's side for a long time. During both the 386 and 486 eras, AMD released processors that rivalled the performance of Intel's, but it didn't fare nearly as well in the Pentium era. Its K5 processor never matched Intel products successfully, ran into production shortfalls, and was plagued with reports of odd behaviour. AMD also adopted the PR, or "Power Rated," system of reporting the part's performance. Under this scheme, a set of benchmark tests is done, then compared to tests run on Intel products. If the results are close, the competing processor is given a speed "Power Rating" (PR) that is more of a marketing number than fact (the actual speed of the processor is less).

Then came the Pentium II and AMD's K6 and K6-2. With these particular processors, AMD was right on the money. The company dropped the PR system and now reports its processors' actual speed. When tested against Pentium II processors at the same speed, the K6 often exceeds the PII's performance, at least with "business applications." Although the K6 includes the MMX instruction set, it doesn't do quite as well with multimedia or floating point operations (but the differences aren't staggering). The K6 is, I believe – Intel's denials notwithstanding – one of the main reasons Intel produced the Celeron.

By mid-1998, AMD had upped the ante with the K6-2. Still able to run on a Socket 7 motherboard, the K6-2 could support a 100 MHz system bus (using the VIA Apollo VP3 chipset or its children). It also adds additional multimedia enhancements beyond MMX, including "3D Now" for in-processor three-dimensional rendering. If AMD keeps to this trend, it will continue to have viable products for some time.

Cyrix

Now for Cyrix and its curious history. I consider Cyrix's marketing practices to be the least appetizing of the non-Intel crowd. You'll remember that Intel stopped using numbers (286, 386, 486) to describe its processors. Cyrix is one of the reasons why.

Intel found it couldn't trademark a number when Cyrix was producing 386 processors and calling them 486s. The part ran just enough of the 486 instruction set to allow it to be identified as a 486 by any software that asked, but functionally it was a 386 in everything but name.

From the beginning, Cyrix has had no fabrication plants of its own (it's a so-called *fabless* manufacturer), which is where IBM comes into the picture. Despite owning some fabrication facilities, Cyrix's new parent company, National Semiconductor, still allows Big Blue to make all Cyrix processors. Then IBM puts its name on some of them and sells them in its low-end systems. In the 486 era, for example, we saw IBM's "Blue Lightning" – a Cyrix 386 chip with another name.

Cyrix has continued its name games into the Pentium era. For example, its 5x86, upon which the MediaGX chips are based, isn't a 586 or Pentium equivalent; it's a 486 that runs some of the Pentium instruction set. The Cyrix 6x86 and M II (formerly 6x86MX) aren't 686 or Pentium II equals, either; they're substitutes for the classic Pentium and Pentium MMX.

Cyrix continues to play the Power Rating game as well. In independent tests, its processors come close to the Pentium MMX in running business applications, even though their actual speed is not the same as the PR number advertised, falling woefully behind on multimedia and floating point operations.

Now we come to the Cyrix-designed MediaGX, which you may still find in some low-end IBM and Compaq systems (although both the MediaGX and 6x86 family were steadily losing ground to AMD as 1998 got older).

On the surface the MediaGX sounds good, but by most definitions it barely qualifies as a processor. This chip, together with a companion chip, provides multimedia services such as video graphics, sound, and telecommunications without the need for additional controllers – a big step toward lowering overall system cost. However, to put it bluntly, the resulting performance sucks.

The MediaGX is based on the 5x86 noted above, which Cyrix's Web site defines as an advanced 486 processor. It doesn't use the traditional processor system bus; it uses the peripheral PCI expansion bus instead, so already it's running on a base speed of 33, not 66, MHz. The overall effect, reported by several benchmark testers, is poor performance. To cite just one example, the MediaGX PR120 performed slower than a 100 MHz Pentium. Its multimedia and floating point numbers were awful. Trust me, this is not the system you want when there are kids around looking for a good multimedia experience.

Centaur/IDT

Whether Centaur/IDT (Independent Device Technology) will remain in the market remains to be seen. Although its initial WinChips, running at just under 200 and just under 233 MHz (the company at least reports actual, not an estimated, speed), did well against similarly performing Pentium MMX systems with business applications, it, too, fared poorly with multimedia and floating point operations. Still, I wish them, and their more recent WinChip-4, luck.

Last, but not least, although Cyrix and AMD have both hinted broadly that they may in future bring Slot 1 design processors to market, both their and the Centaur/IDT products currently use Socket 7. To upgrade to an Intel Pentium II, your only choice will be to replace both the motherboard and most likely the case (to account for the different, ATX form factor used in Pentium II motherboards).

This just in

Just before we went to press, two new developments occurred in AMD's processor plans. Within weeks of this book appearing in stores, AMD will release the K6-3, formerly code-named "Sharptooth." Based on the K6 and K6-2, it will also feature the "3D-Now" instruction set. However, it will start at 350 MHz (rising eventually to 450), use 100 MHz motherboards, and, for the first time in AMD's K6 history, contain an on-die level 2 cache of 256 KB.

Later, "in the first half of 1998," says AMD's published plans, the company will release the K7 processor and introduce a new era. This chip will not use Socket 7; instead it will use "Slot A" designed for the Digital Alpha bus. Initial speeds will start at 500 MHz. The K7 will use **200 MHz** motherboards and come with on-die cache sizes ranging from 256 KB to 8 MB during its life cycle.

Not to be outdone, Intel has also revealed part of its future plans. Before the arrival of the 64-bit Merced in 2000 (or later) and its 32-bit introductory model in mid-1999, the company will introduce a chip currently code-named "Coppermine," based on a 0.18 micron manufacturing process. Initial speeds will start at 500 MHz, and a mobile version, along with a mobile version of the Celeron, is planned.

Processors

Chip	Name	Made by	Long Name	Speeds	Details
Anything earlier than a Pentium	XT, AT, AT-286, 286, 386 DX or SX, 486 DX or SX, DX2, SX2, DX4	Intel, AMD, Cyrix, IBM	eXtended Technology, Advanced Technology, 80286, 80386, 80486	4.77 to 133 MHz	Running older software, primarily DOS character-based. If 386 or better, can run Windows 3.1x. Extending memory to 16 MB, adding faster graphics controller, hard drive controller and larger hard drive could extend your 486 for a few years, particularly if you also add a 486 DX4 OverDrive chip from Intel. Otherwise, these processors are no longer produced and are considered obsolete.
Pentium	Formerly 80586, then P5		Pentium	60, 66, 75, 90, 100, 120, 133, 150, 166, 200 MHz	A fundamental change over the 486-class processor. Runs Windows 9x well enough. The "classic" Pentium without MMX instructions is no longer produced and is considered obsolete.
Pentium P55c	Pentium MMX (would have been 80586 without the name)	Intel	Pentium with MMX (MultiMedia eXtensions) Technology	150/166, 180/200, 233, 266 MHz (Socket 7)	The MMX is faster than the classic Pentium, but still slower than a Pentium II. It is still optimized for 16-bit software, but includes instruction extensions to directly deal with audio, video, 3-D acceleration and telecommunications. All Intel processors now have MMX extensions. The MMX is no longer produced and is supplied from stock. Obsolete.
Pentium Pro	Formerly P6 (would have been 80686 without the name)	Intel	Pentium Pro	150, 200 MHz	Runs pure 32-bit software such as Windows NT, OS/2 or Unix about three times faster than a Pentium or Pentium MMX. Runs 16-bit software, including Windows 9x, slightly slower than a Pentium of the same speed. Now used almost exclusively as multi-processor business servers (see Pentium II, below). Not a consumer product.
Pentium II	Formerly Klamath	Intel	Pentium Pro with MMX Technology	233, 266, 300, 333, 350, 400 MHz and more	Leading edge for consumer systems through to early 1999. To use models faster than 350 MHz requires a motherboard running at 100 MHz and Intel 440BX chipset or more recent. Uses Slot 1, comes in a closed cartridge with up to 512 K of L2 cache running at half the speed of the processor. Due to be replaced by "Katmai," a Pentium II with 70 new multimedia instructions (Katmai New Instructions or KNI) in early 1999. Coming later in 1999: "Coppermine," a smaller "Katmai" (0.18 micron).
Celeron	Celeron	Intel	Celeron	266, 300, 333 MHz (Slot 1)	Pentium II at its core. Celeron is Intel's "Basic PC" processor. Early models at 266 and 300 MHz had no L2 cache, used Slot 1, but came on a bare circuit board, not in a cartridge. Celeron "A" processors at 300 and 333 MHz came on a circuit board, used Slot 1, and had a 128 K cache running at the full speed of the processor. In late 1998 or early 1999, Intel was scheduled to replace Slot 1 Celerons with new models using a 370-pin socket that wasn't compatible with anything else, larger caches and faster speeds (366 and 400 MHz).
Xeon	Xeon	Intel	Xeon	Varies	Also a Pentium II at its core, the Xeon uses Slot 2 on a 100 MHz system bus and is targeted for robust business servers in multi-processor configurations (up to four of them). L2 cache of 512 KB or more will run at the full speed of the processor. Due to be replaced in early 1999 with "Tanner," containing up to 2 MB of cache on a 4-processor system and including the "Katmai New Instructions" (see above).
"Merced"	IA64 (would have been 80787 if Intel still used numbers)	Intel	to be announced	to be announced	"Merced" is the code-name for Intel's long-awaited 64-bit processor (set for release in 2000). Initial releases will be for business servers. The company may release a 32-bit version of Merced in 1999 to allow businesses an upgrade path. Both will use the yet-to-be-released "Slot M." Figure on at least a 100 MHz system bus and fast L2 cache.

Chip	Name	Made by	Long Name	Speeds	Details
5x86	Formerly M1sc	Cyrix, IBM	Cyrix 5x86	Varies	Not really a Pentium-class chip. According to Cyrix it is more similar in operation to a 486 processor, although it does execute some Pentium instruction codes.
6x86	Formerly M1	Cyrix, IBM	Cyrix 6x86	Varies	Using a "PR-scale," Cyrix identifies its chips by the equivalent-to-Pentium speeds they claim, not the actual internal speed. Reports of overheating and incompatibility with certain software.
M II	Formerly 6x86MX	Cyrix/IBM	6x86 with MMX	Up to 300 (sort of)	Matches Pentium MMX performance at rated speed (not actual speed) for business applications, but lags far, far behind in MMX operations and floating point math (affects video speed). A low-end alternative. Uses Socket 7.
Media GX	Based upon 5x86	Cyrix/IBM	Cyrix Media GX	120, 133, 200, 233 MHz (sort of)	Found in the Compaq Presario 2100-/2200 series and some Ambra (IBM) Ispiratis. The 120 MHz version runs slower than a Pentium 100. With companion chip offers a (relatively) low-cost option and provides audio, video, and sound without additional circuit boards. Uses PCI bus, not faster main bus. These systems are not upgradeable.
5x86	K5	AMD	AMD K5	Varies (uses PR rating)	The K5 is AMD's Pentium replacement (equivalent to Cyrix 6x86) with no history of overheating. Still uses "PR" scale to report performance in close to Pentium performance. Many performance and compatibility problems with K5.
K6	K6	AMD	AMD K6 with MMX	200, 233, 266 MHz	The K6 is optimized for both 16- and 32-bit software, is a Pentium II equivalent and stacks up well against the Pentium IIs at the same speed in independent tests running business apps. It doesn't do so well in MMX and floating point operations, but the difference is minimal. Uses Socket 7.
K6-2	K6-2	AMD	K6 with "3D Now"	300 MHz to 366 MHz as of Nov. 1998 (400 coming)	Can run on motherboards with 100 MHz base speeds (see chipset chart). Still uses Socket 7. 3D Now is an in-processor extension to MMX that requires special software to make it work. Faster models (350 and up) use 100 MHz motherboards.
K6-3	AMD K6-3	AMD	formerly "Sharptooth"	350 to 400 MHz	Still uses Socket 7, but on 100 MHz motherboards. First AMD "K6" model with on-die cache, initially at 256 K. Scheduled for release in late 1998 or early 1999.
K7	AMD K7	AMD	AMD K7	500 MHz plus	Due for release in the first half of 1999. Runs on 200 MHz system bus, using Digital Alpha "Slot A" with two 64 KB internal (Level 1) caches, 512 K to 8 MB L2 cache. No indication yet of how well it will run standard software. Watch for a response from Intel.
C6	WinChip	Centaur / Independent Device Technology (IDT)	WinChip C6	Varies	A relative newcomer to the CPU wars. Initial tests suggest comparable performance to Pentium MMX systems of the same speed, but multimedia scores were up to 40% slower. Not yet available in quantity, but if it appears in Canada, it will be in low-priced systems.

7

Motherboards and Chipsets

Motherboards

Everything inside and attached to the outside of your computer is connected in some way or another to the motherboard. If the CPU is the system's brain, the motherboard is the remainder of the computer. After you've chosen a processor, this is the next most important part of the computer to which you'll devote some homework time.

Trends

Although the tables to be found later in this section will mention the top motherboard brands and models popular among local system assemblers as of writing, I am, as ever, reluctant to recommend specific brands. Both I and Walter Gollick, my colleague at the Computer Fest seminars where we talk about upgrading and building custom systems, have been surveying this market for about fifteen years, and one of its quirks hasn't changed in all that time. Choosing a motherboard is a black art because anything we liked last month may not be great next week.

Over the past few years, the shelf life of any particular model of motherboard has been just under three months; then it's replaced by a new model. Even during that time, manufacturers can and do tweak the design, change component suppliers, and update the BIOS software without changing the model designation. Because he custom-assembles systems for his clients, Walter is particular about rate of return (as low as possible), performance (as good as possible), feature flexibility, upgrade potential, and price (as reasonable as the other criteria allow). Most local assemblers seek the same standards, particularly when it comes to that rate of return (or failure, if you prefer). Sadly, we've discovered that just because one model from one manufacturer met those criteria, it doesn't mean that the next model from the same company will meet them – or even that the same model will remain the same during the time it's on the market.

This is why shopping for a reputable dealer with a good history of customer satisfaction is so important, and why, in this instance, you should take your friends' recommendations of motherboard brand and model with a grain of salt. Still, talk to those friends, visit those user groups, and check the Internet newsgroups, but in this instance, look for dealer reputation, not specific motherboard model tips.

Also check Internet Web sites that keep up to date on the latest releases. See pages 10 and 86-87. All are independent sources of reliable data. If these sites are not still available when you check, go to any Internet search engine such as Yahoo, AltaVista, Excite, HotBot, Dogpile or their successors and search on the keyword "motherboard." You'll find lots of links to take you further.

AT v/s ATX

By the time I'm ready to prepare the next edition of *How to Buy a Computer*, I don't expect to be talking about this next topic at all. By then I fully expect the processors involved to have fallen off the market. But during the early period of this book's life, it will still be an issue. If you settle for a system using a Pentium MMX, AMD's K6 family, the M II (formerly 6x86MX) or MediaGX put out by National Semiconductor/Cyrix/IBM, or Centaur/IDT's WinChip processor

family, you'll hit a dead end. You will not be able to upgrade to a
Pentium II, Celeron, or Xeon system unless you change both the
motherboard *and* probably the computer's case.

All processors other than the Pentium II, Celeron, and Xeon use
a motherboard socket designed for the Pentium, known as Socket 7.
They also use a motherboard with what is generically known as an AT-
style form factor. The form factor determines the position of the
expansion slots and external port connections, as well as the motherboard's attachment points relative to the case's openings and attachment points.

Motherboards designed for Pentium II, Celeron, and Xeon processors, which use either Slot 1 or Slot 2 connectors, use the ATX form
factor and require a specially designed ATX case. You cannot put an
ATX board in an AT-style case or vice versa.

In the next two to three years, I expect several things to happen.
AMD, Cyrix, and Centaur will figure out how to produce processors
for Slot 1, or they'll jointly design a motherboard/case combo that is
not Intel compatible. By the time they pick a route, Intel will have
moved on to processors that use its Slot 2, then eventually Slot M,
architectures (for "Merced" processors) – and to keep both competitors and consumers off balance, they may well redesign the motherboard's form again.

Isn't the computer industry fun?

Your homework assignment is to decide now if upgrading your
system to extend its life is even remotely in your plan. Choosing an
AT-style, Socket 7 motherboard now will mean that you'll run out of
performance headroom sooner instead of later, even though some
manufacturers have been producing Socket 7 motherboards that can
run at your choice of 60, 66, 75, 83, 100, or as high as 120 MHz.

Unless you shop very carefully, it is also likely to mean you won't
be able to take advantage of the Accelerated Graphics Port (AGP) slot
and the AGP graphics cards that use it, either. There is not and will not
be (says the company) an Intel chipset that supports AGP on a Socket
7 board, although the Taiwanese company VIA has produced the
Apollo VP3 chipset which does support this feature (see the chipset
table at the end of this chapter).

Choosing an ATX-style, Slot 1 motherboard now means you will have a little more room to grow, but your only product choice among processors in the short term is likely to be from Intel.

There's one more factor to consider. If you want to go the ATX/Slot 1/Pentium II route, you should choose the motherboard's chipset and its corresponding base speed now. For example, the original Celeron-based systems, using the 440EX chipset, were (and may still be) nailed at 66 MHz. And, because of a difference in the attachment mechanism that holds the processors in place, you cannot install a full-blown Pentium II processor on a Celeron-designed motherboard.

If you choose a Pentium II now, but fail to insist that the motherboard have at least Intel's 440BX chipset, you will only be able to use Pentium II processors from 233 to 333 MHz. However, the 350 MHz or faster Pentium II processors will be forever denied to you because they require a 100 MHz motherboard (which the 440BX allows).

Conversely, a motherboard with a 440BX chipset will run at either 66 or 100 MHz, depending on the processor installed in it. According to Intel, Pentium II processors report their design speed when asked. The 440BX chipset asks. If it detects a processor that was designed for a 66 MHz motherboard, it will, says Intel, "downclock" the motherboard from 100 to 66 MHz. Neat trick.

So, you will be able to start with a less-expensive and slower Pentium II, then scale up to a 350 MHz-plus processor later. When you add the faster processor, the 440BX should turn the motherboard's clock speed back up to 100 MHz. Hint: Get the corresponding 100 MHz SDRAM memory modules designed for these boards when you first purchase the system, even if you're not going to run it at 100 MHz right away. When you do add a 100 MHz-based processor later, both the motherboard base speed and memory speed will increase to keep up (otherwise, the slower 66 MHz SDRAM will put the brakes on your system and it will cost you more to replace it). See Chapter 8 for an explanation of exactly what SDRAM is and why it's different from other forms of memory you may be offered (and don't want).

Okay, if the 440BX will query the processor and decide that a Pentium II running at 333 MHz or less should be on a 66 MHz board, that should prevent a less-than-reputable dealer from pulling a fast one. For example, slipping a Pentium II/266 (3.5 internal multiplier) on a 100 MHz board and selling it as a 350 (also multiplied internally at 3.5). Right?

Unfortunately, that's not the case. I am not going to provide details of how it is done here (we don't want to encourage the rascals, so I'm going to be as vague as I can). It is possible to make certain physical alterations that will allow the slower Pentium II processors to be pushed to run on a 100 MHz base plane. Intel is aware of the practice and doesn't like it. The company warns in the strongest terms that such a process will shorten the life of the part (by overheating it). Your only protection is the reputable dealer we discussed at the beginning of this chapter.

So, what to do?

Start by looking at some motherboard design factors, then find the one that meets most of the good criteria and fewer of the bad, cross your fingers, and hope the dealer's reputation for satisfying its customers is justified.

Let's list the good design factors first, starting with Socket 7, AT-style motherboards:

• If you can find a board where the location of the CPU doesn't prevent you from putting a full-length expansion card in any ISA slot without hitting the top of the processor's chip fan or heat sink, that's good (and rare).
• If it has both SIMM and DIMM memory sockets (see Chapter 8), it will provide you with more flexibility if you can use both at the same time, instead of one or the other.
• You'll find out what the most current chipset on the market is (see below) for your particular processor class, and you'll make sure that's the one this motherboard uses. Remember that there's no such thing anymore as a "Triton" chipset of any kind (and hasn't been since mid-1995). If the salesperson insists that's what it has, he or she is either mistaken (and may also be about other things you're being told) or is trying to bamboozle you. Leave the store.

• If it has both PCI and ISA expansion slots, check to find out how many there are of each. This is particularly important if you want to bring older ISA circuit boards over from your previous system. You'll also note how many pairs of slots are so close together that you can use one or the other but not both. One pair of shared slots is annoying, but within current practice. None is better. More than one pair of shared slots will severely limit what you can do later.

• The motherboard has a battery on it. It keeps the clock/calendar alive as well as a special form of memory called the Complimentary Metal Oxide Semiconductor, or CMOS, wherein is stored all kinds of neat information about fine tuning on the chipset, details on your hard drive(s) and other goodies. When the battery dies (as it will, eventually), all that data goes away. *How to Avoid Buying a New Computer* has detailed instructions on how to replace the battery (and the data) when this happens, but your life will be easier if you have a motherboard that allows this battery to be changed or re-routed easily and inexpensively. Ask the salesperson to show you the battery and/or the battery replacement terminal. Run away if he or she responds with a blank expression or tells you it cannot be replaced.

• All Socket 7 processor sockets are not the same. The original Pentium was a 3.3-volt chip. The Pentium MMX uses 2.8 volts to its core and 3.3 volts for input/output operations. In other words, it's a dual-voltage part, and the processor socket has to deliver the right amount to the right places. The AMD K6 family has similar, but different, requirements, and for all I know, the Cyrix M II (6x86MX) may as well (but I don't care and neither should you). You want a board that allows you to use two voltage values and to vary them as needed. At the very least, ask what brand of processors you can use on the board, and if the answer is important, have it written on the sales agreement. If the salesperson doesn't know, ask to see the board's technical manual. If the store doesn't have one, run away and don't go back.

• Modern motherboards have, hardwired to the board, an EIDE/ATA-3 hard drive/CD-ROM controller, floppy drive controller, parallel port connector, two serial port connectors, two PS/2 port connectors, a game controller connector, and USB connectors (two are better). If it has no USB connectors at all, run away. Make sure all surface-mounted

port terminals (as opposed to any that are on separate circuit boards) are actually connected to external connectors at the back of the case. The board may also have an infrared connector, a built-in SCSI controller, and a built-in network interface. It will be expensive if it does.
• If the motherboard also has a hardwired video controller, sound controller, and/or modem, ask how you can turn them off if you want to upgrade any of these controllers in the future by using a version on a circuit board in an expansion slot. Ask how – and more to the point, whether – it will be possible to add more memory to the video controller if you later discover there isn't enough.
• If the motherboard uses a MediaGX processor, you will not be able to upgrade it, and if you become dissatisfied with its performance later, you're out of luck.
• If the motherboard does not have a chipset that supports AGP and there is no AGP slot, you will not be able to add one later.
• If there is external cache memory and if it is soldered onto the board, ask if the amount (whatever the amount) can be increased and, if so, how. If it has none, ask if some can be installed. This is crucial. For example, the IBM Aptiva E26 with AMD K6/233, sold in early 1998, had no external cache and it couldn't be added. The result was a performance drop-off in excess of 20 per cent.
• Ask what is the maximum amount of memory you can put on the motherboard and what type is being offered. If you are not purchasing a system with a chipset designed for Pentium II, Xeon, or Celeron, ask how much of the memory the chipset allows to be cached. If you exceed this amount (usually over 64 MB), the system will slow down. If the board requires parity memory, the memory modules will cost a premium when you wish to add more later. You may want to look at a different model. See Chapter 8 to get your homework assignment.
• Using an AT-style motherboard will prevent you from upgrading to a Pentium II variant that requires an ATX-style board unless you also change the case.

The design features for ATX motherboards are similar, but . . .

• As time goes on, you will have a choice of Slot 1, Slot 2, or "Slot M." The primary difference is that less-expensive processors using

Slot 1 won't physically fit into Slot 2 or Slot M. In Slot 2-based systems, the companion in-cartridge cache module will run at the same speed as the processor, instead of half the speed as it does in Slot 1 products (except, of course, for early Celeron processors, which did not a have a companion cache module and never Celerons with in-processor cache that runs at the same speed as the processor).

• The chipset matters. A board with Intel's 440LX AGP set or 440EX AGP set will be nailed at 66 MHz. If you want to upgrade the processor you will not be able to take advantage of any that require 100 MHz motherboards.

• Conversely, a board with the 440BX chipset, newer 450NX, or 450GX (for Xeon) or better will allow a 100 MHz motherboard and the faster processors. Because it will run at either 66 or 100 MHz, depending on the processor you use, it will also allow you to start with a less-expensive 66 MHz-based processor and work up when the 100 MHz-based varieties come down in price.

• Once you choose an ATX motherboard, there's no going back unless you also change the case; otherwise it won't fit.

• Celeron and Pentium II both use Slot 1, but don't use the same method to attach the part to the slot. You have to decide which family you'll use when you buy the motherboard (you can't interchange them).

Chipsets

Hold onto your seats – this could be a wild ride. There have been logic support chipsets on motherboards for as long as there have been PCs. I'm sure the nature of the chipset affected performance from motherboard to motherboard, but the simple fact is that no one outside the engineering community knew much about what they did or particularly cared about the differences. All we knew was that a 386 used a 386 chipset and a 486 used a different one. That was then and this is now.

Beginning with the first Pentium-based systems, the chipset has taken on an increasingly important role in how – and how well – the whole computer functions. The chipset – so called because it is generally a pair of chips (although for some advanced Xeon-based systems could be as many as nine) – sits on the motherboard's surface. Functionally, it operates between the processor and everything else in the system. Although future chipsets may expand this list, current versions determine the following:

• The type of main system and cache memory the motherboard can use as well as their speed, timing, and the maximum amount of either you're allowed. The chipset also determines how much of the system memory can be cached;
• Whether the motherboard supports the Accelerated Graphics Port (AGP), a special slot and bus that allows the graphics controller direct access to main system memory and to respond to special software instructions that add speed, particularly to 3D-intensive graphics;
• Whether and how the system supports Universal Serial Bus or future connection specifications such as IEEE 1394 (FireWire);
• The type and throughput speed of hard drives, CD-ROM drives, and DVD drives as well as whether the board supports Ultra DMA, a hard-drive specification for EIDE/ATA-3 drives that allows for up to 33 MB/sec throughput;
• How and at what speed the PCI expansion slots and system bus communicate with the processor, as well as how the PCI bus shares processor time with the AGP graphics, memory, and system bus (known as quad port acceleration);
• Which architecture the motherboard supports for attaching a processor (Socket 7, Slot 1, Slot 2, Slot M and so on);
• Whether the motherboard supports advanced power management, including suspend functions and wake on demand, wake on LAN (request from a network), and wake on ring;
• Whether the motherboard supports the Wired for Management initiative that allows for remote sensing and troubleshooting over a wired, wireless or remote network such as the Internet (designed to drive down the cost of ownership in corporate environments).

Over the past couple of years, Intel has released at least one, and often more than one, revised chipset per year. I don't see this pattern changing any time soon.

Your homework assignment is to find out what are the most recent chipsets available for the level of system you choose and to discover what features and support services these chipsets offer. In mid-1998, Intel supplied chipsets for over 75 per cent of the PC market, but it is not the only supplier of these components. You will get information from vendors, particularly those offering alternatives, claiming the non-Intel chipsets are comparable to the Intel brands. Some of them may well be comparable, but if the price on the whole system is ridiculously low, don't bet the ranch that the one you're being offered is. For every claim of equivalency you hear, there are reports of poorer or inadequate performance. The USENET newsgroups that harp on this topic are a good place to hear praises, but they are an even better place to hear gripes.

PC Motherboards

Company	AMI*	Asus			GigaByte	
Model	**781 Olympus**	**SP98-N**	**P2E-B / -M**	**P2B series**	**GA-5AX**	**GA-686EX**
Processor connection	Slot 1	Socket 7	Slot 1	Slot 1	Socket 7	Slot 1
Processors	Pentium II	Intel Pentium, Pentium MMX, (75 to 233 MHz) AMD K5 (PR75-PR133), AMD K6 (PR166-PR266), IBM/Cyrix 6x86 (PR166 ~), M II 6x86MX (PR233)	Celeron, Pentium II	Pentium II	Intel Pentium MMX (90-266 MHz), AMD K5 & K6 (133-266 MHz), AMD K6-2 (266-300 MHz), Cyrix/IBM 6x86, 686L/MX, M II (P150-P300)	Pentium II, Celeron
System Bus speed(s) – MHz	66, 100	66	66	66, 100	60, 66, 75, 83, 100	66
Chipset	Intel 440 BX AGPset	SiS 5598	Intel 440EX AGPset	Intel 440BX AGPset	ALi Alladin V	Intel 440EX AGPset
BIOS options	AMIBIOS 98 (flash?)	Award (Flash)	Award Anti-Virus Flash	Award Anti-Virus Flash	Award Anti-Virus Flash	Award Anti-Virus Flash
Slots (ISA / PCI / shared / AGP)	2 / 5 / 1 / 1	1 / 2 / ? / n/a	2 / 2 / 0 / 1	3 / 4 / 0 / 1	3 / 4 / 0 / 1	3 / 4 / 0 / 1
Max Memory	1 GB SDRAM (512 MB tested)	256 MB (EDO or SDRAM)	256 MB (EDO or SDRAM)	768 MB (SDRAM)	768 MB (EDO or SDRAM)	256 MB (EDO or SDRAM)
Memory sockets	4 x 168-pin DIMM	2 x 168-pin DIMM	2 x 168-pin DIMM	3 x 168-pin DIMM	3 x 168-pin DIMM	3 x 168-pin DIMM
Memory voltage/speed	3.3 v / 66 or 100 MHz	3.3 v / 66 MHz	3.3 v / 66 MHz	3.3 v / 66 or 100 MHz	3.3 v / 66 or 100 MHz	3.3 v / 66 MHz
Max L2 cache	In processor only	512 KB	In Pentium II processor only	In processor only	512 KB	In Pentium II processor only
Form factor	ATX	NLX	Baby AT (P2E-B), ATX (P2E-M)	ATX	ATX	ATX
Onboard I/O						
PCI bus mastering IDE ports	2 (4 Devices,) UltraATA/33	2 (4 Devices,) UltraATA/33	2 (4 devices, max throughput 17 MB/sec)	2 (4 Devices, UltraATA/33)	2 (4 Devices, UltraATA/33)	2 (4 Devices, UltraATA/33)
Floppy port(s)	1 (1.44MB, 2.88MB, LS-120 Support)	1 (1.44MB, 2.88MB, LS-120 Support)	1 (1.44MB, 2.88MB, LS-120 Support)	1 (1.44MB, 2.88MB, LS-120 Support)	1 (1.44MB, 2.88MB, LS-120 Support)	1 (1.44MB, 2.88MB, LS-120 Support)
Serial port(s)	2 (16550A Fast UART Compatible)	2 (16550 Fast UART Compatible)	2 (16550 Fast UART Compatible)	2	2 (16550 Fast UART Compatible)	2 (16550 Fast UART Compatible)
Parallel port(s)	1 Bidirectional (ECP, EPP support)	1 Bidirectional (ECP, EPP support)	1 Bidirectional (ECP, EPP support)	1 Bidirectional (ECP, EPP support)	1 Bidirectional (ECP, EPP support)	1 Bidirectional (ECP, EPP support)

Company	AMI*	Asus			GigaByte	
Model	781 Olympus	SP98-N	P2E-B / -M	P2B series	GA-5AX	GA-686EX
IrDA	none	Fast IrDA Support (TX/RX Header)	no	Fast IrDA Support (TX/RX Header)	no	no
USB	2	Yes (number unknown)	2	2	2	2
Other ports	PS/2 mouse	RJ45, PS/2 Mouse & Keyboard, Video/Audio/Game	PS/2 mouse & keyboard, 1 game port, 3 audio ports	PS/2 mouse & keyboard, 1 game port	PS/2 mouse & keyboard	PS/2 mouse & keyboard
On-board features	ACPI, Doze/Sleep/Suspend Modes, CPU Thermal Protect, CPU / System Fan Control, Voltage Report	64-bit PCI VGA, Intel 80258 Wake-on-LAN Ethernet controller, Yamaha OPL3-SA3 enhanced surround sound controller	Yamaha OPL3-SA3 enhanced surround sound controller	Optional: dual CPU (P2B-D), Ethernet (P2B-L), SCSI (P2B-S), Ethernet & SCSI (P2B-LS), Dual CPU & SCSI (P2B-DS)	CPU Speed Down During CPU Overheats. (OS Independent & Driverless). System Health Status Detect & Report by BIOS, CPU Temperature Monitoring, Poly Fuse for Keyboard Over Current Protection	Power On by PS/2 Keyboard, PS/2 Mouse, LAN, RTC Alarm, Modem Ring & Soft-Power Switch Power Off by Windows 95 Shut down & Soft-Power Switch AC Recovery On/Off Control Supports Fan Stop During Suspend Mode Supports 3 Level ACPI LED
Phone	800-828-9264	510-739-3777			none in North America	
e-mail	none	tmd1@asus.com			info-gbt@giga-byte.com	
Web site: http://www	megatrends.com	asus.com			giga-byte.com	

PC Motherboards cont'd

Company	GigaByte	Intel		Micronics	QDI	
Model	GA-686BX	SE440BX	MU440EX	Redstone	QDI-P6I440EX/ATX Excellent II	QDI-P6I440EX/ATX Brilliant I
Processor connection	Slot 1	Slot 1	Slot 1	Slot 1	Slot 1	Slot 1
Processors	Pentium II (233 to 333 MHz at 66 MHz, 350 to 500 MHz at 100 MHz)	Pentium II (233 to 333 MHz at 66 MHz, 350 to 500 MHz at 100 MHz)	Pentium II up to 333 MHz, Celeron 266 & 300	Pentium II (233 to 333 MHz at 66 MHz, 350 to 500 MHz at 100 MHz)	Pentium II up to 333 MHz, Celeron 266 & 300	Pentium II (233 to 333 MHz at 66 MHz, 350 to 500 MHz at 100 MHz)
System Bus speed(s) – MHz	66, 100	66, 100	66	66, 100	66	66, 100
Chipset	Intel 440BX AGPset	Intel 440BX AGPset	Intel 440EX AGPset	Intel 440BX AGPset	Intel 440EX AGPset	Intel 440BX AGPset
BIOS options	Award Anti-Virus Flash	Intel / Phoenix (flash)	Intel / Phoenix (flash)	no info	Award Anti-Virus Flash	Award Flash
Slots (ISA / PCI / shared / AGP)	3 / 4 / 0 / 1	1 / 3 / 1 / 1	1 / 3 / 0 / 1	1 / 3 / 1 / 1	2 / 2 / 0 / 1	3 / 4 / 0 / 1
Max Memory	1 GB (EDO or SDRAM)	384 MB SDRAM	256 MB SDRAM	384 MB SDRAM	256 MB SDRAM or EDO	384 MB SDRAM
Memory sockets	4 x 168-pin DIMM	3 x 168-pin DIMM	2 x 168-pin DIMM	3 x 168-pin DIMM	2 x 168-pin DIMM	3 x 168-pin DIMM
Memory voltage/speed	3.3 v / 66 or 100 MHz	?? v / 66 or 100 MHz	?? v / 66 MHz	3.3 v / 66 or 100 MHz	3.3 v / 66 MHz	3.3 v / 66 or 100 MHz
Max L2 cache	In processor only	In processor only	In Pentium II processor only	In processor only	In Pentium II processor only	In processor only
Form factor	ATX	ATX	microATX	ATX	microATX	ATX
Onboard I/O						
PCI bus mastering IDE ports	2 (4 Devices, UltraATA/33)	2 (4 Devices, UltraATA/33)	2 (4 Devices,) UltraATA/33)	2 (4 Devices, UltraATA/33)	2 (4 Devices, UltraATA/33)	2 (4 Devices, UltraATA/33)
Floppy port(s)	1 (1.44MB, 2.88MB, LS-120 Support)	1 drive only (1.44MB, 2.88MB, LS-120 Support)	1 (1.44MB, 2.88MB, LS-120 Support)	1 (1.44MB, 2.88MB, LS-120 Support)	1 (1.44MB, 2.88MB, LS-120 Support)	1 – two drives (1.44MB, 2.88MB, LS-120 Support)
Serial port(s)	2 (16550A Fast UART Compatible)	no info	no info	2 (16550 Fast UART Compatible)	2 (16550 Fast UART Compatible)	2 (16550 Fast UART Compatible)
Parallel port(s)	1 Bidirectional (ECP, EPP support)	no info	no info	1 Bidirectional (ECP, EPP support)	1 Bidirectional (ECP, EPP support)	1 Bidirectional (ECP, EPP support)
IrDA	no	no info	no info	Yes (header not specified)	Yes (header not specified)	no
USB	2	2	2	2	2	2

Company	GigaByte	Intel		Micronics	QDI	
Model	**GA-686BX**	**SE440BX**	**MU440EX**	**Redstone**	**QDI-P6I440EX/ATX Excellent II**	**QDI-P6I440EX/ATX Brilliant I**
Other ports	PS/2 mouse & keyboard	no info	no info	no info	PS/2 mouse & keyboard	optional
On-board features	same as at left with 4-level ACPI LED	Single-jumper configuration Advanced Power Management (APM) 1.2 Advanced Configuration and Power Interface (ACPI) 1.0 PCI Power Management Wake on Ring connector	Integrated audio (Yamaha YMF 740-V AC '97 digital controller Analog Devices AD1819A AC '97 analog codec), Integrated video (2X ATI Rage Pro Turbo AGP graphics controller 4 MB SGRAM (graphics memory) DDC2B Compliant)	Optional Ensoniq ES1371 integrated PCI audio (model M1SBR-006), Microprocessor System Hardware Monitor (National LM79), LM75 CPU Temperature Sensor, CPU Fan Speed Monitoring (3-pin header), Chassis Intrusion (2-pin header), Chassis Fan Speed Monitoring (3-pin header)	ATX or SFX power supply support CPU power supply 1.4v to 3.5v adjustable with VID function, meets VRM8.2 spec On board 1.5v and 2.5v regulators Wakeup by PS/2 keyboard, PS/2 mouse, IrDA, Modem or LAN (optional) System monitoring includes 3 fan speeds (controllable) and 7 system voltage, chassis intrusion detector, CPU & system temperature sensed by W83781D (optional) Supports LDCM and ManageEasy (optional) On board 3.5v power supply support for PIIX4EB	Supports slow down, suspend to memory, suspend to hard disk LM80 monitors 2 fans' speed, 6 power supply voltages, chassis intrusion, mainboard temperature. Supports both internal and external modem ring power on. Supports wakeup on LAN
Phone	none in North America	none	none	800-577-0977	905-940-3827	
e-mail	info-gbt@giga-byte.com			none	lily@qdi.ca	
Web site: http://www	giga-byte.com	intel.com (**)		micronics.com	qdigrp.com or qdi.ca	

* AMI = American Megatrends International
** Intel Motherboard Web site: http://developer.intel.com/design/motherbd/

Motherboard and Chipset Features

Motherboard Chipset Features	Intel 430HX	Intel 430TX	Intel 440LX	Intel 440BX	Intel 440EX	Intel 440GX
Processor(s)	Pentium	Pentium, Pentium MMX, AMD K6, Cyrix M II	Pentium II (up to 333 MHz), Celeron	Pentium II (up to 333 MHz at 66 MHz or 350 MHz + at 100 MHz)	Celeron	Xeon
EDO RAM	Yes	Yes	Yes	No	Yes	No
SDRAM	No	Yes	Yes	Yes	Yes	Yes
ECC/Parity	Yes	No	Yes	Yes	No	Yes
System Bus Speed	66 MHz	66 MHz	66 MHz	66/100 MHz	66 MHz	100 MHz
Processor connector	Socket 7	Socket 7	Slot 1	Slot 1	Slot 1	Slots 1 & 2
Universal Serial Bus	Yes	Yes	Yes	Yes	Yes	Yes
Concurrent PCI	Yes	Yes	Yes	Yes	Yes	Yes
QuadPort Acceleration	No	No	Yes	Yes	Yes	Yes
Accelerated Graphics Port	No	No	Yes	Yes	Yes	Yes
Ultra DMA hard drives	No	Yes	Yes	Yes	Yes	Yes
Max memory	512 MB	256 MB	1 GB EDO or 512 MB SDRAM	1 GB	256 MB	2 GB
Max cacheable memory	512 MB	64 MB	all	all	all	all
DPMI (remote diagnostics)	No	No	Yes	Yes	Yes	Yes
ACPI (power management)	No	No	Yes	Yes	Yes	Yes
Multiple Processors	Yes (2)	No	Yes (2)	Yes (2)	No	Yes (2)
Web site: http://www.	intel.com					

Motherboard Chipset Features	Intel 450NX	ALi Alladin V (M1541)	SiS 5597/5598	SiS 5591	VIA Apollo Pro	VIA Apollo MVP3
Processor(s)	Xeon	AMD K6, Cyrix 6x86 and M II	AMD K6 and possibly others	AMD K6 and possibly others	Pentium II, Pentium Pro	Pentium, Pentium MMX; AMD K5, K6; Cyrix 6X86, M II; IDT WinChip
EDO RAM	Yes	Yes	Yes	Yes	Yes	Yes
SDRAM	Yes	Yes	Yes	Yes	Yes	Yes
ECC/Parity	Yes	Yes	no info	no info	ECC	no info
System Bus Speed	100 MHz	75 to 100 MHz	up to 75 MHz	up to 83.3 MHz	66/100 MHz	66 to 100 Mhz
Processor connector	Slot 2	Socket 7	Socket 7	Socket 7	Slot 1 or Socket 8 (Pentium Pro)	Socket 7
Universal Serial Bus	Yes	Yes	Yes	Yes	Yes	Yes
Concurrent PCI	Yes	Yes	no info	Yes	Yes	Yes
QuadPort Acceleration	Yes	Yes	no info	No	No	No
Accelerated Graphics Port	No	Yes	No	Yes	Yes (v. 1 only)	Yes (v. 1 only)
Ultra DMA hard drives	Yes	Yes	Yes	Yes	Yes	Yes
Max memory	8 GB with 4 processors	1 GB (see below)	no info	768 MB (up to 1 MB L2 cache)	1 GB	1 GB
Max cacheable memory	all	512 MB w/ 512 KB, 1 GB w/256 KB	128 MB w/ 512 KB; 64 MB w/256 KB	no info	no info	512 MB
DPMI (remote diagnostics)	Yes	Yes	??	??	??	??
ACPI (power management)	Yes	Yes	Yes	Yes	Yes	Yes
Multiple Processors	Yes (4)	No	No	No	No	No
Web site: http://www.	intel.com	acerlabs.com	sis.com.tw	sis.com.tw	via.com.tw	via.com.tw

The Intel 430VX, 450GX, 450KX, and 450FX have been discontinued from active production
ACPI = Advanced configuration and power interface
DPMI = Desktop Power Management Initiative
OPTi does not provide detailed product feature descriptions
ECC = error correction. Note: if the chipset does not provide parity checking, you'll need more expensive parity memory

8

Memory

Memory, the first thing to go when you get older, can also be found in a number of locations inside today's computers.

There are two basic types of memory in a computer – ROM and RAM. Read only memory (ROM) is also sometimes known as firmware, especially when it's found on peripheral devices. In most cases, ROM chips contain non-volatile memory that doesn't change. "Non-volatile" simply means that the information in the chip stays there, even when you turn the system off.

In a typical PC, ROM chips hold information the system needs to start working. For example, the BIOS (basic in/out system) is stored in a form of ROM that your system reads when it first starts to get the most basic information it needs to function. When you buy a PC, you don't get to specify how much ROM it will have, but you can check to make sure that the BIOS, at least, uses what is known as "flash" ROM. (See the definition of flash BIOS in Chapter 5). These are special ROM chips that can be updated by special software (to service new devices or to handle the Year 2000 problem, for instance).

Other devices that have ROM include virtually all additional services the system provides, including graphics controller, sound controller, and modem. The day you discover that you have flash ROM on all these devices will be a happy one for you. Conversely, the day you discover that you can't upgrade your modem to the new V.90 standard because it doesn't have flash ROM won't be nice at all.

The only time you'll care about how much ROM a device has is when you're purchasing one of the new Palm PCs, a handheld PC (H/PC) or organizer such as the Palm III or Psion. Both the operating systems for these small devices, as well as applications for them, are stored in ROM, so the amount does make a difference.

All other memory in the system will be some form of RAM (random access memory). RAM is volatile, which means that when you cut power to the system, its contents vanish. It's called "random access" because information can be stored anywhere within it, at random. Your system can both read from and write to RAM, and it often does so millions of times per second while you run software. It's found in a variety of locations.

Main system memory lives on the PC's motherboard (or main system board). Usually measured in megabytes (MB), it is, to put it very simply, where programs run when they're on screen (as opposed to your hard drive, which is where they live the rest of the time).

Main system memory (which is what many people, including retailers, simply call RAM) for Pentium, Pentium MMX, Pentium Pro, and Pentium II-based PCs (or their equivalents) is packaged in two physical forms: 72-pin Single Inline Memory Modules (SIMMs) or 168-pin Dual Inline Memory Modules (DIMMs). The average PC sold in 1999 should come with at least 32 MB of main system RAM, with 64 to 128 MB in premium products. As time marches on, don't be surprised if even average systems start appearing with 64 MB or more (I already detect this trend). Systems you're eyeing may have an upper limit for memory of 128 MB, 256 MB, or all the way up to 1 gigabyte (GB). But you're unlikely to ever put that much on it unless (a) you have a *lot* of money, or (b) you plan to use very graphic-intensive programs for such tasks as image retouching or video editing.

Too much RAM?

Yes, Virginia, it is possible to have too much memory in a PC. For
example, if you're planning, for some inexplicable reason, to run
Windows 3.1x on your new system, neither it nor the version of MS-
DOS that ships with it can recognize more than 64 MB of RAM,
regardless of how much your computer will allow you to add.

The same problem doesn't hamper Windows 9x. In theory, it can
recognize up to 4 GB of RAM. In reality, it will stop working if you
have 2 GB of RAM or more and, depending on the system, may
become unstable with more than 768 MB. That's an amount of
memory that none of us is ever likely to have in our computers.
However, there's another factor at work.

If you purchase a used system, or decide to go for the lowest possible cost and get a new trailing-edge system with a Pentium or
Pentium MMX processor, the computer's motherboard chipset (see
Chapter 7) may place a limit on how much memory you can use effectively. If the system contains Intel's 430VX or 430TX chipsets, neither
will cache memory over 64 MB. And, as you'll see below, your computer always runs at the speed of the slowest memory you have. If you
exceed 64 MB, you effectively disable the speed advantage the level
2 cache delivers (see immediately below). You can still use the additional memory, but the whole system will slow down by 20 per cent
or more.

This problem does not occur with the 430HX chipset, nor is it a
factor in chipsets for Pentium II-, Celeron-, or Xeon-based systems.
See the table on pages 86-87 for other chipsets.

External, or level 2 cache memory (L2 cache) also lives primarily on
the motherboard for Socket 7 (e.g., Pentium, Pentium MMX, AMD
K6, Cyrix 6x86) systems. In today's PCs it should total an average of
512 kilobytes (KB), but may be as low as zero or as high in some top-
end systems as 1 MB. In Pentium II or Xeon-based systems, there may
be no L2 cache on the motherboard. Instead, it's in the cartridge with
the processor. In Celeron-based systems, there may be no L2 cache
(early models had none), or there may be an on-board cache module
of 128 KB.

L2 cache memory is much faster than main system memory – almost as fast as the system's central processor (CPU) if it's on the motherboard. It runs at half the speed of the processor if it's part of a Pentium II, and at the full speed of the processor if it's connected to a newer Celeron or Xeon CPU. The fast cache memory forms a bridge between the fast CPU and the slower main system memory. It's a parking area where the CPU can temporarily store the results of calculations it makes as well as any repetitive instructions it receives. Its job is to make the CPU more efficient, and a lack of it can effectively knock the processor down one speed level (which is why "zero" is not a good number if "cache" is the next word you see).

Each time the CPU cycles and nothing happens – an event called a "wait state" – that time is wasted and the processor loses efficiency. In relative terms, main system memory is slow compared to the CPU, and if there is no cache, the CPU constantly has to wait for data to come from and get to that memory. Cache memory is much faster than main system memory. If the CPU can use the cache as a parking area instead, it reduces the number of wait states and performance goes up.

You'll also find cache memory (usually referred to in technical manuals as level 1 or L1 cache) inside the processor itself. The amount varies depending on which processor we're discussing (see Chapter 7). Although its function is similar to that of the L2 cache, there usually isn't enough of it to do a thorough job (which is why you want more).

In some advanced systems, you may also find a small amount of cache memory on the hard drive controller (it's not unusual to find it on a SCSI adapter at the high end) or on the hard drive itself. In both cases, this cache memory is used to speed up data retrieval and has a similar function to the caching that used to be provided by Windows 3.1x through a program called Smartdrive and is now integrated into Windows 9x. Unlike all the other types of memory we've discussed so far, whether the controller or drive has memory is a choice you make when you buy them; they can't normally be upgraded. See Chapter 10 for more details.

More memory will also be associated with your graphics controller and, possibly, with your sound controller, too.

The function of the memory for the graphics controller is primarily to provide higher colour values as you increase resolution. For example, it takes only 1 MB of graphics memory to produce 24-bit colour (16.7 million shades) at a resolution of 640 by 480 (640 horizontal pixels by 480 lines of them). To get that many colours at 800 by 600, you'll need 2 MB of graphics memory; 4 MB will be required to get it at 1024 by 768.

Most people don't need 24-bit colour at these high resolutions, although arch gamers, designers, desktop publishers, and artists can benefit from 16.7 million shades. So, why do some of the more recent graphics controllers have 8 MB? Three-dimensional rendering and acceleration can also use memory – and the more of it that newer cards can get, particularly those using the new Accelerated Graphics Port (AGP), the better.

There will be memory present on a sound controller if it's one that uses wave table synthesis. The memory is used to store actual sound samples from which all other sounds are extrapolated. On low-end sound controllers, the memory will be ROM. On higher-end sound controllers it will be a form of RAM, allowing you to add more sounds. Certain models from Turtle Beach, Advanced Gravis, Diamond Multimedia, Creative Labs, and perhaps others may allow you to add memory to them.

We'll be discussing the types of memory currently available below, but new variations are always appearing. Your homework assignment is to find out what type of L2 cache and main system RAM the motherboard's chipset supports, as well as how much of the main memory is cacheable. You'll also want to read on a little more to find out how the popularity of a memory type can affect its price relative to other forms. As part of your upgrade strategy (or if you have a system you want to upgrade now), the following will also come in handy.

Memory prices go up and down like a yo-yo. In the latter half of the 1990s memory has been less expensive than at any previous time. Several times in the past few years, faster memory has actually been less expensive than older, slower types, simply because of supply and demand. For example, in early 1998, SDRAM was actually less expensive than EDO RAM. Also, 168-pin DIMMs were less expensive per megabyte than 72-pin SIMMs, which were, in turn, less expensive per meg than the old 30-pin modules for 486 systems. When purchasing memory, it really does pay to shop around.

There is a simple rule to follow when adding more memory to any of the parts of your computer that allow you to do so (typically motherboard, graphics controller, and possibly sound controller): *Find out what you have already and get more of what you've already got.* Mixing types of RAM on the same device will almost invariably lead to what technicians call "unexpected and undesirable results."

For detailed notes on adding more memory, please see *How to Avoid Buying a New Computer*.

Memory Types

Memory Types	Found where?	Description
DRAM	motherboard, graphics controllers, printers, audio controllers	Pronounced dee-ram. Dynamic RAM: Single-port random access memory with only one data path. Unlike Video RAM (VRAM), which can be read from and written to simultaneously, DRAM can only perform one function at a time. When a graphics board uses DRAM instead of VRAM for bitmap data transfer, you may want to wallpaper the bathroom while waiting for the screen to redraw. DRAM gets the name "dynamic" because the electrical charges used to store memory states are provided by capacitors which store, then release, the charge. They have to be continuously refreshed (hence the term "dynamic"). DRAM is the commonly used type of memory that makes up the and conventional extended memory detailed above and is normally sold in single inline memory modules (SIMMs). Two wait-states.
SRAM	L2 cache	Static RAM (ess-ram) is unlike DRAM in that it doesn't have to be constantly refreshed, but holds its contents until released (or until you turn the computer off). This makes it considerably faster than DRAM, and because SRAM cells often contain four transistors instead of one, much more expensive. When you see a computer advertised as having 128 K, or 256 K of cache memory (or external or L2 cache memory), it's an indication of how much SRAM is in the system.
SDRAM	motherboard, graphics controllers	Synchronous DRAM. Its timing is synchronized to the system clock. By running in sync to an external clock signal, SDRAM can run at the same speed as the CPU/memory bus. This results in a memory system without wait-states to slow everything down. At the same speed, SDRAM is about 10% faster than EDO RAM, but newer versions of it are significantly faster, running at 10 ns instead of the 60 ns common for EDO RAM. SDRAM now also comes in two distinct types: for 66 MHz motherboards and for 100 MHz boards using Intel's new 440BX chipset and faster (350 and 400 MHz) Pentium II processors. At any speed, your system's chipset must support it explicitly before you can use it. 100 MHz SDRAM is the most expensive of the memory types currently available, but 66 MHz SDRAM is often the least expensive of the three mainstream varieties. SDRAM comes in 72-pin SIMMs and 168-pin DIMMs.
Synchronous SRAM	L2 cache	Older, asynchronous SRAM reads and writes sequentially, with one operation completed before the other begins. Pipelined, synchronous SRAM lets a second data access begin before the first is completed, permitting burst transfer rates as high as 100MB per second. Synchronous burst SRAM can cut cycle time to roughly 10 ns, an easy match for a 66 MHz bus. Will faster cache memory be useful on a 100 MHz motherboard? You betcha!

Memory Types	Found where?	Description
EDO-RAM	motherboard, graphics controllers	Extended data out random access memory (EDO RAM) and its cousin, Burst EDO RAM (BEDO RAM), controllers are anywhere from 4 to 15% faster than FPM-DRAM. EDO RAM gets its name by extending the time during which data can be read from memory, because the available read time doesn't become invalid until an additional signal is sent to the chip. By contrast, conventional DRAM normally discharges its contents after each read and must be refreshed before another read can occur. EDO RAM takes one processor wait-state, which led some publications to claim it was 50% faster than FPM-DRAM. It isn't. In order to use so EDO RAM, your motherboard's chipset must explicitly support it. The memory market fluctuates constantly, so EDO RAM is now usually more expensive than FPM-DRAM, but less expensive than SDRAM. EDO RAM comes in 72-pin SIMMs and, occasionally, on 168-pin DIMMs (dual inline memory modules).
FPM-DRAM	motherboard, graphics controllers, printers, audio controllers	With the introduction of newer types of computer memory, such as EDO RAM and SDRAM, standard DRAM has now been dubbed "Fast Page Mode" or FPM-DRAM.
Weird Memory Types		
CDRAM	motherboard	Cached RAM, invented by Mitsubishi Electronics, combines an SRAM (static RAM – see above) cache with 4 or 16 MB of DRAM within a single chip. This onboard SRAM can be used as either a cache or a buffer and gives the RAM an approximate 15 ns access time. Because the RAM does not have to send its information to an external SRAM cache, overall system performance is improved considerably.
EDRAM	motherboard	Enhanced DRAM. Like CDRAM, it also incorporates an on-chip SRAM cache. Developed by Ramtron International Corp. (Colorado Springs, CO). By improving the DRAM's performance to 35 ns, and combining it with a 2KB, 15 ns SRAM cache, a DRAM chip with a 15 ns access time is created. In contrast, CDRAM uses a much larger 15KB, 15 ns cache and DRAM with a much slower 70 ns access time.
RDRAM	graphics controllers	Rambus DRAM, developed by a company of the same name. Currently being toyed with by Toshiba and Samsung, it's similar to SDRAM (see above), but faster, says Rambus. You're more likely to find it appearing on accelerated graphics cards and the Nintendo N64, but I wouldn't be surprised to see it show up on somebody's PC, eventually.

Memory Types	Found where?	Description
Graphics Memory Types		
FPM-DRAM, EDO RAM, SDRAM	graphics controllers	All of these standard memory types may be found on a graphics controller, too, but it won't be as fast as if it used one of the types below.
SGRAM	graphics controllers	Synchronous graphics RAM, a form of DRAM for graphics controllers and printers that is synchronized to the system clock and, according to one manufacturer, Fujitsu, produces data bandwidth up to five times that of standard DRAM.
VRAM	graphics controllers	Video random access memory. Pronounced vee-ram. The oldest of the so-called "dual port" memory types that allow the graphics processor to read from memory and redraw the screen simultaneously, eliminating the problem plaguing single-ported memory types (i.e., DRAM), where the memory can only be read from or written to at one time (and the graphics engine must wait each time the screen is updated). With single-port memory, the higher the refresh rate, the resolution or the colour depth used, the more times per second the RAMDAC (the device that converts the graphics card memory's digital contents to an analog signal) will have to read from the frame buffer, and the slower the system.
WRAM	graphics controllers	Window RAM, developed by Samsung Electronics and most likely to show up on a Matrox. graphics controller and others. According to Advanced Imaging (June 1996), "when considering the benefits of WRAM over VRAM memory, one must bear in mind that WRAM memory is both faster, offering a 50 percent performance increase, and less expensive, 20 percent lower cost per bit, than VRAM memory."

9

Notebooks and Other
Small Computers

Notebook or desktop?

Your daily life may require that you do computing on the road or cart
your computer from home to office and back again. If that's the case,
there's no debate here. Buy a notebook. The rest of us, however, will
find that notebook computers have both attractions and disadvantages.

Notebooks (also known as laptops and portables) are small and
light compared to desktop systems and require very little desk space.
They're highly portable and quite powerful. On the downside, the light
weight and high portability make them eminently stealable (add insurance to your costs). They are 50 to 100 per cent more expensive than
a comparably powered desktop system, and yet they trail behind desktops in technology. For instance, while there were new models using
Intel's "Deschutes" Pentium II processors in 1998, the speed topped
out at 300 MHz, compared to 450 MHz for desktops, and there
weren't any notebooks using the 100 MHz motherboards with 440BX
chipsets, although the 440BX was also a mobile chipset.

Notebooks have a limited upgrade potential; their obsolescence
is built in. New models arrive about every six months and their high

cost drops like a stone in a very short time. The same factors that affect the need to replace or upgrade desktops (see Chapter 3) also affect notebooks.

Last, but not least, notebook computers hurt. You can either have the screen or the (often cramped) keyboard at the right height to avoid strain injuries, but not both. Every ergonomic and workplace safety expert I've interviewed or whose work I've read has thrown their hands up and merely suggested exercises to lessen the effects.

These are concerns for adults, but teenagers and beginning university students seem to love to talk parents into buying these products using the arguments of lightness and portability, but adding a few wrinkles of their own.

Most parents know what to do with the "But everyone else has one" argument. Here are a few more strategies. If your son or daughter claims they can use the computer to take notes in class or go to a friend's house to do homework, ask not only how fast they can type, but also how many teachers or professors will allow a notebook to be used in class. If everyone else has one, ask where the notebook will be plugged in when the batteries (usually good for a couple of hours at best) run out.

When the notebook can't be taken to class (during gym class, for example, or when a cranky teacher won't allow it), ask your offspring where it *will* be kept. Ask how secure a school locker *really* is and how long it would take them to get into someone else's locker if they had an urgent need. What will happen to the expensive notebook if it's left unattended anywhere in the school for longer than ten seconds? How many times have things taken to school never, ever, been seen again. On this same note, ask how safe they will feel carrying it to school or to a friend's house. It's a sad commentary on the times in which we live, but the answer may vary depending on what type of neighbourhoods your children have to cross to get there and the transportation method used.

As noted above it may, because of job requirements, be a necessity for an adult to put up with the physical stress associated with notebook use. But homework, like rust, never sleeps. Does it seem reasonable to subject a growing body to these strains night after night after night? Yes, on this topic, I'm a cranky old poop – and proud of it.

Notebook, Handheld, or Palmtop?

Okay, let's assume that, despite arguments to the contrary, you still want a notebook or at least some form of small computing device. Within broad categories, you get some choice. "Notebook" in this context has a specific meaning. We're discussing a unit with a screen, keyboard, mass storage, and some multimedia capabilities that runs the same operating system(s) and software as a full-sized desktop PC (or PowerMac). However, there are two other categories of small devices (actually three, if you want to get picky).

A handheld PC or PC companion, also known as an H/PC, is a unit with a small screen, small keyboard, and rudimentary storage that runs Windows CE (currently in version 2.1). Although most people think of WinCE as Windows 9x Lite, Microsoft insists that it was written from the ground up and that the similarity to the Win9x interface is merely cosmetic and functional. WinCE runs special versions of Win9x software that, while similar, are designed to fit within WinCE's smaller environment.

H/PCs are made by many of the same companies that make full PCs, such as Compaq, NEC, and Hewlett-Packard, as well as by some who previously made proprietary electronic organizers, such as Sharp, Casio, Hitachi, and others. H/PCs may have screens in black and white, sixteen shades of grey, or colour (and that choice alone will affect their price). They currently cost around $1,000 Cdn, which may account for their relative lack of popularity compared to the next group.

Early in 1999, Microsoft will release another version of WinCE with a more robust feature set. Code-named Jupiter, it is designed for larger H/PCs that approach the functionality of full-blown notebook systems. These new units have already been dubbed Jumbo H/PCs, and Hewlett-Packard was said to be well advanced in developing one.

A **Palm PC** has no keyboard and usually accepts input via stylus, using one form or another of handwriting recognition. There are two broad classes of Palm PC. The most recent runs a version of Windows CE 2.1 and stripped-down versions of Win9x applications. Palm PCs, like H/PCs, are made by a variety of companies. However, the most popular versions use proprietary operating systems and software that will only run with the proprietary product.

By far the most successful is the PalmPilot from USRobotics (now owned by 3Com). It set the market for these "palmtops," and its successor, the Palm III, shows every sign of continuing this process.

A British company, Psion, also makes a Palm PC. Others such as Sharp, and Casio continue to market lower-cost proprietary organizers of their own (our tentative third category). Hewlett-Packard, once heavily into this market, has abandoned it in favour of WinCE products. Apple, the company that started all this with its Newton personal digital assistant (PDA), has left the small-format market entirely. None of these proprietary systems is compatible with anything else.

Prices of palmtops vary, but the most popular, the 3Com products, usually sell for just under $600 Cdn.

Notebooks

As with every other class of products in this book, you can expect the notebook market to keep changing. As noted earlier, the average shelf life of a particular notebook model is about six months before it is replaced by a newer version with a more powerful processor and more features. Your homework assignment will be to find out whatever is new.

The trend for notebook prices doesn't follow the desktop model, where the grid showing prices for top-of-the-line models down to the trailing edge has remained constant with ever-more-powerful systems filling each niche.

Between 1996 and 1998, the top price for notebook systems fell about $1,200 Cdn, with manufacturers announcing price cuts almost monthly (see the examples below). It's a trend we can only hope will continue.

At the low end of the notebook price scale, we've not seen the same changes that have occurred in the desktop market. For example, the introduction of Intel's Celeron, AMD's K6 family, and, to a lesser extent, various products from National Semiconductor/Cyrix/IBM meant that the low end of the desktop market provided new, albeit slower, technology for those on a tight budget, the so-called entry level. Prior to this, the low end for desktops meant trailing-edge products that proved woefully inadequate in a short time.

In the notebook sector, however, the trailing edge of the price structure *is* the trailing edge of the technology, often literally last year's technology.

There are other differences, too. For example, earlier, when I was explaining the difference between nationally advertised brand-name products and locally assembled desktop systems, I noted that the consumer market was split about fifty-fifty. I also said it largely didn't affect performance, reliability, or stability. The same is not true for notebooks.

To begin with, notebooks, as opposed to handheld and palmtop systems, aren't really considered to be consumer products. Their price and the uses to which they are put make them primarily business products, and businesses tend to favour national brands (businesses represent about 85 per cent of the total market for all types of systems). In the notebook sector, this preference is marked: nearly 95 per cent of notebooks purchased by businesses will be from nationally advertised brand-name manufacturers.

It's not just superstition that gives national brands this edge. Designing and building a notebook computer involves some very high-end engineering. Notebooks are full of proprietary solutions to achieve the amount of miniaturization required to pack a lot of power into a small package, and, frankly, local assemblers usually don't have the type of budget or expertise to get it right. Locally assembled or no-name brands do exist, but in my experience they tend to be heavier and, if not demonstrably less reliable, at least a little more fragile. There are also some legitimate concerns when it comes to warranty protection for some parts and after-warranty service on others.

One of the questions you should always ask about a notebook, particularly when it has a thin film transistor (TFT, or active matrix) screen, is just what the warranty covers and when you become eligible for warranty service. (See below for more detailed definitions and explanation.)

Notebooks also use batteries when they're not plugged into an electrical outlet. Some types of battery outlast others but all of them stop working eventually. The vast majority of them are proprietary in at least shape and connector type. Unless you bought a spare at the time you purchased the original system (not a bad idea), you'll need to find a replacement that fits your system. You'll want to be able to get one from either the original manufacturer or from a third-party supplier, and your chances of being able to do so are higher if it was from a well-known brand that is still in business.

While we're on the topic, it's a good idea to pick up all kinds of extra parts when you purchase the original system because these parts tend to be in rather short supply not long after the notebook is considered an old model. These extras include batteries, extra hard drives, optional floppy drives and CD-ROM drives, battery charger adapters, automobile power adapters, external port extenders, and full docking stations, as well as any proprietary cables required to connect the notebook to a PC or a printer.

If this is true for notebooks, it is doubly so for H/PC and Palm PC products.

Notebook market overview

The story about notebook computers in 1998 can be summed up in one word: price. Not only had notebook prices fallen across the board since 1997, but what you received for what you paid was considerably more. In 1997, 373,000 notebooks were sold in Canada, according to IDC Canada's market analyst, George Bulat – a 21.9 per cent growth over 1996. By comparison, the desktop computer market grew by only 9.3 per cent in the same period. Figures for the first half of 1998 show a similar jump: over 20 per cent more units shipped than in the first half of 1997.

However, it's when we look at the value of the market that the issue of price becomes more evident. Total Canadian 1997 notebook sales of $1.22 billion represented only 14.5 per cent growth over 1996, and the expectation is that we'll see the same disparity between unit sales and dollar value during 1998.

More specific examples came from IDC's price analyst, Kevin Ritchards. In March 1997, the most you could spend for a notebook computer bought you a Toshiba Tecra 740 CDT, with built-in multimedia, CD-ROM drive, and a 133 MHz Pentium MMX processor. It would have set you back $10,300 Cdn on the street. Competing with it closely in performance and price was IBM's Thinkpad 380E, a 150 MHz Pentium MMX-based unit.

A year later, that same Tecra 740 CDT was selling on the street for about $3,810 Cdn, while the Thinkpad 380E, when you could find it, was about $2,000. In six months, previous trailing-edge systems, based on 133 or 150 MHz MMX processors, will have dropped off the market, says Ritchards. Pentium processors at 166 MHz were the new entry level by summer 1998, and they will give way to 200 MHz notebooks – likely by fall. The lowest price tier for brand-name systems (about $1,800 to $2,200) isn't expected to change.

All the change in price ranges for notebooks is taking place at the high end. For example, we've already noted that Toshiba's 1997 high-end model cost $10,300. In April 1998, it was replaced by the company's new performance leader, the Tecra 780 DVD with 266 MHz Pentium II processor, which was selling for about $9,000 Cdn. In the fall, the performance bar went up again, with 300 MHz Pentium IIs forming the new top end, and at a similar price. IBM, Compaq, Dell, and a host of others also have Pentium II-based models. IBM's Thinkpad 770e with 8 GB hard drive was selling in spring 1998 for about $8,000, Compaq's Armada 7800 without DVD for $7,830, and the HP Omnibook 7100's "average street price" was $7,895.

The 1997 Canadian market leaders were Toshiba (24.1 per cent), IBM (20.3), Compaq (16), Dell (6.9), Packard Bell/NEC (6.3), Ottawa-based Eurocom (2.9), and Apple (2.9). Companies with less than 2 per cent market share included AST, Acer, Computron, Digital, Gateway 2000, Hewlett-Packard, Impulse (which has since gone), Panasonic, and Vancouver-based Sidus. Others with shares too small to calculate included Bondwell, Fujitsu, Hitachi, and a variety of locally assembled and no name products (total 13 per cent). All figures from IDC are based on units shipped.

New features at the high end

In February 1998, Intel began shipping its "Deschutes" mobile Pentium II processors. These allowed business notebook users to run the more robust and corporately favoured Windows NT operating system without a hitch. When Intel released its 440BX chipset for 100 MHz desktop motherboards as well as 350 and 400 MHz Pentium II processors in April 1998, it also announced that the 440BX would come in a notebook configuration. You can expect the company to follow the 266 MHz Pentium II notebook processors with 300 and 333 MHz models running on 66 MHz notebooks even sooner, and I wouldn't be surprised to see even faster versions soon afterwards. In fact, as noted above, 300 MHz models had already arrived in the fall.

Top-end systems shipped with 64 MB of at least EDO memory, if not the faster synchronous DRAM (SDRAM).

Built-in digital video/versatile disc (DVD) drives, while still not available from all companies, were increasingly common in this price range. Alternative CD-ROM drives ranged from 16X to 24X drives. Hard drives had respectable capacity, too, with 4.77 GB to 7.63 GB (and higher) options widely available.

There were no dual-scan screens in this price range (see below). All models at the high end come with bright TFT (thin film transistor, aka active matrix) screens. Screen sizes range from 13.3-inch diagonal (most high-end models) to 14.1 inches (Thinkpad 770E).

The days of being stuck at 640 by 480 resolution and 256 or fewer colours were over, too. Graphics accelerator controllers are everywhere, and having 4 MB of memory for them isn't uncommon, producing 16.7 million colours at 1024 by 768 without having to attach an external monitor.

Other multimedia items to be found include MPEG-2 decoding in hardware – virtually a requirement if the model ships with a DVD drive – as well as Dolby Digital (formerly AC-3) sound support. Fully packed units include NTSC (television) and S-video output ports as well as full stereo sound output. The Tecra 780DVD also sports its own camera for video conferencing.

Expandability features include PC card slots (see below). A single slot holding two Type II cards or one Type III card is standard, and the card slots will include both CardBus (a faster implementation) and ZV (zoomed video) port support. Universal Serial Bus ports (two of them) are becoming a standard, and today I wouldn't consider a new computer of any kind that didn't have USB.

Desirable options to seek include user-serviceable memory slots and use of industry standard memory components for easier and less expensive upgrading. Of even more value are hot-swappable bays (that allow you to insert or change a component while the system is running and have it recognized immediately) or connectors for attaching a floppy drive (if it isn't built in), extra hard drive, or second battery.

Speaking of batteries, the high end has gone almost exclusively to Lithium Ion (L-Ion) in preference to the older Nickel Metal-Hydride (NiMH); see below.

And at the other end . . .

By fall 1998, Intel hadn't leaked any plans to follow its low-end desktop processors, the Celeron line, with an equally low-cost notebook version, nor had we heard anything from the Intel wannabes. The low end of the notebook price scale still represented last year's technology.

I mentioned above, for example, the Toshiba Satellite Pro 440 CDX with an approximate street price of $1,796 (according to IDC, although at the same time its list price on Toshiba Canada's Web site was $3,929). For the price, you got a 133 MHz Pentium MMX processor, 16 MB of EDO RAM (considered low for running Windows 95) and 256 KB L2 cache. It included a 1.35 GB hard drive (small), a 12.1-inch dual scan (DSTN) screen, and a graphics controller with 2 MB of memory (upper resolution of 800 by 600 at 65,535 colours), a 10X CD-ROM drive, built-in sound system, L-Ion battery, PC card slot, and one USB port, but a modem was extra.

Another example came from IBM. The 150 MHz 380E was no longer featured at the company's Canadian direct-purchase Web site (www.can.ibm.com/hc), but a similar model, the 310ED, priced at $2,199, was. It came with 166 MHz Pentium MMX processor, 32 MB of EDO RAM, and 2.1 GB hard drive (smallish). It also included a built-in sound system and speakers, 20X max CD-ROM drive, 56 Kbps modem, NiMH battery, 12.1-inch DSTN display (only 1 MB of video memory), and PC card slot, but no USB port or L2 cache were mentioned.

This still leaves a broad spectrum between $1,800 to $2,200 at the low end and $7,800 to $9,000 at the top. You'll find that the price differential translates directly into processing speed, hard drive capacity, memory, screen size and type, graphics speed and colour range, and add-on components. This price gap also provides some alternative directions.

For example, Toshiba is no longer alone in the mini-notebook field. Its diminutive Libretto line has been joined by similar products from Hitachi, Fujitsu, Mitsubishi, and NEC (although not all models are available in Canada). In spring 1998, the most recent Libretto, the 100CT, boasted a 166 MHz Pentium MMX processor, 3.03 GB hard drive, 32 MB of EDO RAM, 7.1-inch TFT screen. It weighed in at 2.3 lbs. with an L-Ion battery. Canadian list price was $3,999.

On the other hand, if your job puts you (or your computer) in harm's way, there's always Panasonic's "ruggedized" line to consider. With a metal case and sealed keyboard, it, too, is in the mid-price range.

Notebook batteries

Batteries play a big part in your use of a notebook system. You'll want to know how long the battery will keep your system alive, how long it lasts before it dies completely, and how quickly it recharges. Look at how much it costs to get a backup or replacement when the original wears out, and whether this model's battery is easily available either from the original manufacturer or from other vendors (batteries for some of the lesser-known brands can sometimes be difficult to find).

Modern notebook computers use one of three, possibly four, battery types, but before we get to details, I need to describe "memory effect," a phenomenon common to all types of rechargeable battery. With most rechargeable products you need to fully discharge the battery before you recharge it. Otherwise, you will shorten its life. What happens is that after a while, the battery "remembers" the level to which it was discharged, and it will no longer discharge past that point. Over time, the level moves up until one day it won't discharge, won't recharge, and simply won't work. It's dead, Jim, and you need to replace it.

As for the types you'll likely encounter:

Nickel Cadmium (NiCad) batteries are the oldest in terms of technology. They're also the least desirable because they're most likely to suffer from memory effect. NiCads also discharge more quickly than the other types, limiting the length of time you can use your system on battery rather severely. You'll only find NiCads in old, used notebooks (at least, I haven't seen any on the market for a couple of years now). However, you may still find this type, which is the least expensive to produce, in some electronic organizers, palmtops, hand-helds, and digital cameras.

Nickel Metal-Hydride (NiMH) batteries also go flat fairly quickly and suffer from memory effect, although they take a little longer to die than NiCads. Several companies have worked on the NiMH technology to extend the length of time you can go between charges and the point at which they die, but treat all claims that a par-ticular company's brand "doesn't suffer from memory effect" as good marketing, but a little light of reality. You're more likely to find NiMH batteries in budget systems, and they are far more common in hand-helds, palmtops, and digital cameras.

Lithium-Ion (L-Ion or Li-Ion) batteries last a long time between charges; however, they die more quickly if you deep-discharge them. Unlike NiCad and NiMH batteries, L-Ion batteries love short charges. You'll find them in nearly all leading-edge notebooks, but they are not yet common in handhelds, palmtops, or cameras, and will probably push prices up when and if they ever are.

In the first edition of *How to Buy a Computer*, I talked about a new battery type that was being discussed in the notebook community: Zinc-Air. I said at the time that no one had produced a system using this scheme and, to my knowledge, no one ever did. Today there is yet another new type in the offing, Lithium Polymer, but I suspect it will actually come onto the market by early 1999.

Lithium Polymer (L-Poly) is a battery type currently being developed by Toshiba and others. It shares a love of short charges with

L-Ion, but has the added attribute of being mouldable, just like Silly Putty. Notebook engineers rub their hands together anticipating thin batteries that could fit behind the screen, or oddly-shaped batteries that can fit around other components. While L-Poly may make the dual tasks of miniaturization and fitting an increasing number of devices into the same space easier, it may also make finding a replacement – when and if the battery dies – a real challenge. We'll see.

As you add toys to a notebook, you'll find that concerns over battery life will dominate your choices. An active matrix colour screen eats power like candy compared to the less-gorgeous dual-scan screen. The size of a hard drive isn't relevant to battery life, but adding a floppy drive, CD-ROM or DVD drive, sound system, devices in the PC card slots, devices connected to a USB port, and other gizmos all take a toll. Ask about how the model you're eyeing handles power management (such as turning selected devices and ports off when they're idle or not in use).

Notebook screens

There are four types of notebook screen currently on or about to go on the market, but we're going to talk about only two of them in detail here. I'll briefly discuss the one that isn't here yet and save the one that's fallen away from notebook use for the following discussion of handhelds and palmtops. By the way, unlike desktop monitors, notebook screens really are the size advertised.

There are no monochrome (black and white or shades of grey) screens left in the notebook market. You're going to get colour. The discussion that's left is how bright the colour will be, how many people will be able to watch it at the same time, how many colours you'll see, and at what resolution you'll see them.

The most popular (and most expensive) screen technology is called **active matrix** (also referred to as thin film transistor or TFT). TFT is a type of liquid crystal display (LCD). Each picture element (pixel) is composed of three crystal cells representing red, green, and blue. As power is applied to a crystal, it twists to allow more or less light through it to produce colour shades. If the crystal can twist through eight variation, each pixel can produce one of 16.7 million shades. The fast refresh rate of an active matrix screen is achieved by powering each cell with its own transistor (which is why we also call these things thin-film transistor screens. Some notes:

• In order to achieve a stated resolution (1024 x 765, for example) there have to be as many pixels as that resolution requires (786,432 in this case). Where the display may suffer is when you run it at a lower resolution than the maximum. You'll either get a black border, or, if the system stretches the image to fill the whole screen, it may be blurry.

• There is space between the pixel cells corresponding roughly to the dot pitch on a desktop monitor. In a notebook, the range is 0.28 mm to 0.31 mm. There is also space between the pixels themselves. Depending on the model, the pixel pitch could be as low as 0.02 mm or as high as 0.20 mm.

• NEC uses a scheme that places the transistors on the sides of the cells, where they block less light. The company claims the result is a brighter screen.

TFT screens produce bright colours and are viewable even if you're at an angle to the screen. If you're engaged in colour-sensitive work on the road, such as preparing electronic slide presentations, the colour fidelity is worth the added cost. If you use your notebook to share information with clients (real estate, insurance, and so on), the wide viewing angle is very useful.

In 1998, TFT screen sizes ranged from 7.1 inches viewable (Toshiba Libretto sub-notebook) to over 14 inches (virtually the same viewable size or more than you'd get from a 15-inch desktop monitor). High-end models offered 24-bit colour and on-screen resolutions up to 1024 by 768 without the need for an external monitor. (See Chapter 13 for detailed definitions of terms such as pixel, 24-bit colour, and resolution.)

The other LCD variation in current use for notebooks is also known by several names, such as **Dual Scan**, DSTN (dual supertwist nemonic), FSTN (fast supertwist nemonic), or the more generic **Passive Matrix**.

Like TFT screens, passive matrix screens are composed of three-cell pixels. Again, the crystal cells twist to permit backlight to come through them. The difference is that the cells are not independently powered. Instead, there is a row of transistors across the top of the screen and columns down the side, which anchor a grid (or matrix) of wires that intersect at the cells. To apply power to one cell, for example, the system might count 20 lines down, 150 cells over. The term Dual Scan is used when a second row of transistors runs across the middle of the screen, allowing the top and bottom halves to be refreshed simultaneously. This is what you get at the low end of the price scale.

Gas Plasma is the technology that may appear before the next edition of *How to Buy a Computer*. Toshiba, among others, has demonstrated this technology, but primarily in large flat monitors designed to be hung on the wall (at about $14,000 US). If the technology improves to the point where (a) it can be applied to a small screen, (b) it can be used without draining the batteries in a second and a half, and (c) it's affordable, we may see it on a notebook sometime in 1999 or later. One of Gas Plasma's better features may allow it to be detachable, improving on the ergonomic concerns discussed above.

PC cards

What we now call PC cards used to have a much longer name: PCMCIA cards (which stood for Personal Computer Memory Card International Association, or People Can't Memorize Computer Industry Acronyms, whichever you prefer). These miniaturized hardware devices are still the main way you add capabilities to a notebook. In essence, PC cards solve the problem created because notebooks don't have the expansion slots found in desktop systems (unless there are some in a full-sized docking station).

There are hundreds of PC card devices on the market. They are used to add multimedia components to an older notebook that doesn't have them, modems, network interfaces, scanners, removable mass-storage devices, SCSI adapters, video cameras for desktop conferencing, more memory, small hard drives, NTSC (television) input and output devices, and lots more.

Because of the flexibility of PC cards and the direct connection of their 68-pin connectors to the system bus, they usually provide good performance. New standards for them, such as CardBus and Zoom Video, have made them better. But all PC slots in notebooks are not the same. While the majority of systems will include one Type III slot that's able to accept one Type III card or two Type I or Type II cards, you may find models at the low end that won't allow more than one card of any type. (A PC card's "Type" is generally defined by its thickness, which in turn is a function of how much is packed into it. I'm sure there are long technical descriptions of the difference, but simple, or thinner, cards such as modems, sound cards, SCSI adapters, network cards, and the like, tend to be Type II. Hard drives on a card tend to be thicker Type III cards. To my knowledge, there aren't many older Type I cards still in general circulation.)

As with any other computer component, the quality of any individual PC card device may vary. Some of them are better than others at being "hot-swappable" using Windows 9x "plug and play" (also known as "plug and pray"). A cable that often connects a card to an external device (such as a drive or set of sound input/output ports), generically known by the curious name "dongle," may last longer from some companies than from others. As with any other separately purchased component, you'll want to choose one that has a technical support system with either telephone (or better yet) Internet contact points to get updated drivers or service when applicable.

Some points to ponder

When you're checking various notebook models, you'll find that you have lots of choices. Screen sizes will vary. Multimedia components will vary. So will your choice of pointing devices and keyboards. For example, an "eraser head" mouse embedded in the keyboard, plus a shelf on which to rest your wrists, or a touchpad pointer, will provide less grief to your wrists and your pocket than a trackball or a mouse (they die).

Some sub-notebooks save space by leaving out little things, such as external ports for a full-sized monitor, keyboard, or mouse. Others don't include a floppy disk drive, and you'll have to check carefully to see if an external model is (a) available and (b) included in the price. If you can connect an external floppy (a) in addition to a built-in CD or DVD drive and (b) while the notebook is running, you'll like both options. Keyboards with the Windows key should be standard by the time you read this. So should at least one USB port.

Virtually all notebook and sub-notebook manufacturers offer some sort of external docking port to allow you to keep connections for various devices back at the office and to hook them up quickly. Some of the ports cost hideous amounts, are almost as big as a full desktop system, and offer only a skimpy list of connectors. Others have small port extenders or replicators that cost much less and may include SCSI and Ethernet network connectors along with the full complement of external monitor, serial, parallel, and PS/2 connectors for mouse and keyboard.

How big are your fingertips? When you make something smaller, something usually suffers. Pay attention to the keyboards and your habits. Notebook systems often make compromises about the size of function keys and cursor controls, and the software you normally use might make the compromises built into a specific model awkward. Cramped keyboards are the bane of notebooks. Hunt-and-peck typists may have no problem with them, but anyone who can touch type is going to have trouble adjusting. Key sizes and placement vary wildly from brand to brand and model to model. You'll need to see the model and try it out.

If your system is loaded to the gills with toys, you'll want to be able to save as much battery as you can. Power management features have become pretty much standard, but they vary from model to model.

How many things you can power off, whether the notebook will enter "suspend" mode and wake up successfully, or whether it will wake up on a modem ring or a local area network command is a combined function of the system's BIOS (basic in/out system), the chipset used on the motherboard, and the operating system (Win98 is better than either Win95 or NT4.x – you may have to wait for NT5.0 to take advantage of these features if Windows NT is what you wish to use).

Warranty: What happens when your notebook breaks? Various manufacturers have different warranty policies dealing with everything from active matrix screens (how many transistors powering cells have to die and in what combination before it's considered defunct) to catastrophic failure. Fixing one if you're in Winnipeg or San Francisco – either through on-site service, short-turnaround courier service, or by carrying it into an authorized technical depot – may not be a problem. But the type of service offered and how you'll access it are things you'll want to consider carefully if you're planning to visit Prague, Pago Pago, or Rangoon.

Memory expandable to xxx: the number doesn't matter. Whether you can use industry standard memory modules (rare) does matter. Expect additional memory to cost a lot more than for desktops.

"Brand" may be a fine distinction: Despite what I've said about name-brand products, only Toshiba makes its own notebooks. Everyone else gets the parts from original equipment manufacturer (OEM) suppliers. To find out who makes what, check Per Lyngemark's Notebook Jungle (http://www.lyngemark.com/jungle/). Other Internet resources for the comparison shopper include Emanuel P. Brown's Portable Computing Center Status Report (http://www.enteract.com/~epbrown/), James Omura's The Moving Target (http://www.pathcom.com/~jimomura/), and Scott Watson's Lapland (http://www.ccia.com/%7Ewsw/lapland/index.htm). If one or more of these sites is inactive when you check, use any Internet search engine (Yahoo, Alta Vista, Excite, Hotbot, Dogpile or their successors) to search for notebooks and reviews. You'll find new sites.

Colours and resolution: You're bound to see specs that show 65,535 or 16.7 million colours available on your notebook screen at 800 by 600 or higher. Hold that thought. Some models will display 800 by 600, but most can show only 640 by 480 unless you hook up to an external monitor. Ask what the specification *really* means, especially at the low end of the price scale.

I'm going to live overseas. Should I buy my notebook in North America or will it be cheaper abroad?

I didn't address this question in the first edition of *How to Buy a Computer*, but a few folks who bought the book did contact me to ask. I checked with a few manufacturers and got the following answers.

All computer products are less expensive in the North American market than they are elsewhere. That's just the way the world works. Perhaps more importantly, the on-screen instructions and manuals are almost always written in the language of the country where the unit is sold, so unless you're fluent in the host country's language . . .

Yes, but what about differences in electrical currents? Toshiba, NEC, Compaq, Dell, and IBM say that the power supplies for their notebooks are "universal." You may have to acquire a converter for the wall-plug part of the plug-in cable, but it should work. Nevertheless, it never hurts to ask the vendor and to have the answer clearly written on the sales agreement just in case this practice doesn't continue for every new model.

Where you're more likely to run into trouble is if you're a Canadian customer and you buy your system in the United States (desktop or notebook). Quite often, the Canadian operation of a national brand is a separate company. It may not honour the warranty. Sometimes the distinction isn't obvious. For example, IBM Canada won't honour the warranty of a unit purchased in the States unless you're an American citizen on a visit. Go figure.

Budget Notebooks

Model	Compaq Presario 1200	Compaq Presario 1600 series	Compaq Armada 1500 series	Dell Inspirion 3000 M200ST	Dell Inspirion 3200 D233XT	Eurocom 6200
Processor	Cyrix MediaGX/200	AMD K6 233 MHz	Pentium MMX 166 to 266 MHz	Pentium MMX 200	Pentium II 233 MHz, Mobile 440BX chipset	Pentium MMX 200 or better
L2 cache memory	none	512 KB		512 KB	512 KB	512 KB
Architecture	MediaGX	PCI	PCI	PCI	PCI (66 MHz motherboard base speed)	PCI (60 MHz system bus)
Standard/max. RAM	32 MB (SDRAM) / 80 MB	32 MB (SDRAM) / 96 MB	16 MB (SDRAM) to 80 MB or 32 MB (SDRAM) / 96 MB depending on model	32 MB (SDRAM) / 144 MB	32 MB (SDRAM) / 144 MB	32 MB (EDO) / 128 MB
Expansion options	One PC Card slot (2 Type II, 1 Type III). No USB.	One PC Card slot (2 Type II, 1 Type III). No USB.	Two PC Card slots (2/II, 1/II)	PC Card (2/II, 1/III), 3.3 and 5 v. cards supported, hot-swappable. Removable hard disk drive, optional port replicator	Modular options bay accepts CD-ROM or floppy (both included) or 2nd battery	PC Card (2/II, 1/III), port replicator
Ports	serial, parallel (EPP), PS/2 mouse or keyboard, RJ-11 phone jack, headphone, line-in, microphone, SVGA out	serial, parallel (EPP), PS/2 mouse or keyboard, RJ-11 phone jack, headphone, line-in, microphone, SVGA out	Audio line-out, mic-in, headphone out, enhanced parallel (EPP), serial, SVGA out, PS/2 keyboard in	serial, parallel, PS/2 keyboard/, mouse, USB (1),	serial, parallel, PS/2 keyboard/mouse, USB (1), headphones, line-in, microphone, SVGA out, cable (supplied) for simultaneous CD/floppy operation	parallel (ECP/EPP), serial (16C550), VGA out, MIDI/Game port, docking port, mic-in, line-in, line-out
Hard disk drive	2.1 GB	2.1 GB	2.1 to 4 GB	2.1 GB IBM	3.2 GB	2.1 GB
CD-ROM drive	20X max	20X max	20X max	20X Max	24X Max	20X max
Floppy drive	1.44 MB included	1.44 MB included	1.44 MB included	1.44 MB included	1.44 MB included	1.44 MB included
Pointing device	Touchpad	Touchpad	Touchpad	Touchpad	Touchpad	TrackPad
Display	128-bit integrated graphics with processor, 64K colours @ 800 x 600, MPEG (no version stated) software emulation. 12.1" "HPA" (high performance addressing)	128-bit integrated graphics with processor, 64K colours @ 800 x 600, MPEG (no version stated) software emulation. 12.1" "HPA" (high performance addressing)	32-bit PCI local bus graphics, 1 MB EDO RAM (64 K colours), 12.1" DSTN or 12.1" TFT	12.1" TFT, 16M colours, 64-bit NeoMagic 2160 controller, 2 MB EDO RAM	13.3" XGA active matrix (TFT), 128-bit graphics accelerator. Note: quoted price includes 17" Dell 1000LS external monitor	12.1" DSTN or 12.1" TFT

Model	Compaq Presario 1200 series	Compaq Presario 1600 series	Compaq Armada 1500 series	Dell Inspirion 3000 M200ST	Dell Inspirion 3200 D233XT	Eurocom 6200
Sound	Integrated with processor, includes JBL ProAudio speakers	As at left, plus ability to play audio CDs without booting the PC	16-bit "Compaq PremierSound"	16-bit, Yamaha wave table, 3D surround sound, SoundBlaster compatible	3D surround sound with Yamaha software wave table	Stereo speakers, no other details given
Docking stations	none	optional port replicator	(optional) Convenience Base with or without Ethernet	Optional port replicator	Optional port replicator	Optional port replicator
Integrated modem (all may have optional PC card modems) Shows "None" if extra $$$	56Kflex (no mention of V.90 upgradeability)	56Kflex (no mention of V.90 upgradeability)	56Kflex (no mention of V.90 upgradeability)	USR X2, 56K PC card included in price of M166ST (but not in M200ST)	optional	None
Zoomed Video/ CardBus support	no / no	no / yes	Yes (in bottom slot only) / Yes	No / No	not mentioned	Yes / No
Infrared Port	none	none	IrDA 1.1. (4 mbps)	IrDA 1.1. (4 mbps)	IrDA 1.1. (4 mbps)	Yes (spec not noted)
Battery	NiMH	NiMH	L-ion (standard) will also support NiMH	L-ion	L-ion	NiMH (Duracell DR-36) or L-ion
Size (LWH – inches)	10 x 12.2 x 1.93	10 x 12.2 x 1.93	9.6 x 12.2 x 2.1	9.21 x 11.77 x 1.65	9.21 x 11.93 x 2.03	9 x 12 x 2
Weight (lbs.)	7.3	7.3	7.6 to 7.97	6.4	6.9 with CD drive	7.5
Warranty	1 year parts, 1 year carry in labour	1 year parts, 1 year carry in labour	1 year carry-in, 2 year extension available	1 year, extendable to 3 yrs	"A variety of custom support plans are available to suit every need."	1 yr, extendable to 2 yrs
Price**	Starting at $2,921 Cdn list	Starting at $3,718 Cdn list	Starting at $2,549 Cdn list to $4,419	$3,199 direct price	$2,999 direct price (special advertised Aug/98)	Starting at $1,999 Cdn list
Company	Compaq Canada			Dell Canada		Eurocom Canada Ltd.
Phone	800-567-1616			800-544-5056		613-224-6122, 905-282-9744
Web site: http://www.	compaq.ca			dell.ca		eurocom.ca

Budget Notebooks cont'd

Model	IBM Thinkpad 380D	IBM Thinkpad 560	NEC Versa LX VL210	Toshiba Satellite 300CDS	Toshiba Satellite 4000CDX	Toshiba Libretto 100CT
Processor	Pentium MMX 150 MHz	Classic Pentium 133 MHz	Pentium MMX 233 MHz	Pentium MMX 166 MHz	Pentium II / 233 MHz	Penium MMX 233 MHz
L2 cache memory	256 KB	None	512 KB	256KB	512 KB	None
Architecture	PCI 2.1	PCI	PCI	PCI	PCI	PCI
Standard/max. RAM	16 MB (EDO) / 80 MB	8 MB (EDO) / 40 MB	32 MB (??) / 192 MB	16 MB (EDO) / 144 MB	32 MB (SDRAM) / 160 MB	32 MB (EDO) / 64 MB
Expansion options	n/a	PC Card (2/II, 1/III)	Two PC card slots (2/II, 1/II)	Same as right, CD-ROM and floppy are both integrated	Same as left, plus PC Card (2/II, 1/III), dedicated Toshiba memory expansion slot, optional port replicator with 2 Type III CardBus PC Card slots	PC Card (1/II), dedicated Toshiba memory slot, optional port replicator with 1 Type III PC card slot
Ports	PC card (2/II, 1/III), parallel (ECP/EPP), serial, PS/2 keyoard/mouse, SVGA out, audio line in/out	parallel (ECP/EPP), serial (16550A), PS/2 keyboard/mouse, SVGA out, docking connector, external floppy	serial, Enhanced parallel (EPP), SVGA out, PS/2 keyboard/mouse, USB (1)	SVGA out, serial, parallel (ECP – may not work with some inkjet printers), PS/2 keyboard/mouse, USB (1), port connector, ext mic in, line in, headphone	SVGA out, serial, parallel (ECP – may not work with some inkjet printers), PS/2 keyboard/mouse, USB (1), port connector, ext mic in, line in, headphone	SVGA out (in included I/O adapter), parallel (ECP – may not work with some inkjet printers), replicator connector, External keyboard/mouse port and USB only available through optional replicator
Hard disk drive	2.1 GB	2.1 GB	2.1 GB	2.02 GB	3.82 GB	3.03 GB
CD-ROM drive	8X	None	24X max swappable	16X max	24X max	None
Floppy drive	1.44 MB included	1.44 MB included	1.44 MB included	1.44 MB included	1.44 MB included	1.44 MB external (included)
Pointing device	TrackPoint III (eraser head)	TrackPoint III (eraser head)	Touchpad	AccuPoint Pointing Stick (eraser head)	AccuPoint Pointing Stick (eraser head)	AccuPoint Pointing Stick (eraser head)
Display	12.1" TFT, 64 K colours, NeoMagic MagicGraph controller with 128-bit accelerator, 1.125 MB iDRAM	12.1" TFT, 64K colours, Trident Cyber9382, 64-bit SVGA accelerator, 1 MB VRAM	12.1" SVGA TFT (64 K colours @ 800 x 600), 4 MB SGRAM, ATI 3D Rage LT Pro	12.1", "enahnced" STN, 64 K colours at 800 x 600, 2 MB EDO Video RAM	12.1", "enahnced" STN, 64 K colours at 800 x 600, 2 MB EDO Video RAM	7.1" TFT (16.7 M colours @ 800 x 480), 1 MB EDO video RAM

Model	IBM Thinkpad 380D	IBM Thinkpad 560	NEC Versa LX VL210	Toshiba Satellite 300CDS	Toshiba Satellite 4000CDX	Toshiba Libretto 100CT
Sound	Crystal Semiconductor 16-bit, FM synthesis. 1 internal spkr & mic. line-in/out	16-bit ESS 1688, OPL-3 (Sound Blaster Pro) compatible, internal spkr, mic, line in/out	16-bit Sound Blaster Pro compatible, Maestro 2E PCI audio accelerator, stereo speakers, line-in, spkr out, mic in	16-bit, 48 KHz sampling, stereo spkrs	16-bit, 48 KHz sampling, stereo spkrs	16-bit, 48 KHz sampling, stereo headphone out
Docking stations	optional port replicator or convenience docking with 2 CardBus slots	optional port replicator	optional port replicator	optional port replicator with 2 type III PC card CardBus slots	optional port replicator	optional port replicator
Integrated modem (all may have optional PC card modems) Shows "None" if extra $$$	None	None	None	None	None	None
Zoomed Video/ CardBus support	Yes / only with optional docking station	No / No	Yes (both slots) / Yes	Yes / Yes	Yes / Yes	Yes / Yes (with port replicator)
Infrared Port	4 mbps IrDA 1.1	IrDA 1.0 (115 kbps)	Yes (no other details)	4 mbps IrDA 1.1	4 mbps IrDA 1.1	4 mbps IrDA 1.1
Battery	LiIon	L-ion	L-ion	L-ion	L-ion	L-ion
Size (LWH – inches)	9.2 x 11.8 x 2.4	8.7 x 11.7 x 1.2	10 x 12.1 x 1.8	9.4 x 11.9 x 2.2	9.4 x 11.9 x 2.1	5.2 x 8.3 x 14
Weight (lbs.)	6.9 with battery	4.1 with battery	7.2 with CD-ROM installed	7.7 with battery, floppy and CD-ROM drives	6.8 with battery, floppy and CD-ROM drives	2.3 with battery
Warranty	1 yr limited, international service and EasyServ (door-to-door courier)	1 yr limited, international service and EasyServ (door-to-door courier)	1 yr return-to-factory	1 yr parts & labour	1 yr parts & labour	1 yr parts & labour
Price**	$3,699	$3,499	$2,499 US	$1,979 Cdn list	$3,129 Cdn list	$3,289 Cdn list
Company	IBM Canada	IBM Canada	Packard Bell NEC, Inc., Canada	Toshiba Canada	Toshiba Canada	Toshiba Canada
Phone	800-IBM CALL (426-2255)	800-IBM CALL (426-2255)	888-8NEC NOW (862-3669)	800-387-5645	800-387-5645	800-387-5645
Web site: http://www.	can.ibm.com/hc/	can.ibm.com/hc/	nec-computers.com	toshiba.ca	toshiba.ca	toshiba.ca

* Dell prices do not include shipping
** All prices are Canadian list or direct purchase prices except where noted (NEC does not publish Canadian prices).
Digital Equipment Corp. is now owned by Compaq

10

Storage Devices

Storage devices are where you park your operating system, applications, and whatever you've created with them when they are not in use. They include hard drives, floppy drives (and their alternatives), CD-ROM and DVD drives, and removable backup storage devices. But before we start, I want to explain the difference between the words "disk" and "disc," in order to avoid confusion later.

"Disk" is short for diskette and today describes media on which data is recorded magnetically. These include hard disks, floppy disks, and media for drives that use similar formats. "Disc" is the term used to describe optical media, such as compact discs (CDs) and digital video/versatile discs (DVDs).

I didn't make up these definitions, but I am going to follow them. About the only time we run into real confusion is with devices that employ lasers in some form, but record magnetically, such as magneto-optical drives and the modified floptical drive known as the LS-120 (see under "Cheap at the price," below). I've chosen "disk" as the short form for the media for these drives.

All other devices use removable media that come in sealed cartridges.

The days when a computer program would fit on one floppy diskette are gone forever, and the time when you could buy a computer without a hard drive passed long ago. Today, it's rare to get one without at least a CD-ROM drive, and it isn't a good idea to try. Most applications come on CD-ROM, because it costs less to produce a single compact disc than a single 1.44 MB diskette. If you use a CD-ROM drive for nothing else except to listen to music and install software, it will still be worth having. Otherwise, you'll be spending a lot of time waiting – and it will cost you extra – to have the company that sells the software ship you diskettes instead.

The questions we'll try to answer in this chapter include how much capacity a hard drive in a new computer should have and whether it's better to use the enhanced IDE type of drive or one that employs the small computer systems interface (SCSI). We'll deal with CD-ROM technology to explain what the numbers (16X, 24X, and so on) mean and delve into the difference between CD-ROM, CD-R, and CD-RW drives. Should you get a DVD drive now or wait for DVD recordables? Should you stick with the old 1.44 MB floppy, or opt for one of the alternatives such as Zip, LS-120, or Avatar? For backups, should you rely on tape or something else?

Ready? Here we go.

Hard Drives

A hard drive (also called a hard disk, or, if you work for IBM, a hard file) is so called because the magnetic recording medium is on hard, inflexible platters (in floppy diskettes the medium is flexible). One truism in the computer world is that data will always expand to fill the container, and the best overall advice is simply to get the highest capacity hard drive you can afford, then start saving up for another one. Throughout this section, I'll be using the words "size" (and descriptors such as "bigger" and "smaller") and "capacity" interchangeably. When I do, I'm referring to how much data the drive can hold, not its physical dimensions. Unless you're looking at a special device that is too rare (or old) to be mentioned here, internal hard drives are 3.5 inches wide by just under an inch thick.

How big?

When you buy a new computer, it's unlikely you'll be offered a choice of hard drive type unless you persist (more on this below), but you should be able to choose the hard drive capacity.

Capacity is a measure, usually in gigabytes (GB) in today's market, of how much information the drive will hold. This should not be confused with the amount of memory (RAM) the system has, but I admit that the way Windows uses available blank space can make the distinction hard to determine. Nevertheless, the salesperson who tells you that you don't need much memory in your system because you've got a large hard drive is either technically inept or is trying to scam you. Run away.

To use a car as a very crude analogy, think of the computer's central processor as the engine, the amount of memory as the gas, and the hard drive as the interior, the trunk, and, under certain circumstances (more fully described in Chapter 8), as a reserve gas tank. The processor and memory determine how fast and how far you can go. The hard drive mostly determines how much you can take with you and how much you can bring back, but that storage capacity can also assist when you run low on gas.

As you become more familiar with what your computer can do, you'll find yourself adding ever more programs. With those programs you'll create and then need to store data – all your business accounts, the kids' homework, your homemade Christmas cards, "saves" in the games you play, and that rotating 3-D diagram of the whatsit you invented. *You will never get a hard drive that has too much capacity.* I repeat: get the largest you can afford, then start saving for another one. Still, like all other things in life, there is often a difference between what we'd like and what we can afford.

In 1998, hard drives at the low end typically held around 3.2 GB. If you've been this route before but haven't been paying attention for a few years, that sounds like a lot – and it is compared to bygone days when a 528 MB drive was considered huge. However, a couple of trends have developed. One, the cost of storage has fallen like a rock as capacities have risen and technology has improved. Two, software demands more space than ever, a condition that has led some grumpy folks to start calling it "bloatware." The operating systems want more space (Windows 98, for example, will take 195 to 295 MB of hard drive space, depending on how many of its features you install). Applications also want more space and the documents we produce require more space to store them, as well (a function both of additional information stored with them by the application and the complex objects we can insert into them).

How high can you go? Well, even if you stick to the less-expensive EIDE type of hard drive (see below), I've seen models advertised with capacities as high as 16.8 GB at the extreme high end. Average in an entry-level PC by the end of 1998 at the price "sweet spot," where the cost per megabyte was the lowest, was 4-3 to 5-7 GB.

As with all other components, all hard drives are not identical. Nor does the number sold by any particular company over a period of time indicate anything about its quality (except whether return rates are low and prices are reasonable). Nevertheless, the typical and better-known brand names you'll find in the hard drive market include (in no particular order for now) IBM, Fujitsu, Seagate, Western Digital, Maxtor, Quantum, and Samsung.

EIDE versus SCSI

You can forget all about the obsolete drive technologies such as ST-506 (MFM or RLL) and ESDI (but if you want details, hunt up a copy of the first edition of *How to Buy a Computer*). By the end of the 1990s only two generic types of hard drive have survived. SCSI (small computer systems interface – pronounced "scuzzy") drives come in several sub-flavours we'll describe later, but for the most part have a recognizable name. When we come to EIDE drives, however, the number of different terms applied to describe them will turn your hair green – so we'll start there.

EIDE: The name given to non-SCSI drives changes depending on who's talking. Consumers and most retailers know them by the popular term EIDE (enhanced integrated drive electronics), which distinguishes them from an older standard (known simply as IDE). The "enhanced" was added when this generic drive type underwent a fundamental change in early 1995.

The confusion arises because engineers have an entirely different name for these drives. Even when IDE was the popular term, the people who build these things called them AT (Advanced Technology – the same term given to the "AT-286" PCs) Attachment devices (ATA for short). When they revised the original ATA standard in 1995, it was dubbed ATA-1, and the new set of rules became ATA-2 (what we know as EIDE). Those rules have been modified twice since although they're still called ATA-3 – but an ATA-4 standard is in the works. (One of the more interesting things about computer industry "standards" is that there are so many of them.)

Under ATA-1, IDE hard drives were limited in capacity to 528 MB. There was only one IDE drive controller with a two-connector cable in a PC, allowing up to two hard drives in a system. Only hard drives fell into the IDE standard, and typically they could move data (that is, provide a data transfer rate or throughput) at around 1 MB/sec at the high end, although the theoretical limit was 3 MB/sec.

Under ATA-2 (EIDE), the capacity of this type of hard drive jumped to 8.4 GB. It supported two drive controllers, each with its own two-connector cable. Now you could have four IDE devices in the same system. Theoretical maximum throughput rose to 13 MB/sec, but few models actually delivered this much. A substandard began to evolve at about the same time, called AT Attachment Packet Interface (ATAPI). It would run CD-ROM drives and eventually other devices.

Under ATA-3 and its current revisions, other devices were added to the main standard including CD-ROM, tape, Zip, and other removable storage devices. A new technique was introduced, called Ultra DMA (dynamic memory allocation), which, as long as the system had a motherboard chipset to support it, could drive throughput up to 33 MB/sec. One of the latest developments allows for drives larger than 8.4 GB, although no one partition on the drive is allowed to exceed this figure. (See *How to Avoid Buying a New Computer* for a thorough discussion of partitioning a drive, why you'd want to do so, the methods, and the implications.)

Throughout these revisions, one drawback and one advantage have remained constant. The drawback is that the EIDE/ATA standards remain as internal specifications only. That is, the device is mounted in one of the bays inside the computer case. There are no external EIDE devices. External versions of EIDE products tend to use the computer's parallel port to connect to the motherboard, with a large drop in throughput rates as a result (usually topping out at 1.25 MB/sec). Ultimately, these parallel port devices will evolve and use Universal Serial Bus (USB) instead.

The advantage of EIDE is that its devices tend to be less expensive than their SCSI counterparts. Because of this and because EIDE controllers are built into today's motherboards, new consumer computers tend to come with EIDE hard drives and CD-ROM drives by default. That's why I said when we began that you may have to be persistant, and you will have to pay extra, if you want a SCSI adapter and drives in your new computer.

In the first edition of *How to Buy a Computer*, based on e-mail conversations I'd had with engineers involved in developing the ATA standards, I warned that devices being sold at the time may have been unstable. I also cautioned that retrofitting older, pre-EIDE systems with EIDE drives was fraught with traps. With some qualifications I'll discuss under CD-ROM drives (see below), I'm glad to report that today's EIDE/ATA devices are stable – and you should have no difficulties with them in a new system (but the traps still exist for pre-EIDE system retrofits).

Today, all Pentium-class systems handle EIDE/ATA-2 devices. However, only newer Pentium-class systems using Intel's 430TX chipset or equivalent can use the ATA-3 variants using Ultra DMA. Pentium II-class systems must have the 440LX AGPset or something more recent to use Ultra DMA devices (see the chipset table on pages 86-87).

One note for the future: In 1998, I came across several non-Intel chipset manufacturers claiming to support a new upper speed limit for Ultra DMA drives. Dubbed "Ultra DMA/66," it implied a doubling of the EIDE transfer rate from 33 to 66 MB/sec. As of October 1998, Intel has yet to release a chipset supporting Ultra DMA/66, nor had the standards body, the X3T10 committee, officially announced a new speed limit. This, however, doesn't mean it won't happen.

SCSI: You don't hear a lot of debate over SCSI versus EIDE any more now that the EIDE/ATA standards have settled down a bit. SCSI, first developed for the Mac platform, is more flexible than EIDE. It allows both internal and external devices. Depending on the type of SCSI adapter you choose, you could have up to seven internal and seven external devices attached to the same controller, and nothing prevents you from putting more than one controller in the same system. While we're on the topic, nothing prevents you from adding one or more SCSI controllers to a system that already has EIDE, and many people do.

SCSI hard drives can have far larger capacities than EIDE drives, and at the high end, when several are chained together, they're preferred for use in network servers or specialized uses such as broadcast-quality video editing. SCSI controllers and drives can be faster (higher data transfer rate or throughput), too. They also don't rely on the motherboard's chipset to achieve high throughput – up to 40 MB/sec at the high end.

Where SCSI can get complicated is that it comes in several flavours and uses a variety of connectors. These include 8-bit,16-bit, and 32-bit SCSI. There are also SCSI-FAST, SCSI-WIDE, and SCSI-ULTRA. Some controllers can provide multiple flavours, such as SCSI-ULTRA/WIDE.

Two of the best-known SCSI adapter manufacturers are Adaptec (the market leader) and Future Domain. When you shop for an adapter, you'll want to know what type of SCSI devices you already have, and you'll also want to note what type of connector each device requires. For an external device, it could be a 25-pin connector similar to a parallel connector, 50-pin Centronics, 50-pin SCSI-2, or 128-pin WIDE connector. There are different internal connectors, too, depending on whether it's a SCSI-WIDE device or not. If you're a SCSI device user, you'll soon have a collection of fairly expensive cables with a variety of connector combinations to get all your devices hooked together.

The primary disadvantage of SCSI, aside from its multiple flavours and "connector, connector, who's got what kind of connector" games, is the cost. You can shell out over $300 Cdn for a top-of-the-line controller card, and the devices themselves tend to cost around 30 to 40 per cent more than a comparable EIDE device.

Frankly, with the introduction of devices (scanners, removable storage drives) that will share the parallel port or use USB, and the maturation of EIDE-based internal devices of many kinds, the need for SCSI – simply to get access to non-standard devices – has diminished. There is no difference, for example, between the performance characteristics of an EIDE-based CD-ROM and SCSI-based CD-ROM drive, aside from price. While there was a time when it looked as though SCSI would move into the mainstream, it pretty much remains the preserve of power users.

Performance: Once you've decided how much hard drive capacity you can afford and have made the choice between EIDE and SCSI drives, you're down to sorting out the differences among specific models. Price will, of course, be a factor, but performance characteristics and the manufacturer's reputation for quality will also be important. Specifications aren't hard to find, but if you rely solely on computer ads to make your choice, they may be scarce (see Chapter 3). You can get tips from your friends, but hard drive models change faster than most other components, so last month's fave brand may not be all that good next month.

Your best source of up-to-date information is the USENET newsgroups dedicated to hard drives.

So, what's fast? Hard drive performance is measured two ways: Average access speed is a combined figure that includes the length of time it takes to find data on the disk surface (seek time) and the time it takes to get the data off the surface and on its way to you (latency). Average access is quoted in milliseconds (ms). In the late 1990s market, 12 ms is slow, 10 ms is about average, and 8 ms or less is very fast indeed.

Access speed is affected by a couple of factors. The speed of the drive's read/write head is one factor, but the drive's rotational speed is the other. For example, one of the fastest drives on the market in early 1998 was Seagate's Cheetah – a drive that rotates at 10,000 rpm. It and similarly quick models are expensive and also tend to be noisy, but when power is the name of the game, what's a little rumble?

The second measurement is transfer rate or throughput (although "throughput" is more properly applied to the drive's controller, it is often indiscriminately swapped for the term "transfer rate"). The transfer rate is the rate at which data, once it is found, gets through the drive's circuitry and out into the real world. It also covers the rate at which data moves through the drive on its way to be written to the disk. The measurement is in megabytes per second (MB/sec).

There are some fine points to understand about the transfer rate. First, it is generally quoted in two different circumstances. The "burst" rate indicates the drive's top speed, while the "sustained" transfer rate is the average you get during normal operations. You want to see both figures. The second item to ponder is that the upper speed limit of a particular standard (33 MB/sec for Ultra DMA; 40 MB/sec for SCSI-FAST and SCSI-ULTRA) represents only the *theoretical* maximum. Only top-end products will come close to the maximum. Others will fall short by degrees that vary from brand to brand and from model to model within brands. Transfer rate is also affected by the motherboard's chipset and the quality of its on-board controller. Translation: Simply because a drive is advertised as an Ultra DMA model, it does not necessarily mean it will provide a data transfer rate of 33 MB/sec. (Gotcha, again!)

Care, feeding, and maintenance

As the technology improves, it has become harder to hurt hard drives. In bygone days, the read/write head(s) would crash onto the surface of the drive platter(s) when power was turned off, causing physical damage and scrambling the data in the damaged sector(s). Today, EIDE and SCSI drives come with what are called floating heads. When the computer is turned off, they hover away from the drive surface; power is required to bring them close enough to read or write to the disk (the heads don't ever touch the platter surface, but they get very close).

What is more likely to damage a hard drive is dirty power. In Chapter 14 there's a discussion of power conditioners and uninterruptible power supplies (UPSs). These devices prevent electrical spikes and surges from ripping into your computer and wreaking havoc. UPSs also prevent brownouts and blackouts from scrambling your data just as it's about to be written to disk.

Something else happens to hard drives that you don't hear too much about. They get tired. The surface of the platters is covered with a thin layer of a metal oxide, the molecules of which are lined up magnetically. That's how data is stored, in molecular patterns in the oxide layer. The patterns are created by a weak electrical current and read later by the change in current detected by the heads. Over time, the magnetic force dissipates and the patterns begin to lose their coherence. How long a time depends on many factors: how much power is flowing through the system, the temperature and humidity, static discharges, and the whims of the gods.

It's a good idea, particularly with older drives, to periodically make a backup of all of the data and to reformat the drive. I try to do it every couple of years. It's a pain to take the time, but no more painful than discovering that something I've spent days writing is in the "sector not found."

Other things that retire hard drives before you're ready include failure of drive motors, misalignment of drive spindles, and the curses of passing wizards (they just die, is all).

Removable Storage

"I've just bought a new computer with a humungous hard drive, almost 8 GB capacity. I keep reading in your column and elsewhere that I should keep backup copies of my data, but the idea of owning, never mind using, around 8,000 floppy disks isn't my idea of a good time. What are the alternatives?"

This quote pretty much sums up several letters I've received. Anyone who has owned a computer long enough to experience the gut-wrenching anxiety of losing all your data when a hard drive goes south will tell you that having a backup copy of the programs and data stored on the drive is the only thing that saved their, er . . . bacon.

The day *your* hard drive goes AWOL, you will not panic. After doing whatever you must to get it back up and running or replaced, you'll merely reach for your most recent backup and continue. The alternatives are too sad to contemplate. Experts make backups all the time. It's only novices who fail to do so until after their first disaster.

Before we get too deeply into this, I should mention floppy drives. Unless you buy an iMac, which has none, you'll get one, a single 3.5-inch, 1.44 MB drive, and in today's environment, that's all you'll need. The 5.25-inch floppy is well and truly history. But the fact is that so little work remains for any kind of floppy disk drive, apart from carting the occasional file back and forth to the office, it just hasn't noticed that it's nearly dead, too.

When hard drives were small, it wasn't uncommon to make backups on floppy disks. Since those halcyon days, drive sizes have increased exponentially – and there hasn't been a floppy-based storage scheme that's stuck since the introduction several years ago of the 3.5-inch, 1.44 MB diskette drive with AT-286 systems.

We went through a brief bridge period when hard drives topped out at around 528 MB. Streaming tape cartridges that held 250 MB of compressed data were just bearable. The cost of tape drives and their media, plus one other important factor, made them get really old, really quickly. Unlike hard drives and diskettes, where data is stored at random all over the surface and can be retrieved randomly, too, information on tape is recorded sequentially. If you wanted to recover data from the end of the tape, followed by some in the middle, you had to wait and wait and wait while the drive found what you wanted – then you had to wait some more. Today, tape drives still exist, and they can hold large amounts of data, but their only practical use is for backing up networks – it's the only time when large-capacity tape drives pay for themselves.

I'm also not going to spend a lot of time on magneto-optical (MO) drives. They have a long and deserved reputation for reliability and durability (they use a laser to melt a special coating on the disk surface before the magnetic media can be changed – making them ideal for secure storage, particularly in areas where there may be stray magnetic fields). However, the prices of the MO drives are ridiculous, and both CD-R (recordable) and CD-RW (rewritable) drives are pricing them out of the consumer market (see below).

I am going to discuss three tiers of products you can add to your system: the least-expensive floppy alternatives, the mid-range CD and CD-like alternatives, and the slightly more expensive removable mass-storage devices. When we get to the comparison table, you may want to note not only the cost of the drive and the media, but also how the cost per megabyte of storing data drops the more you use each device.

Cheap at the price

In the inexpensive category we'll start with the Zip drive, initially developed by Iomega Corp., because it's the most popular to date. The Zip can currently handle up to 100 MB cartridges and can be found at most retail outlets. In 1998 it came in two flavours and four versions.

Zip drives can be external or mounted internally in a computer. External Zips attach either via the parallel port or through a SCSI (small computer systems interface) adapter. Both retail for between $189 and $199. Internal Zips can attach either to a SCSI adapter (about $169) or to the same "ATAPI" or EIDE connector used by a CD-ROM drive (about $149). Individual Zip cartridges sell for between $18 and $19, and are available in two-, three-, and ten-cartridge packs.

At the beginning of 1998, Iomega released a new category of Zip drive, the Zip*Plus*, which is basically the same as the original external model except that it can be used on either parallel or SCSI connections. It's also a little faster, comes with a decent bundle of multimedia software, and sells for about $50 more.

Although Zips can handle up to 100 MB of data, Zip drives need special software, available primarily from Iomega, to be used successfully to back up large hard drives. The backup software which was part of Windows 95, for example, although it sees the drive as a removable device, can't store data across several cartridges. The program stops when it reaches the end, saying "disk full." According to Microsoft, the backup applet in Windows 98 can handle a wider variety of backup device types. However, when I installed Win98 on my system, it not only couldn't find the Zip drive, but it also failed to find my floppy drive, a SyQuest SyJet and an HP/Colorado T1000 tape drive. So I'm not sure it's an improvement. Microsoft may have patched this problem by the time you read this.

Some third-party products, notably Cheyenne backup software, can also handle Zips, but don't automatically assume you can use a Zip drive as a backup device. Talk about it with the vendor, or check that there's a compatible backup application in the box. Zip drives can only read and write to their own proprietary cartridges.

Another candidate in the "inexpensive" category is from SyQuest. Best known among Mac users, SyQuest has been trying hard to make inroads into the PC camp for some time. Its older product, the EZ-135, didn't do well against the Zip, but its latest, the EZ-Flyer 230, just might. The price is a little higher ($230 Cdn), but the EZ-Flyer 230 boasts higher speed and more than twice the capacity. The only drawback to the EZ-Flyer is that it has only one version, an external model that requires the presence of a SCSI adapter that will cost extra (SyQuest may have released alternate EIDE, parallel, or USB versions by the time you read this).

A third entry in the "inexpensive" category is a new player in the storage field. The Avatar Shark 250 is aimed squarely at notebook users. The Shark is the physically smallest and lightest contender in its category, yet it's no lightweight. The tiny cartridges it uses hold up to 250 MB of data, and the drive itself can either attach to a parallel port or via a PC card to a notebook. When used in its PC card mode on a notebook, the Shark doesn't need a separate power supply – it gets enough from the PC card slot to operate. Although its 12 millisecond (ms) access time is impressive, the 1.25 MB/sec throughput – while about 4.5 times faster than a Zip – is still not great. Sharks sell for around $250 Cdn, with media priced at $50 to $60 per cartridge, making it one of the most expensive drives per megabyte in this roundup.

Finally, we come to the LS-120 drive, initially developed by a consortium of companies including Matsushita (Panasonic), Imation, O.R. Technology, and Compaq. The LS-120 holds 120 MB of data and is the only alternative removable storage device available that is backward compatible to existing 3.5-inch diskettes (it will read and write to 720 KB and 1.44 MB diskettes as well as its special high-density media).

The LS-120 drive uses a laser as a guide to keep the drive's read/write head precisely focused on the disk surface, allowing for more data tracks in a smaller area. Internal LS-120 drives were retailing in 1998 for around $159, and the special media, sold by both Imation and Maxell, were about $19 per disk.

According to Panasonic Canada's product manager of storage products, Robert Kwong, the LS-120 is only the beginning of where the technology will go. In 1999, there will be higher density (240 to 500 MB capacity) and faster drives. The newer drives will read older media, but of course anyone with an older LS-120 drive won't be able to use the new high-density media designed for the new drives. This story will be familiar to anyone who ever owned one of the first 720 KB, 3.5-inch disk drives.

Mid-range "CD" devices

Panasonic has another technology it's quite keen on. Marketed under the "PD" (phase-change dual) label, these are "rewritable optical" cartridge drives that can also read CD-ROM discs. PD drives are SCSI devices. In 1998, there were two Panasonic PD drives, an external model with a suggested retail price of $599 and an internal version for $499. The 650 MB cartridges cost about $27 each. A new PD model with a 24X CD-ROM reader would be released later in the year. One drawback to the PD drives is that while the drives will read CD-ROM discs, the recording medium is not a CD, it's a cartridge that can only be read by another PD drive.

Also in the 650 MB-capacity ballpark are the CD-R (one-time recordable and not erasable) and CD-RW (CD-rewritable) drives. In early 1998, there were several CD-RW drives on the market from companies such as Yamaha (CRW4260), Smart & Friendly (CD-RW 426), and Hewlett-Packard.

HP's SureStore 7200 was doing well in Canada. The external 7200e model uses the PC's parallel (printer) port and had an estimated street price of $870. The internal 7200i had a suggested retail price of about $712 (although I've seen them quoted at closer to $525 on the street). The price of the recordable CD media will depend on what you want to do with the results. If you just want to distribute the discs to others, CD-R (recordable but not rewritable) media cost about $3 per disc. However, if you want to be able to write, erase, and rewrite, the CD-RW discs will set you back about $37 each.

Before we get much further along, we need to discuss some technical aspects of compact discs (and part of this discussion will also pertain to recordable DVD when we get to that topic below). When you look at the side of the compact disc that doesn't have a label, it's silver-coloured and appears to be shiny. In fact, the surface is covered with a mixture of dark areas (pits) and shiny areas (lands), laid out in a circular track that starts at the centre and spirals out to the outer edge. In your drive, a laser is pointed at the disc surface and a lens in the drive reads the difference between the light reflected from the dark pits and from the bright lands. A laser didn't burn the disc you have in your drive; only a master disc was subjected to this procedure. All of the copies are stamped out.

When we come to CD-R and CD-RW drives, they too have lasers to read reflected light, but the lasers are also used to record data. Once again, however, there's no burning. Sandwiched between clear plastic layers is a layer of photosensitive dye (either emerald green cyanine or yellow-green pthalocyanine). The recording process darkens some areas of the dye, in effect creating false pits. This process has a technical name: phase change. It's the same process used for Panasonic's PD drives (described above) and for some DVD recordable solutions (described below).

Now, back to where we left off. One advantage of CD-R and CD-RW drives is that you can read their discs in most recent CD-ROM drives that employ an automatic gain control to step up the laser intensity. Many models manufactured earlier than mid-1996 may have trouble because the light reflected from the green or yellow-green CD-R/RW discs isn't as bright as from standard silver CDs. You can also read them in a second-generation DVD drive or better. First-generation DVD drives could not read CD-R or CD-RW discs because the light reflected from the green or yellow-green recording layer was the wrong colour (i.e., had the wrong wavelength) to be "seen" by the drive's reader. Later models corrected the problem by using two lasers with one or two separate lens arrays. Look for the term "MultiRead" or specific reference to the ability to read these discs if it's important to you.

One disadvantage of a parallel port-based device is that the data throughput is never going to be as fast as either a SCSI or ATA/EIDE drive, or one connected through a USB port. There's also a potential problem of conflicts with existing printers or other devices that share your parallel port, such as a low-cost scanner.

Fat city

Now we're going for the gusto. Beginning in late 1997, a war over high-capacity storage devices broke out between rivals Iomega and SyQuest. Iomega had four versions of its SCSI-based Jaz cartridge drive. There was a high (2 GB) and low (1 GB) version in both external and internal formats. The 2 GB external drive would set you back about $899 (1 GB, $435). The 2 GB internal Jaz sold for about $799 ($399 for 1 GB). None of the prices included a SCSI adapter. Media for the Jaz drive were pricey at $240 for a 2 GB cartridge and $179 for the 1 GB version.

SyQuest had two entries in the 1 GB-or-more class. The SyJet holds 1.5 GB per cartridge and requires a SCSI adapter, while the slightly-less-expensive SparQ holds 1 GB per cartridge and attaches through a parallel port. (Both models may have alternative connection methods by the time you read this.)

I had mixed results with the SparQ. Although I was able to get the second unit the company shipped to work on both my Dell Dimension and a visiting Toshiba laptop, nothing the SyQuest engineers and I could do would make either one function on an IBM Aptiva E26. (However, one correspondent tells me that her SparQ did work on another Aptiva model.) My *We Compute* colleague Murray Soupcoff also had a problem and had to send his first SparQ back. Subsequently, SyQuest went out of business in late 1998, partially blamed on the SparQ's instability.

Ups and downs

The good news is that the computer industry is developing fast, large-capacity devices to replace both the 3.5-inch floppy drive and tape drives as methods of removable storage for the consumer market. There's a positive side to this for consumers, too, as this competition will bring prices down.

The downside, of course, is that this is really the bleeding edge of technology. If I had to make a decision, I'd play safe. I believe the Zip drive will survive, and that CD-RW will be around for some time to come. I'm not as confident about the others. Bearing in mind such dead ends as the floptical drive and the 2.88 MB floppy, I'd buy as much of the storage media as I could afford while it was still available.

What about recordable DVD?

Because I'm writing this in mid-1998, some of the following information may have changed by the time you read it. One of the great promises of DVD (digital video – or versatile – disc), aside from its extremely high capacities compared to CD-ROM, was that we'd eventually be able to use the devices to record our own data. Unfortunately, an abundance of generations and confusion over standards – not to mention a noticeable shortage of products – have held up the widespread acceptance of the technology.

When DVD was in its infancy, two different groups of companies were pushing two incompatible standards. After the section of the entertainment industry that was supposed to supply content knocked some heads together (saying, in effect, "We're not going to have a VHS versus Beta argument here!"), one common method of creating DVD-ROM playback units emerged.

The grumbling didn't stop, however, and with recordable DVD, the knives are out again. As of late 1998, there were four different "standards" fighting for survival.

DVD-RAM was approved by the DVD Forum – the consortium made up of the DVD-ROM manufacturers – in 1997, but it seems that everyone at the table except Panasonic had their fingers crossed.

Panasonic's parent company, Matsushita Electric, is the main proponent of this phase-change design (see above). In its current format, DVD-RAM will hold 2.6 GB per side on single- or double-sided discs, which require a special cartridge to hold them. Panasonic claims that its first model, due out in late 1998, will also read its PD cartridges (see above under "Mid-range CD devices").

Hewlett-Packard, Philips Electronics, and Sony are behind a second scheme dubbed **DVD+RW**. All three are members of the DVD Forum. However, they prefer this approach because, they say, it will eventually be able to write to CD-R discs as well as DVD, giving users the ability to produce discs for the huge installed base of CD-ROM drives for portability and distribution. Also a phase-change device, DVD+RW discs would have a higher capacity (3.02 GB per side on a single layer) and wouldn't require a cartridge to hold the discs.

Both camps are silent on whether the discs produced by either DVD-RAM or DVD+RW will play back on standard DVD-ROM drives, but early indications aren't good. (Gotcha!)

Pioneer, which has been a player in the CD-ROM market for some time, is developing what it calls **DVD-R/W**. Based on existing CD-RW technology, it uses a random-access medium storing up to 3.95 GB of data. Pioneer says its approach will lead to discs that can be read by existing DVD-ROM drives and TV-only DVD players without modification. It also says the product isn't intended for consumers, but for content developers.

Last, but not least, is **MMVF** (multimedia video file format) from NEC. The company says its goal is to fit a complete two-hour movie on one side of the disc. With 5.28 GB capacity per side, it would hold more data than any of the competing schemes. There's no indication whether it will require a cartridge holder.

As for CD-ROM drives

I know, I skipped over CD-ROM drives. Does this mean I think they're going to disappear? As a matter of fact, I do, but I don't think this will happen during the life of this book until and unless the mess over DVD recordables gets sorted out.

Removable External Storage

Company	Hewlett-Packard	Iomega		Panasonic		SyQuest		
Product	CD-RW (SureStore 7200)	Zip	Jaz	LS-120	PD	EZ-Flyer 230	SyJet	SparQ
Capacity	650 MB	100 MB	1 or 2 GB	120 MB	650 MB	230 MB	1.5 GB	1 GB
Price	$712 (internal), $870 (external)	$149 (internal IDE), $169 (internal SCSI), $189-$199 (external, parallel or SCSI)	$399 (1 GB internal), $799 (2 GB internal), $435 (1 GB external), $899 (2 GB external)	$159 (internal)	$499 (internal), $599 (external)	$229.99 (external, SCSI or parallel, internal ATAPI/EIDE)	$448.99 for all models	$299.99
Average Access Speed (ms)	32 ms	29 ms (SCSI)	16 ms (SCSI)	70 ms	no info	13.5 ms	12 ms	12 ms
Throughput	300 KB/sec write (2x write, 6x read)	275 KB/sec	7.38 MB/sec (SCSI)	300 KB/sec	no info	SCSI: 10 MB/sec, EDIE: 11.1 MB/sec, EPP: 1 MB/sec	SCSI: 10 MB/sec, EDIE: 12 MB/sec (16.6 in burst mode), EPP: 1.25 MB/sec	SCSI: 10 MB/sec, EDIE: 12 MB/sec (16.6 in burst mode), EPP: 1.25 MB/sec
Media	CD-R or CD-RW discs	Proprietary cartridge	Proprietary cartridge	Special 3.5" diskette, standard 1.44 MB or 720 KB disks	Proprietary cartridge or CD-ROM discs	Proprietary cartridge	Proprietary cartridge	Proprietary cartridge
Media unit price	$3 (CD-R), $37 (CD-RW)	$18.99 (also available in 2-, 3- and 5-packs)	$179 (1 GB), $240 (2 GB)	$19	$27	$39.99 ($89 for 3-pack, $149.99 for 5-pack, $299.99 for 10-pack)	$119.99 ($299.99 for 3-pack)	$59.99 ($149.99 for 3-pack, $449.99 for 10-pack)
Interface	Parallel (external), IDE (internal)	Parallel or SCSI (external), EIDE or SCSI (internal)	SCSI	Floppy controller	SCSI	Parallel or SCSI (external), EIDE or SCSI (internal)	Parallel or SCSI (external), EIDE or SCSI (internal)	Parallel (external)
Cost for 1st GB*	$749 ($0.73 per MB)	$339 ($0.33 per MB)	$399 ($0.39 per MB)	$349 ($0.34 per MB)	$526 ($0.51 per MB)	$390 ($0.38 per MB)	$449 ($0.44 per MB)	$299 ($0.29 per MB)
Cost for 10 GB*	$1,304 ($0.13 per MB)	$2,049 ($0.20 per MB)	$2,010 ($1.96 per MB)	$2,040 ($0.20 per MB)	$931 ($0.09 per MB)	$2,030 ($0.20 per MB)	$1,289 ($0.13 per MB)	$899 ($0.09 per MB)
Cost for 100 GB*	$6,558 ($0.06 per MB)	$19,130 ($0.186 per MB)	$18,120 ($0.177 per MB)	$19,140 ($0.186 per MB)	$4,765 (.05 per MB)	$18,070 ($0.18 per MB)	$8,729 ($0.09 per MB)	$6,299 ($0.06 per MB)
Contact #	1-800-276-8661	1-800-MY-STUFF (697-8833)		905-624-5505		no pre-sales phone number		
Web (http://www.)	canada.hp.com	iomega.com		panasonic.ca		syquest.com		

* cost per GB/MB includes cost of drive. Cost for first GB takes into account that you usually get one recordable disk, disc, or cartridge with a new drive. Cost for 10 and 100 GB do not include the first free media example

* cost is also based on least expensive model when there are several. In the case of the HP SureStore, cost per GB/MB is based on CD-RW discs. The cost will be significantly lower using CD-R discs

Prices quoted are based on manufacturer's suggested retail price or list price in Canadian funds the week of April 20, 1998, and may fluctuate by dealer and/or region

In the meantime, if you find a software application or movie or anything else you just have to have, and it's available only on DVD, that's a good excuse to get a DVD drive. Similarly, if the market has reached the point where DVD and CD-ROM drives are competitively priced, and the problem with generations is solved, why not get a DVD?

However, until then, CD-ROM drives are they way to go, so let's deal with the current issues around them. The first is a little matter of speed. CD-ROM drives running at up to twelve times the speed of the original models (12X) used a technique known as Constant Linear Velocity (CLV). Newer drives (16X and above) use something called Constant Angular Velocity (CAV).

As noted earlier, data on a compact disc is laid down in a sequential track beginning in the centre of the disc and spiralling outward. As the drive spins, the read head moves in a straight line while it follows the track. As the disc spins, its centre portion moves more slowly than its outer edge. In a CLV drive, the spin rate changes constantly as the drive attempts to have the data flowing over the read head at the same speed, no matter where it is on the disc. The data transfer rate is the same, no matter where the data is located. A 12X delivers data at twelve times the speed of first-generation CD-ROMs.

CAV drives don't alter their spin rate (except for music – I'll get to that in a moment). They are slower in the centre than they are at the outer edge, and only the fastest speed is advertised. That's why you see many of these drives now advertised as "24X max." However, the average performance of the drive is usually about half the advertised number. What's more, you seldom reach the maximum speed (most data CDs are less than half full, so you seldom visit the outer edge).

So, when you're assessing which drive is faster, the "X" factor isn't as reliable a guide as it once was. Average access speed is a better guide, but because it is relatively slow compared to a hard drive, it is not as important an indicator. Transfer rate is a better indicator of performance, but once again, you want to discover the average transfer rate, not the rate at the drive's top speed.

What's this about music? Unless it's encoded as part of a software program, sound from the audio CDs you can play back on your drive has to play at the speed of the original ("1X") CD-ROM drives. Otherwise the music will speed up and everything will sound like

Alvin and the Chipmunks (go ask your parents). The reason is quite simple. The information on an audio CD isn't digital; it's analog. The laser is reading a pattern of smooth areas (lands) and pits, almost the way a needle on an old vinyl record player did. Surprise!

Here's a quick quiz you may be asked to take by some salesperson with more charm than knowledge. Which is better: a CD-ROM drive with 500 MB capacity, 650 MB capacity, or 720 MB capacity?

Time's up. If you picked any of the answers above, you're a candidate for pocket-picking. The drives have no capacity at all. All the capacity is on the compact discs. (Gotcha!)

So, what should I ask for?

Some of players in the CD-ROM market are also in the DVD game. Leading manufacturers include Sony, Toshiba, Philips, Pioneer, Panasonic, Mitsumi, NEC, Plextor, and Teac. As with hard drives, however, their sales volume doesn't necessarily reflect the quality of their products.

The debate about internal versus external drives pretty much went away when CD-ROMs became standard equipment in new computers. Most CD-ROM drives on the market (except for some of the CD-R and CD-RW models) are internal EIDE/ATA devices – and there's really no reason to seek an alternative.

One last note: The pattern on any magnetic media (tape or disk) begins to fade over time. With tape, it's even more fun; the patterns not only fade, they mix between layers. After about three years, the deterioration may make reading the data difficult. After five years, it may not be possible at all.

If you have vital data you want kept safe from all hazards, you should have more than one copy, kept in more than one location, on more than one medium. Today, at least one of the storage methods should be either magneto-optical (see above) or compact disc, which do not deteriorate with the passage of time. Each time you switch to a new storage method (technology will *keep* changing), you should make another copy on the new medium. Otherwise, the day may come when you get a nasty surprise.

11

Multimedia and Telecommunications

It burbles, it chirps, it plays the tarantella. It's multimedia computing. You can thank Microsoft and, to a lesser degree, the Internet for creating an appetite for sound and moving pictures in the PC market. Before the advent of Microsoft Windows (and, to a lesser extent, IBM's now nearly defunct OS/2), these treats were virtually the exclusive preserve of Apple (the Macintosh line), Commodore (the Amiga), and Atari – all dead or nearly dead computer systems. But, once PCs could use a graphical interface, that all changed. You'll have to fight to get a PC today that doesn't have a sound controller, CD-ROM drive, speakers, and accelerated video controller.

It's here where classifying various components and peripherals gets murky. Although CD-ROMs and DVD drives could be considered multimedia, I've dealt with them as storage devices in the previous chapter. Here, we're going to discuss the remainder of the topics that fall under multimedia. Sound controllers are here because there is a difference in quality among them and choices to make (not to mention some marketing games to expose). Telecommunications in the 1990s means the Internet, especially the World Wide Web portion of it, which features images and sound. It falls squarely into the "multimedia" framework, so we'll also talk about modems and alternative hardware technologies for access to the Web.

Just to round things off, we're going to look at two other methods of getting pictures into your computer – digital cameras and scanners. Products to get television (video and sound) into – and out of – a PC are in Chapter 13.

Sound

You've probably noticed that I describe the devices that produce sound in your computer as "sound controllers." The terms "controller" and "adapter" show up a lot in this book. In the first edition of *How to Buy a Computer*, I tended to call these devices "cards" or "boards." The difference is easily explained. Back then, you had to fit a circuit board or card into an expansion slot on the motherboard to be able to hear sound or dial up the Internet. Today, it is becoming more common for the circuitry to be embedded directly into the motherboard itself. "Controller" and "adapter" are now the more accurate terms, and they cover both contingencies.

Composer Claude Debussy said music is "the arithmetic of sounds as optics is the geometry of light," and you have to wonder if he was prescient. He couldn't have anticipated today's computer sound controllers, could he? Sound on your computer *is* arithmetic – what your controller is doing is reading and playing digital code.

As with every other component in your computer, all sound controllers aren't equal. Having a sound controller that works well is fun; having one that doesn't work with the game you just bought, or that only works in Windows, or that produces tinny, unnatural sound with a slow sampling rate is not fun. Similarly, tacking $10 speakers onto a $4,000 PC may provide more disappointment than rapture.

Tech stuff

Little has changed in sound controller technology over the past few years, but there are some interesting changes coming – not least of which is a new (for sound controllers, anyway) method of connecting them to a PC. There is a movement afoot in the PC industry to do away with the industry standard architecture (ISA) expansion slots, which have been on PC motherboards since the AT-286, by July 1, 1999. They have limited bandwidth (16 bits per cycle) at 8 MHz, no matter the speed of your motherboard or the architecture of your processor is. Both Intel and Microsoft complain that improving "plug 'n' play" is impossible so long as these slots exist. Bandwidth? This is a description of both the size of the data packet (16 bits) and the speed at which it is carried (8 MHz). Bandwidth is a term you'll also hear associated with the Internet, usually accompanied by the qualifier "limited."

A new set of specifications for a basic PC, dubbed PC 98 and initiated by Microsoft, Intel, and Compaq, came into effect July 1, 1998. To be compliant with the PC 98 specification, no ISA device is to ship with a new system after that date. So, finally, sound controllers will move to the PCI bus (Peripheral Component Interconnect).

This is going to provide sound controller manufacturers with both opportunities and headaches. The PCI bus, at 33 MHz, is significantly faster than ISA, providing more bandwidth for 32- or 64-bit peripherals. Among other things, the PCI bus can provide up to nine simultaneous audio channels. However, it has no direct access to memory (DMA), nor does it have access to interrupt request (IRQ) channels, both of which are required for the "Sound Blaster compatibility" that is so important for games.

Bandwidth has another role, but up until now, most of the discussions about it have centred on graphics controllers. If you've already read Chapter 13, you'll know that binary math (numbers with one and zero) can only describe a certain number of events. Eight bits of data give you 256 choices; 16 bits provide 65,536; 24 bits give 16.7 million; 32 bits give 4.2 billion; and so on.

Sound controllers sold in 1998 were 16-bit devices, allowing for a maximum of 65,536 "shades" or variations of sound at any one time. This provided better sound than the now obsolete 8-bit products, but still can't come close to the nuances we can distinguish with our ears in the real world. Will 32- and 64-bit PCI-based sound cards provide billions or trillions of sound nuances? Maybe so, maybe not – but the extra bandwidth can be used to do all sorts of tricks we haven't heard yet.

To describe what I'm getting at, we have to use another computer product that we'll be exploring in more depth below – scanners. Again, if you've read Chapter 13, you'll already know that 24-bit, 16.7 shade colour is the best you can see from any current graphics controllers. But there are all manner of 30-, 32-, and 36-bit scanners on the market. In fact, they do see billions of shades, but the marginal shades are discarded so the scanner can produce the purest colours and the densest black. I suspect a similar scheme will emerge from sound controllers with the extra bits used to fine-tune the results.

Why are the "shades" of sound important?

Sound is composed of a rich variety of nuances. It has resonance and harmonics. It has pitch. The higher the frequency of the vibration, the higher the pitch. In music, low-frequency vibrations produce low notes and high frequencies produce high notes. Sound has tremolo (oscillation of pitch), volume, and vibrato (oscillation of volume). Sound also has timbre – the quality of sound that distinguishes it from other sounds of the same pitch and volume, such as the distinctive sound of a particular musical instrument. Finally, it also has tone (a combination of pitch, intensity, and quality).

What this has to do with sound controllers will become clearer after I explain two other terms first: "analog" and "digital." Analog means a one-to-one representation of real events as they happen in the world around us. When you use a microphone, a membrane in the device vibrates and is translated into a pulsed electrical signal, which in turn vibrates a speaker membrane somewhere else. One-to-one relationship: analog. This is the sound we get when we play those old vinyl albums.

When an analog event gets translated into numbers, it becomes digital. For instance, when I use the microphone attached to a sound controller, it is an analog process right up until it gets to the chips on the board. Then it hits an analog-to-digital converter (ADC), which, together with some other circuitry on the board, converts the electrical impulses into numerical data and passes them on to the computer's CPU, which in turn passes them on to the hard disk, where they are stored.

Going in the other direction, the digital data comes off the hard drive, through the CPU, to the sound controller, where yet another chip – this time a digital-to-analog converter (DAC) – turns it back into electrical signals, out to a speaker plug, through speakers and into my ears.

There is no "sound" stored on your hard disk; there are only numbers describing it. The higher the bit-depth of the sound controller, the more numbers it can use to describe the sound. Rather than leaving out high and low frequencies, you get a wider range. Sounds are fuller, less tinny. But that's not the whole story, either.

The next characteristic you'll hear used to describe a sound controller is it's sampling rate. Converting analog sound into digital form takes time, and it can also produce lots and lots of data. Those are two factors determining how often the sound controller "samples" the instructions you're feeding it. When you and I hear noises, we hear them in a continuous stream – no gaps or pauses (unless our hearing aids are on the blink or we're under twenty and an adult is talking).

Quite simply, the human brain is a great multitasker. It can listen to sound, process all of it, and read a book at the same time. Computer hardware is much slower, and the average PC can't do two things at once, so the sound controller has to read the instruction, process it, send it to the CPU, then go back to read or "sample" again.

Low sampling rates are 8 and 11 KHz (8,000 to 11,000 times per second). Mid-range and high sampling rates are 22 and 44.1 KHz, while some high-end controllers can sample at 48 KHz. At low sampling rates, the accuracy of the reproduction suffers and the sound gets fuzzy. At higher rates the accuracy improves, but 16-bit sound sampled at 44.1 KHz in stereo will eat up space on your hard drive at a rate of about 11 MB per minute.

Bit-depth and sampling rate together largely determine the quality of the sound processed by the controller, but there are a few other issues as well – and here, I'm afraid, we're going to get a bit technical.

If you're getting a sound controller simply to play back Windows' sound files or to tinker with voice recognition or telephony (voice mail), the following won't matter much to you. If you want to take full advantage of both the voice *and* music tracks in high-end DOS games, or use your sound controller to create MIDI music, it will matter a lot.

MIDI: Musical Instrument Digital Interface – a protocol for connecting electronic musical devices to computers, which covers both hardware and software standards. Used for electronic musical instruments, computers, and other devices. MIDI commands contain all the information a sound controller needs to reproduce the desired sound and the files produced can be quite small.

General MIDI and Roland GS (General Synthesizer) are two overlapping specifications for defining the standard sets of MIDI sounds that are associated with specific commands. Most sound cards have a standard MIDI port on the mounting bracket, but most gamers use it for its other purpose: as a game port for joysticks, gamepads, steering wheels, and other game controllers. Watch for the introduction of Universal Serial Bus to change all this, soon.

FM synthesis: Most mid-level to low-end sound controllers use a process known as FM (frequency modulation) synthesis to support MIDI. Invented over twenty years ago, FM synthesis, usually produced by a Yamaha OPL2, OPL3, or compatible chipset, synthesizes musical instruments, drums, special effects, or the human voice, by mathematically manipulating two to four sine waves. (Sine wave: see your kid's mathematics textbook.) The result is only a loose approximation of the real thing, but the advantage to sound controller developers is that the technology is inexpensive.

A MIDI file is small, because it is a simple data file that merely tells the synthesizer when to play which notes and for how long. This makes MIDI popular with game developers. FM synthesis makes neat bleeps and bloops, but is awful when trying to duplicate the sound of traditional acoustic instruments, especially brass (trumpet, trombone) and woodwind (saxophone, clarinet) families. You need it for some game compatibility, but don't want it to be the only reproductive technique the controller uses; otherwise your parents and/or spouse and neighbours will want to bury you in an unmarked grave.

Wave table synthesis: Instead of manipulating sine waves, adapters with wave table synthesis use digitized recordings of the real thing, stored in memory on the controller (either ROM or RAM), as a basis for creating sounds. For example, it could have a piano's middle C, plus a C one octave higher. Using technomagic, the controller will compare the signal it receives to its built-in table, then extrapolate the rest of the notes in between. One item for you to check when you're shopping is to find out how many notes are compared. You'll get a better result if the controller is checking two notes – before and after – not just one. High-end products from Creative Labs, Turtle Beach, Diamond Multimedia, and Advanced Gravis may store samples in RAM, instead of ROM, which will allow you to add sounds. You may even be able to add more RAM, and more sound samples, to the wave table for greater accuracy and a wider range of reproduction.

Physical modelling synthesis: A new alternative to wave table and FM synthesis for generating sound by emulating the impulse patterns of real-world instruments using a software model instead of a hardware chip. Developed by engineers at Stanford University. Physical modelling is attractive because it is easily implemented in software, it can theoretically produce consistent results on different machines, and the coded algorithms are quite short; but *fast processors are needed* to synthesize such sounds in real time.

Creative Labs was one of the first audio controller vendors to implement physical modelling in an end-user product. In addition to 4MB of traditional wave table samples, Creative Labs' Sound Blaster AWE64 Gold board has fourteen instruments recreated through physical modelling.

Yeah, but what do all these gizmos *do*?

To give you a benchmark to aim for, check the following quote from Creative Labs' description of the advanced wave effects synthesis used in their Sound Blaster AWE32 board:

The Sound Blaster AWE32 supports 32 channels with 32-voice polyphony [keep this number "32" in mind for later – MW]. It utilizes a 6-part *amplitude envelope*, an additional 6-part *auxiliary envelope* for independently controlling pitch and timbre, and distortion-free *pitch shifting* techniques. It also contains *resonant filters* which change the timbre of each instrument when played at different dynamic levels or with different types of articulation, two *low frequency oscillators (LPOs)* for independent control of *vibrato* and *tremolo*, and advanced effects like chorus and reverb which add richness and ambience to the sound.

Here's a quickie explanation of these terms: Most sound controllers use some form of amplitude envelope when producing musical sounds. It allows sounds to be manipulated four ways: attack, decay, sustain, and release. During attack, the amplitude of the sound rises to its highest point, then it dies down a little (decay), holds for a while (sustain), then fades out to nil (release). How these states are handled can change how an instrument sounds. For example, if you eliminate the attack of a piano, it begins to sound like a string instrument being bowed. Creative Labs' auxiliary envelope uses the same techniques to hone pitch and timbre independently.

Pitch shifting changes the frequency of a sound. For example, a recorded F note can be made higher ($F^\#$, G) or lower (E, E^b, or D). By storing one note and turning it into five, the amount of memory you need for your wave table is drastically cut.

Two low-frequency oscillators per voice allow for independent control of vibrato and tremolo. Vibrato and tremolo add life to the sound, and you can only do one at a time if there is only one LPO per voice channel.

Now you are probably getting the point of why extra bits of data should make digital sound sampling more interesting in the future. It also brings us to the programmable digital signal processor (DSP). Regardless of who supplies them (several companies do, with Crystal Semiconductor and its Cirrus Logic division being among the more active in the late 1990s), these little marvels are to sound controllers what video accelerator chips are to video controllers. They are special processors tuned to handle the mathematics of digital audio, and their purpose is to cut down on the amount of time your computer's CPU has to spend feeding your sound controller. Creative Labs sometimes calls its DSP an ASP (audio signal processor), but it does the same thing.

Last, but not least, we come to some new features provided by today's sound controllers, all designed to use your two stereo speakers, but which, by applying various forms of legerdemain, appear to be "three-dimensional." Also known as "positional" audio, the techniques involve both special DSPs and application programming interfaces (APIs). Some of the better known names include QSound, SRS, AD3, Digital Dolby – formerly AC3 – and Microsoft's DirectSound3D. See the "Jargon" section below for more detail.

Does adding a DSP make a sound controller more efficient and provide more things it can do? Yes. Does having one of the new "3-D" schemes cost more money? You betcha.

Marketing madness and other traps

There is one marketing trick that affects existing 16-bit products. If you've followed the explanations above (*good* for you!), you've detected that we get more nuances as we move from 8 to 16 to 24 to 32 bits and beyond. I've also said that all sound controllers available in early 1998 were 16-bit devices. So, what about Creative Labs' Sound Blaster AWE32, AWE64, and so on? Does the existence of these products refute what I've just said? Well, no, it doesn't, but it is great marketing on the company's part.

In fact, the "32" and "64" in the product names refers to the number of MIDI voices the controllers can handle. They have nothing to do with the number of bits used to formulate data. (Gotcha!)

Ads for sound controllers, particularly for the Sound Blaster AWE64, are notoriously vague about which version of the AWE64 is being offered for that low, low price. At last count, there were several: "Value," "Gold," "Gold P'n'P," "Gold PCI," and the ubiquitous "OEM" (original equipment manufacturer) version that is sold to system assemblers. That low price may not provide as much memory as you expected, the architecture (i.e., ISA or PCI) you expected, the features (such as physical modelling) you expected, the software bundle you expected, or even the on-board components you expected for the price advertised.

Without finding out which version the vendor offers, you cannot make a price comparison based on ads that merely say "Sound Blaster

AWE64." Similar considerations apply to product lines from Turtle Beach, Diamond, and Ensoniq (or any other brand, for that matter). Without the brand, model name, and *version*, the price quoted is meaningless.

While there are some peripheral players in the sound-card market, four brands dominate the scene, and I've selected four of their products for the comparison table below. Creative Labs' Sound Blaster line has long been an industry leader and it continues to maintain the largest market share. Closely grouped around what's left are Diamond Multimedia, Turtle Beach Systems, and a relatively new player, Ensoniq. That doesn't mean these are the only participants, however. There are a variety of companies producing digital signal processors for sound technology, as well as the new 3-D sound schemes noted above and detailed in the "Jargon" section below.

Prices can range from $50 to over $200 and will be a factor of whether the card uses FM, wave table, physical modelling synthesis, or some combination of the three. It will reflect how much memory is on the card and what kind, and, if it does use wave table, the quality of the recordings that went into the table. Price is also based upon whether or not it employs a digital signal processor, has support for stereo embellishments (positional or 3-D audio effects), and the quality of the software bundled with the device.

Compatibility buzzwords

• Sound Blaster compatible: Mono FM synthesis, just enough compatibility to play most, if not all, games that require Sound Blaster compatibility. Won't work so well in high-end gaming products.
• Sound Blaster Pro compatible: Stereo FM synthesis, just enough compatibility to play most, if not all, games requiring Sound Blaster Pro compatibility. May not work so well in high-end gaming products.
• Business audio: Stereo FM synthesis, just enough compatibility to work within Windows for business applications, such as presentation programs or Internet downloads, but all bets are off if your high-end game requires DOS.

Beware of the bite

Don't take anyone's word for how good the sound controller is. Read the ads, the reviews, and the marketing bumph, but then go to the store and listen to the controller. Take some headphones with you to cut out the distractions. If it sounds good, has drivers for your operating environment, supports the software you plan to use with it, and you can afford it, jump on it.

If the salesperson or the manufacturer's bumph says the controller does "CD-quality recording," ask to hear a sample. Does it sound like a CD or an AM radio? Check your headphones. Are you hearing stereo or mono?

Beware of tricks. Some naughty folk may play you selections directly from a CD-ROM drive and suggest that the sound is being produced by the sound controller. That's a no-no. You don't need a sound controller to play a CD-ROM (you can pipe it directly to an amplifier). If, during the demonstration, you see the CD-ROM drive light come on, thank the salesperson for the demo of the CD-ROM and then ask to hear the controller playing a file from the hard drive.

What you'll need if you want your sound controller for high-end DOS games is one that uses both FM *and* wave table synthesis, because many games use both techniques for voice and music. Also, even though a sound controller may use wave table synthesis to play back previously stored MIDI recordings, that doesn't mean it also has a MIDI connector that allows you to plug in a keyboard. Controllers designed specifically for the MIDI market may produce rich sound and they will have a MIDI port, but they may not have a microphone connector.

Gamers should take note that there are several standards for game sound. Read the box copy or you could end up wondering what the game really sounds like. Also keep in mind that while the Windows Sound System 2.0 claims DOS-Sound Blaster/AdLib compatibility, you won't like how it – or other controllers that work the same way – does the job.

The Windows Sound System 2.0 controller, and others advertised as "business audio," works well in Windows, and if all you're planning to do is to use it for business applications and games within Windows, it's okay. For DOS games and MIDI music, look elsewhere.

A sound controller manufacturer offering FM synthesis as the sole MIDI synthesizer is hoping you're tone deaf.

Make sure you can return the controller within a reasonable period if you're not satisfied with its performance – particularly if the store didn't allow you to listen to it first, or if the actual performance of the controller doesn't match its hype.

Speakers

What are you going to do for speakers?

A few sound controllers pre-amplify their output, and tiny speakers come as part of the package. Most don't. Check what your choice does and shop accordingly.

Price doesn't always determine quality, but it doesn't make a whole lot of sense to hook your computer to a pair of $20 speakers with a one-inch diameter diaphragm. You may want to splurge a little here. You'll want to do some homework, applying the same tests to speakers that you do to the sound cards themselves.

There is one caution worth noting, however. Speakers usually contain magnets. Unless they've been specially shielded, having them right next to your monitor may produce unpleasant results, and you may have to learn what "degaussing" means. Placing them too close to floppy or hard drives and using them as a place to pile up diskettes is a bad idea, too.

Jargon

As you navigate through the world of PC sound controllers, you're liable to encounter the following additional terms:

3-D sound: A blanket term for technologies that alter the way sound is distributed in real-world space. Spatialization broadens the soundstage (the area in space where the sound seems to be coming from), making it more dramatic and spacious, and gives the illusion of pushing it beyond the physical location of the speakers. Positional audio uses encoded audio streams to position sounds realistically in the space around the listener when the sounds are played back on compatible equipment. See A3D Interactive and DirectSound3D, below.

A3D Interactive: A powerful, proprietary 3-D-positional audio algorithm developed by Aureal Semiconductor that makes it possible to position and move audio events (gunshots, door slams, engine noises, and so on) in a three-dimensional space using only two speakers. Aureal also developed an API (application programming interface) called A3D, which presaged Microsoft's DirectSound3D (see below).

AC3: The former name of what is now called Digital Dolby.

AC '97: Intel's recommended standard or *audio codec* for PC audio circuitry. The specification reduces noise by partitioning analog and digital components into separate modules.

ADPCM: Adaptive Differential Pulse Code Modulation. Refers to the process by which sound waveforms are compressed and converted into digital data.

Algorithm: A mathematical, step-by-step procedural description of an event (such as a software program).

API: Application Programming Interface – a set of rules that provide a framework within which a programmer can access hooks in the operating system environment to produce consistent, device-independent results. In other words, a method that should, if followed properly, allow the same results from any software, regardless of the source of the hardware – or how two different sound controllers can be made to produce the same sound.

Audio accelerator: You can't make sound go faster, otherwise everything sounds like Alvin and the Chipmunks (go ask your dad). An audio accelerator is designed to offload audio processing from the CPU. New tools, such as A3D Interactive (see above), DirectSound and DirectSound3D, QSound, and SRS (see below), require some kind of hardware to do number crunching. Audio accelerators take on that processing load to free up the CPU for other tasks. See "Yeah, but what do all these gizmos *do*?" above.

Chorus: An audio effect that duplicates a sound, slightly changes and delays it, then overlays it on top of the original to add complexity and character.

Decibel: Most commonly seen in its abbreviated form: dB. A unit that measures the strength of a signal. Good audio controllers produce a signal-to-noise ratio (see below) greater than 80 dB. *Really* good products punch this higher to greater than 90 dB

DirectSound3D: Microsoft's 3-D-positional audio API, first introduced with DirectX 5.0, that makes it possible to position and move audio events (gunshots, door slams, engine noises, and so on) in a three-dimensional space, even if you have only two speakers.

DirectX: Game developers prefer DOS because it gives them direct access to hardware such as video and audio controllers. Windows 9x hates this and Windows NT won't allow it at all. DirectX is a set of Microsoft Windows APIs designed to provide software developers with direct access to low-level functions on PC peripherals to get around all this. DirectX is actually a suite of drivers including DirectDraw, DirectSound, DirectSound3D, DirectPlay, DirectInput, and DirectSetup.

If you want a broad idea of what they're designed to do, think about printers. In the DOS era, every software developer had to ship umpteen dozen printer drivers and each printer manufacturer shipped a gazillion software drivers in the hopes that a poor end user could get at least two products working together. Windows introduced "device independence" by providing the print routine, and, if a printer was supported, the software developers didn't have to worry about it any more. DirectX is the same sort of thing for multimedia devices. The suite was in version 5.0 when in Windows 98, but by October 1998 had already been updated to version 6.0, which indicates the rapidity with which Microsoft got complaints about earlier, buggier versions.

DLS: Downloadable samples (or downloadable software samples). A wave table sound controller (see above) that supports DLS has a functionally infinite library of waveforms at its disposal because new sounds can be loaded into memory – either system memory (a PCI controller) or local memory on the controller itself (an ISA adapter).

Dynamic range: The sound frequency range (the lowest-pitched sound to the highest-pitched sound) that a sound controller is able to digitize and reproduce.

Full duplex: When applied to sound controllers (as opposed to modems), a full duplex sound adapter can receive and transmit sound simultaneously – something you'll want if you plan to use it to make

Internet "phone" calls. Otherwise, get used to saying "Over," just like in the old shortwave radio days.

IEEE 1394 (FireWire): Something to do with International Electrical Engineers. FireWire is an internal and external communications bus with a much higher bandwidth than USB (see below). Already in use for some digital cameras, it could connect the disk and disc drives of the future, as well as other external sources. How much of an impact it will have on the sound controller market remains to be seen. See the discussion of ISA, next.

ISA: Industry standard architecture, the standard 16-bit expansion bus created for the original IBM PC-AT. This bus can carry data at only 8 MHz (no matter how fast your motherboard or processor may be) and by mid-1998 was typically used only by sound cards and modems (and older technologies).

The cons of the ISA bus, aside from the difficulty of implementing full plug 'n' play, include its limited bandwidth of 2 to 6 Mbps (megabits per second). A stereo-CD data stream at 1.4 Mbps, along with sound effects and a MIDI voice or two, could easily gobble 40 per cent of the available bandwidth – leaving precious little for whatever else you may have wanted to do.

The PCI bus, with its 100 MBps (megabytes per second) bandwidth (or higher), hardly works up a sweat, even with multiple audio streams running concurrently. And run concurrently they can – up to nine of them – just ducky for producing the effects desired in positional sound strategies. PCI also allows for a higher signal to noise ratio (over 90 dB instead of around 85 dB for ISA).

However (and these are biggies), ISA cards are less expensive to implement. And ISA cards use dynamic memory allocation (DMA, also known as direct memory access) channels and interrupt request (IRQ) channels to move audio from memory. PCI has no direct access to memory or IRQs, so to maintain compatibility with Creative Labs' Sound Blaster for DOS games and other legacy programs requires some fancy workarounds the industry was just creating as this book went to press.

Mono sound: Sound or music that is reproduced over only one sound channel, even though it may be played through two (or more) speakers. Short for monaural.

PC 98: A set of standards for basic, business, and entertainment computers devised by Microsoft, Intel, and Compaq, but now endorsed by most computer manufacturers. Among other things, it calls for new computers, in order to achieve certification, not to ship with any ISA devices after July 1, 1998, and for new ISA devices to cease being sold after July 1, 1999. Most affected by this will be sound card and modem manufacturers. See ISA, above, and PCI, below.

PC speaker sound: Beeps produced by the PC internally and output through a speaker inside the computer. This is the standard sound system that exists on every PC-compatible computer, whether it has a sound card or not. It's awful.

PCI: Peripheral Component Interconnect, an expansion bus standard slated to replace ISA (though it coexists with the older bus in nearly every PC currently on the market). The PCI bus is much faster than the ISA bus (half the speed of the motherboard up to 33 MHz) and is a boon to digital audio, but sound controller manufacturers had only just begun to migrate to the PCI bus in mid-1998. It's difficult to maintain Sound Blaster compatibility without ISA (see above).

PCM: Pulse Code Modulation. Refers to the process by which sound waveforms are converted into digital data.

Positional audio: See 3-D sound, above.

Reverb: An abbreviation of the word "reverberation" (which in turn is a long word for "echo") and designed to simulate environmental acoustics. Without it, the sound is flat. With lots of it, you might pretend the sound was produced in a large, wood-panelled hall.

S/N ratio: Signal-to-noise ratio. Refers to the proportion between the recorded audio (the signal) and the hiss, distortion, and other contamination (the noise) present in an audio stream. Signal-to-noise ratios are expressed logarithmically in decibels (dB). The higher the signal-to-noise ratio (the dB figure in the marketing bumph), the less artifacts you hear along with the screaming space boogers or your favourite band (see Decibels, above).

Sequencer: A computer program that co-ordinates and controls the input and output from musical instruments, usually via MIDI interfaces.

SRS: Sound Retrieval System, a proprietary algorithm developed by SRS Labs that is designed to expand a stereo soundstage. Unlike with DirectSound3D or A3D Interactive (see above), a soundtrack need not be pre-recorded or pre-processed with SRS. Critics of this technology, however, maintain that SRS distorts a recording artist's intent because of the way it manipulates audio frequencies.

Stereo sound: Sound or music that is recorded and reproduced over two separate sound channels, left and right. See 3-D sound, above, to see why today's stuff ain't your daddy's stereo any more.

Synthesized sound: Sound created by electronics or computer equipment. Synthesized sound is created by duplicating the components that make up sound – frequency, waveform, attack, decay, sustain, release components, etc. (see above).

USB: Universal Serial Bus. Watch for the full driver support for USB in Windows 98 to have a profound effect on all external peripheral devices, including game controllers and MIDI hardware. By the time you read this, Altec Lansing should have released speakers using USB in mid-1998. Also see IEEE 1394, above.

Waveform: The "picture" of sound you see on an oscilloscope. This is actually what the sound card "samples."

Telecommunications

In 1998 and 1999, unless you opt for one of the competing technologies listed below, you'll be looking at POTS (plain old telephone service) modems offering 56K speed for accessing the Internet.

While modems are still optional equipment in some low-end systems, I expect them soon to join sound controllers and CD-ROM drives as standard equipment. Before long you'll be wondering how people could ever have purchased a computer without one.

There was a fairly thorough discussion of the war between competing "56K" standards and the terms of the peace treaty in the ad primer (Chapter 5). If you haven't read that section yet, go there now; then come back. What we're going to discuss here are the different methods available to you to access the Internet.

Sound Cards

Product	Creative Labs Sound Blaster AWE64*	Diamond Multimedia Monster Sound MX80*	Ensoniq AudioPCI	Turtle Beach Malibu Surround 64
Street price (Cdn$)	$79 - $139	$199	$79	$129
Bus architecture	ISA or PCI	PCI	PCI	ISA
Supports Windows 95/NT 4.0 / 3.x	Y Y Y	Y N N	Y Y Y	Y Y Y
Supports DOS	Y	N	N	Y
Audio chip set	Creative V 32D	Analog Devices 1843	AKM-4531	Crystal Semiconductor 4237
Sound Blaster Pro–compatible	Y	N	Y	Y
DirectSound support	DirectSound 5.0	DirectSound 5.0, 3-D	DirectSound 5.0, 3-D	DirectSound 3.x
Hardware/software wavetable synthesizer	Y Y	Y N	Y Y	Y Y
ROM for on-board samples	4MB	16MB	None	4MB
Maximum parts (simultaneous timbres)	16	15	32	16
Maximum voices (simultaneous tones)	64	32	32	64
Number of MIDI instruments/drum kits	503 / 24	240 / 80	128 / 10	128 / 64
Claimed signal-to-noise ratio	>90 dB	>92 dB	>90 dB	>92 dB
Claimed 16-bit sampling range	5-44.1 kHz	8-48 kHz	5-48 kHz	5-48 kHz
DSP model	E-mu EMU8000	Analog Devices 2181	Ensoniq AudioPCI ES1370	Crystal DSP (optional)
Primary DSP function	Real-time effects, wave table synthesis	A3D positional audio	PCI-bus control, real-time effects, wave table synthesis	Dolby Digital audio, wave table synthesis
MIDI output effects	Reverb, chorus, delay, expanded stereo, E-mu's 3-D positional audio	Pan, time-varying filter, vibrato	Chorus, reverb, 3-D positional audio	Chorus, reverb, SRS expanded stereo
Microphone-in / Line-in / Line-out	Y Y Y	Y Y Y	Y Y Y	Y Y Y
MIDI or joystick / Internal CD audio	Y Y	Y Y	Y Y	Y Y
Mixer rack	Creative Mixer	Willow Pond	Voyetra AudioStation2	Voyetra AudioStation2
WAV recorder	Creative Sound LE	Willow Pond	Voyetra AudioView	Voyetra AudioView
MIDI sequencer	Voyetra MIDI Orchestrator Plus	Willow Pond	Voyetra MusicWrite	Voyetra MIDI Orchestrator Plus
Sound editor	Creative Wave Studio	Willow Pond	Voyetra AudioView	Voyetra AudioView
Wave table sample editor	Vienna SoundFont Studio 2.1	None	None	None
Warranty	1 Year	3 Years	3 Years	1 Year
Toll-free technical support	N	N	N	N
Web site: http://www.	soundblaster.com	diamondmm.com	ensoniq.com	tbeach.com

*There are several AWE64 configurations: Value, Gold, Gold P'n'P, and PCI, as well as an "OEM" version. Without the full model name in the ad, you can't tell what you're being offered or whether the price is competitive. Diamond's Monster Sound also has two versions, the MX200 (64-voice wave table, quad speaker support) and MX80 (32-voice wave table)

MoDefinitions:

MODEM (*MOdulator/DEModulator*): Traditionally, a device which converts analog phone signals to digital computer data and back. However, today it means any device that connects your computer to a remote location, primarily the Internet. Several of the alternatives below don't convert from digital to analog at all, but they're still called modems.

POTS (*Plain Old Telephone Service*): As of early 1998, the international standard for "56K" data transmission was called V.90. Any modem you purchase offering 56K speed should be fully V.90 compatible.

Your homework assignment here is to find out if the V.90 standard has changed or been replaced by something faster. One hint: If you begin to see something called V.90*bis* or V.90*ter*, it means the standard has been revised. "Bis" and "ter" are abbreviations of German words meaning two and three. So, V.90*bis* is like saying, "V.90, the sequel." If the promotional material says V.90*terbo*, it isn't a misspelling; it's a play on words. In any event, the modem you choose should have "flash" ROM or "flash" BIOS (see Chapter 5 for an explanation). This will allow you to take advantage of any changes or improvements to its firmware via software upgrade during the time you own it.

In early 1998, mainstream brands with telephone and Web-based technical support included 3Com (USRobotics), Motorola, AT&T, GVC, and Diamond Multimedia (Supra). There was a host of other suppliers, some we've never heard of before. Regardless, if the product doesn't have telephone or Web-based support, or if it doesn't mention how to contact the manufacturer anywhere in the documentation, you don't want it.

POTS modems will offer fax send and receive, preferably at 14.4 kilobits per second (Kbps). They may also offer voice services so you can use your modem as an automatic answering machine. As long as your computer has a sound controller, you don't need voice services on the modem itself to make Internet long-distance "phone" calls (but you will need a microphone to connect to your sound controller).

POTS modems use a standard touch-tone telephone line. Despite claims to the contrary, I've never met a modem or a software application that succeeded in allowing it to share a single residential line with the other uses you'll have for it (such as turning down annoying salespeople who call during dinner). If you're running a small business from your home, plan to use the Internet a lot, and put your fax number (or e-mail address) on your business card, you'll want to have two phone lines (which will up the cost of operation slightly).

The cost of connecting to an Internet Service Provider (ISP) varies from company to company and from region to region, as well as with the level of service you require. But the Canadian price range of $15.99 to $29.99 per month in early 1998 was the cheapest of the methods described here. POTS is also likely to be available from every ISP in most locations throughout North America and elsewhere, which is not something that's true of any other method listed below.

Despite the alternative methods of Internet connection discussed below, you may still need a POTS modem for fax service.

Shotgun: At the beginning of 1998, Diamond Multimedia (Supra, Supra Express) introduced an exclusive technology it called Shotgun. It ties two 56K, V.90 POTS modems together, using two standard phone lines, to produce *up to* 112 Kpbs download speeds (an older 33.6 Kbps, V.34*bis* modem, plus one of Diamond's Shotgun modems can produce up to 89 Kbps. A 28.8 Kbps modem in the mix drops the top download speed to 84.8 Kbps). A Shotgun modem dials out on one line and only invokes another if it detects a large download. If a voice call comes in during a download, Shotgun releases one of the lines (and the speed drops) to take the call. (You can get more information about it at http://www.diamondmm.com.) Although the SupraExpress with Shotgun cap works with other brands of modem, no other company has yet embraced the scheme – and I urge you to consult your ISP to see if the service is supported before making a commitment to a second line or a second modem. My suspicion is that this, like ISDN below, will eventually fall prey to one of the other emerging technologies.

ISDN (*Integrated Services Digital Network*): Considerably faster than standard POTS, ISDN requires special phone lines (two of them), a special modem, and, if you want to use it, a special telephone. If your current ISP doesn't provide ISDN service, you need one that does if you want to use ISDN technology. If your local telephone company doesn't provide ISDN service, you'll need to move to another town. Upload and download speeds range from 64 Kbps, if you use one of the two lines, to 128 Kbps, if you use both. Problems with ISDN include setup (it can make you crazy) and cost.

The phone company will charge you to initiate service ($150 to $300 Cdn in early 1998), a special monthly fee ($50 in Toronto for residential, $100 for business), and if you don't already pay the higher business-phone rate, an additional per-minute line charge. You will have to purchase a separate (and expensive) ISDN modem ($300 to $500). The ISP may charge you for initial setup and the monthly service charge will be higher than for a POTS hookup. ISDN is for experienced users with substantial budgets only, but may lose out to the following and eventually vanish.

Fax? Nope, there's no such thing as an ISDN fax modem (and if there were, you probably couldn't afford it).

The WAVE (*Cable TV modem*): This is provided by local cable TV companies, and is neighbourhood specific (which means it's not available in all cities or in all neighbourhoods). Under this scheme, your cable company becomes your ISP. It may offer a more limited set of Internet services or even censor some material on the Internet. WAVE setup requires a special network card to be installed in your system, which may conflict with older equipment or existing network interface cards. Because the computer is *always* connected to the Internet whenever it's on, some people have had concerns about security.

Setup charges vary, but the typical monthly fee in Canada in 1998 ranged from $45 to $60 per month. Upload/download rates vary from 1 to 27 *mega*bits per second (Mbps), but the number of users on any one node affects speed. A large number of users can slow transmission to less than 28 Kbps.

Some of my local computer press colleagues who have WAVE (it's not yet in my neighbourhood) rave about it compared to POTS service. However, as I write this, there are very few opportunities for a direct comparison to the next method on the list, so none of us have been able to do head-to-head trials.

Fax? You have to be kidding.

xDSL (*Digital Subscriber Line*): All Digital Subscriber Line variations are asymmetric. That means the speed of transmission is less from you to your ISP than it is coming back to you. North American telephone companies and others worldwide have been experimenting with DSL. The two methods most often talked about are ADSL (asymmetric DSL) and HDSL (high-speed DSL – although it, too, is an asymmetric standard). There is also another version, VDSL (very high-speed DSL), but it isn't talked about much other than as a fantasy.

ADSL uses standard POTS phone lines (no special modifications required) with upload speeds from 128 Kbps to 1 Mbps and download speeds from 600 Kbps to 7 Mbps. The speed you get is directly related to how close you are to your nearest telephone office (and the need to build local offices in rural areas is the main reason the phone companies give for the delay in implementation). ADSL requires special modems, and ISPs (most likely to be the telephone company) must support it with appropriate server modems. Expect a premium rate from everyone. If ADSL is to compete with cable it must be priced competitively, but so far that has not been the case. Where it has been available, Bell and other Canadian telephone companies have charged higher rates than the cable TV companies have for WAVE.

Fax? Not likely from any xDSL modem, but. . . . One of the more interesting aspects of ADSL is that you can use a single line to send and receive data while holding a phone conversation. I don't see why fax transmission couldn't also be possible, but you'd have to have a separate POTS fax modem.

Digital satellite: Also not widely available yet in Canada. It's asymmetric – both in speed and technology – and uses phone lines and standard POTS modem to upload at rates of 14.4 Kbps and up. Download is via satellite dish at 400 Kbps to 6 Mbps. Early systems are expected to cost around $1,000 or more to set up, plus a variable (average $100) monthly charge, plus ISP fees. Probably best for use in remote communities.

Fax? Use your POTS modem.

PCS wireless: Also not widely available. PCS (Personal Communications Service – a digital form of cellular technology that uses the 1800 KHz band instead of cellular's 800 KHz band for transmission) has the theoretical potential for 1 to 27 Mbps transmission in both directions, but, like xDSL, requires repeater stations at closer intervals than cellular technology. This may delay implementation, particularly outside major metropolitan areas. PCS is still an emerging technology, and use of it for data communication is still experimental. The monthly fees, the identity of the ISPs, and technical requirements hadn't been established in early 1998. Expect it to be offered by telephone, cellular, and PCS companies.

Fax? Maybe.

Other weird schemes: Just before this book went to press, there were several reports of experiments in both Canada and Britain using electrical transmission lines (yes, the ones from your local Hydro company) to carry telecommunications signals. Upper speed, modem type, cost, and methods of implementation are still in the highly experimental realm. I can, however, report that the British experiment was put on hold when people noticed that the streetlights were flickering when a communications session was in progress. Back to the drawing board. Check the third edition of *How to Buy a Computer* to find out how this one works out.

Digital Cameras and Scanners

While they are two quite different products, both digital cameras and image scanners share one feature, TWAIN, that deserves to be discussed first. There's a simple rule here. If you're contemplating any device that's used to put still images into your computer and it doesn't have a TWAIN driver, run away.

TWAIN

TWAIN is not what you yell at someone sitting on the twacks. The exact definition of the acronym, "TWAIN," depends on who is doing the telling and when they told you. Originally, TWAIN stood for Technology Without An Independent Name (this is true; I have the document). Then it was claimed that it wasn't an abbreviation at all. Instead, it stood for the meeting of hardware and software (in this case, the twain did meet). Some folk have started calling it Technology Without An Interesting Name. Pick one.

Names aside, TWAIN results from a rare case of clear thinking by two segments of the computer industry. In a nutshell, the early purveyors of scanner hardware and the folks who developed software likely to use scanned images (Adobe led the pack) got together, looked at what was then the printer market, and shuddered. Back in the pre-Windows days, each software application had to support multiple brands of printers (and vice-versa). Without a compatible printer driver – the software that translated an application's output into instructions the printer could understand – it was dead easy to buy a printer you couldn't use with the software you had or to get new software that couldn't talk to your existing printer. And the problem could compound if you upgraded either one. The scanner hardware and software companies rightly figured that if they went the same route, it would make everyone crazy and consumers would be reluctant to buy their products.

TWAIN was an elegant solution. At its core, it's a common driver designed so that it doesn't matter whose scanner you use or with which product. If both are TWAIN compatible, you can use one to scan directly to the other. There were no digital cameras when this was first being hammered out, but they have since joined the TWAIN "community."

Make no mistake: Not all TWAIN drivers are alike. They are usually specific to a particular model of scanner (or digital camera) and come with the hardware device. To my knowledge, only Corel and Xerox have attempted to create a "universal" TWAIN driver that is hardware independent. Some hardware companies are better than others when it comes to creating software, so some TWAIN drivers are capable of (or better at) automatically determining image type (colour, greyscale, line art) and size. Some let you select a custom scan area and/or zoom to a selected area. Some don't. Some will guess at and/or let you set colour temperature (gamma), contrast and brightness, hue, and saturation before you scan – as well as providing other pre-scan services (mirror image, negative image, rotated image, and so on). Again, some either don't provide these services, or don't do a terrific job when they do.

In short, when researching your scanner or digital camera options, paying attention to reviews that mention the quality of the TWAIN drivers is often as important as assessing the quality of the hardware.

One thing TWAIN drivers don't – or shouldn't – do is to care about which software is calling the TWAIN driver, and by and large, the drivers are remarkably good. Today you can scan, through TWAIN drivers, directly into a growing number of products, including word processors, presentation programs, Web design tools, spreadsheets, databases, fax programs, optical character recognition (OCR) software, desktop publishing programs, children's "storybook" applications, and image manipulation programs beyond number and for all skill levels. With one notable exception I discovered in early 1998 from a pair of Agfa Snapscan models (300 and 600), no company had screwed it up yet beyond the occasional instance of bad programming and bugs that plague all computer technology from time to time.

Changes due?

Not long ago, I asked John Warnock, CEO and co-founder of Adobe (developers of PostScript and a wide variety of image manipulation and desktop-publishing software) about the current status of TWAIN, and – particularly given Agfa's "accomplishment" of providing an incompatible driver – whether it was time to reconvene the TWAIN committee.

Warnock found the idea intriguing. "A thing about computer industry public standards," he said, "is that they seem to take forever to find wide adherence, and they're always subject to problems if the programmers don't read the documentation, fail to understand it, or simply decide to ignore it. You're right when you say TWAIN has had broad success, but this isn't the first instance we've encountered with a problem, although fortunately they're rare.

"The other problem with standards is that once they become entrenched, it's very difficult to change them. One of the shortcomings of TWAIN, particularly as it is implemented on digital cameras for example, is that it is single-minded. You can't process multiple images in batches through the TWAIN acquire routine. So, given all these things, perhaps you're right. It may be time for another pass at TWAIN."

Your homework assignment is to find out whether there is now another version of TWAIN on the horizon that does, for example, allow batch processing.

Scanners

A lot of computer peripheral products have come down in price over the last few years. But few have dropped so dramatically as scanners. As late as spring 1997, Canadian consumers would still be paying between $750 and nearer to $2,000 for a good flatbed model. Even today, high-end professional products from Hewlett-Packard, Agfa, Kurzwell, and others, hover closer to the $1,000 mark or more. However, the widespread use of images on Web sites, plus the success of TWAIN, has made image capture a popular sport and has brought prices down sharply.

The drop in scanner prices to under $500 Cdn (as low as $199 for some models) has killed at least one venerable product. The hand-scanner, which used to sell in the same price range, has disappeared.

Instead, for those who can't bring themselves to give up desk space to a flatbed model or even a small-footprint sheet-fed scanner, a new genre of consumer scanner – intended strictly for photographs, has emerged. Depending on the maker, they can fit in a 5.25-inch drive bay (Storm's unique PhotoDrive) or sit on your desk in about the same space a 5 x 7-inch photograph would need (such as Polaroid's PhotoPad).

You can still find some sheet-fed scanners, the format of choice for those who plan to use the device purely for optical character recognition, but stay away from them if your plan is to save money. Sheet-fed units, once less expensive than flatbed models, are now by and large *more* expensive. Also keep in mind that scanners at the very bottom of the price range are often one-page-at-a-time models that will eat up your time.

Today, flatbed scanners dominate the market. There are plenty of models from many companies and a wide choice of options and prices. They remain the most flexible of the model types, and can scan even tiny objects (if you can see it, you can scan it). They're the only kind of scanner suitable for small-profile, three-dimensional objects. I've been able to scan hand tools, circuit boards, memory modules and full motherboards. This should interest coin and jewellery collectors or those who'd like to scan pressed flowers (just to name a few options). Flatbeds are, of course, suitable for photos and documents, but they will also handle over-sized objects such as newspaper pages, bulky objects such as books (you *will* watch those copyrights, won't you?), and fragile mementos such as old photos or clippings.

My descriptions above may already have painted a picture of the difference between sheet-fed and flatbed scanners, but just in case they didn't. . . . In a sheet-fed scanner, the material to be scanned is fed, through a series of rollers, over a fixed lens array. This kind of device lends itself to the use of automatic document feeders (ADFs) that can hold multiple sheets of originals. They're best for scanning documents for optical character recognition when there are many pages to process at a time and do well with standard page sizes. Because of the rollers, however, they have problems with thick or bulky objects, don't do three-dimensional objects, and are likely to eat newspaper clippings or fragile photographs. If you want another machine with which to compare a sheet-fed scanner, think of a stand-alone fax machine.

Flatbed scanners have a lid hinged on either a long or short side which you lift up. Objects are placed one at a time on a glass plate and the scanning head moves under them. The action is similar to that of a large photocopier. Flatbed models can be equipped with automatic document feeders, but ADFs for flatbeds are often larger than the scanner itself and may cost more, too, when they're available (they aren't for many low-end models). Unlike sheet-fed scanners, they are eminently suitable for objects that are thicker, larger, or smaller than a standard business or legal sheet of paper, but they can also be used for optical character recognition for small-lot jobs and generally come with the software that allows you to use them this way.

Something had to go

In order to bring the price down and the scanning speed up, many of the low-price models make sacrifices. For example, in my arbitrarily chosen price range of under $500 Cdn, it is far more common to find A4 (8.5 x 11.7-inch) scan beds instead of full 8.5 x 14-inch beds (models from IBM are a happy exception). It's also not uncommon for the scanning lamps on these units to stay lit whenever the power is on to reduce warm-up time. Last, but not least, a significant number of them connect to a PC through its parallel printer port, instead of a faster SCSI adapter usually shipped with the more expensive SCSI models (similarly, many aren't available for Mac users).

Nearly all parallel-port models in the comparison table (below) require an enhanced parallel port (EPP), which is both bi-directional and faster than the standard parallel port (SPP) found on most older systems. Two notable exceptions are the products from Visioneer, which will use the SPP if it is also bi-directional and that's all you have, as well as Storm Technologies' ImageWave 250, a flatbed model that provides an optional Universal Serial Bus (USB) converter kit. You can expect parallel port models to slowly disappear as more USB models begin to ship.

Who's in and who's out

If I've missed your favourite brand in the table, ah well. It's hard to find information on some of the lesser-known bargain "brands." Epson and Umax aren't here, because they were late to jump into the low-price market. Logitech is also missing because it sold its scanner line to Storm Technologies.

Scanner shopping specs

Thirty- or **36-bit colour**: The highest number of colours you're ever likely to see on your computer monitor is roughly 16.7 million. Also known as 24-bit or "True" colour, it is, according to some, the maximum number of colours the human eye can discern. To get the 24 bits, 8 bits are assigned to each of the three (red, green, blue) colour channels. So what happens to the extra bits? Thirty- and 36-bit colour can provide billions of shades you can't see. Instead, a combination of the scanner hardware and software looks for the bits containing the most noise, then discards them to optimize the 24 bits that are left. It gives richer colours on screen as well as helping to provide details to edges and shadows.

Ten- or **12-bit greyscale**: The same with images in shades of grey. With a few exceptions, greyscale images are optimized for 8 bits (256 shades). If the scanner actually uses all ten bits to provide 1024 shades, you may not see them unless you render the result to colour, because most photo image software is limited to 256 shades.

What did he say? In most TWAIN drivers, if you set the type of picture you want to "greyscale," the scanner will only "look" for a limited number of shades of grey and will only send the best 8 bits to produce the 256-shade rendering of the image to your computer. However, even if the image you have is originally in shades of grey (e.g., a black and white photo), and you override the settings to capture colour, the scanner will attempt to render all the subtle variations it "sees," using up to 16.7 million shades to do so.

Scanning speed: I've left this particular specification off the table below, primarily because the figures provided by the manufacturers are often incomplete. They often quote a figure (i.e., "x" seconds per scan). But only rarely do they divulge the resolution used, the size of the original image, whether the speed quoted came from a colour or greyscale scan, or whether it includes computer processing time – all of which affect the time it takes to scan an image. Some (likely out of embarrassment) avoid the topic altogether.

Optical versus "interpolated" resolution: The scanner hardware produces optical resolution. The figure quoted represents the number of collection points across the scan head's charge couple device (the first number in the table below), by the number of samples in an inch taken during a scan. Keep in mind that for screen rendering (background wallpaper, images on the World Wide Web), you'll seldom want to use more than 75 dots-per-inch (dpi) and for most other operations, 150 dpi is more than adequate. You only need high resolution to scan really tiny objects on a page.

The scanner software produces interpolated resolution. In effect it averages out the values between two data points and guesses what was missed. Again, most consumers seldom use these high resolutions. If you're wondering what is the equivalent is in dots-per-inch to Agfa's "points-per-inch" quoted in the specifications and "lines-per-inch" used in the documentation and software, you're not alone; not even an Agfa Canada spokesperson could tell me.

LE, SE, and Express: If you find these terms on the software that comes with the scanner, it indicates that you're getting the "lite" or limited version – not the full thing. It may be time limited (it stops working after a certain date or number of times it is used), function limited (it doesn't do some of the things the full version does), or both. It's really promotional demoware (not such a great deal, after all). The time to worry about this is not when you see these terms, it's when you don't. Unless the marketing material indicates you get the full (or "Pro") version of a product, start asking questions and have the answers specified on the sales agreement, just in case.

TWAIN compatibility is still not universal enough to be taken for granted. If the product is TWAIN compatible, the package should say so. If it is not, *you do not want it*. I have studiously avoided mentioning products which I know are not TWAIN compatible in the table.

Scan size: While the maximum scan size is always useful to know, you don't care about the minimum scan size for a flatbed (f you can see the object, you can scan it). On anything with rollers, however, particularly if the object to be scanned gets pulled into the unit (as with the photo scanners), minimum size is important. I've tried to get the companies to be precise, but while most could give me outside dimensions, they found it harder to come up with minimum and maximum *thickness*. The average minimum is 0.004 inches, while the maximum thickness is about 0.050 inches.

Low-Cost Scanners

Company	Agfa	Adara		Hewlett-Packard		Microtek
Model	SnapScan 310	StarLight I	ImageStar I	ScanJet 5s	ScanJet 5100c	ScanMaker E3
Type	Flatbed	Flatbed	Flatbed	Sheet-fed	Flatbed	Flatbed
Interface	SCSI*	EPP**	SCSI	EPP	EPP	SCSI
Platform supported	PC/Mac	PC	PC/Mac	PC	PC	PC/Mac
Ships with adapter/cable	Yes/Yes	n/a	Yes/??	n/a	n/a	Yes/No
Alternate Interface(s)	Parallel	none	none	none	USB (model 4100C)	none
Footprint (L x W x H)	17.5" x 13" x 4.1"	17.3" x 11.5" x 3.2"	19.1" x 14" x 4.7"	13 " x 5" x 4.5" (without ADF)	19.1" x 12" x 4.9"	19.1" x 14" x 4.7"
Weight lbs/kg	not specified	11 / 5	16.5 / 7.5	3.5 / 1.6	12.5 / 5.7	16.5 / 7.5
Image sensor	CCD cold cathode	Linear array CCD /cold cathode	Linear array CCD /fluorescent	not specified	CCD/Xenon lamp	Linear CCD with daylight fluorescent lamp
Optical resolution	300 x 600 ppi	300 x 600	300 x 600	300 x 300	600 x 600	300 x 600
Interpolated resolution	4,800 x 4,800	4,800 x 4,800	2,400 x 2,400	600 x 600	1,200 x 1,200	4,800 x 4,800
Colour bit-depth	30-bit	30-bit	24-bit	24-bit	36-bit	24-bit
Greyscale bit-depth	10-bit	10-bit	8-bit	8-bit	8-bit	8-bit
Max scan size	8.5" x 11.7"	8.5" x 11"	8.5" x 14"	8.5" x 30"	8.5 x 11.7	8.5" x 13.5"
Min object size	n/a	n/a***	n/a	2" x 3.5"	n/a	n/a
Doc feeder	none	none	optional	built-in (10 pages)	not yet (summer '98)	optional
Transparency adapter	none	none	optional	n/a	none	optional
Software bundle	Caere OmniPage LE (OCR), Visioneer Paper Port, iPhoto Express	Caere OmniPage LE, Ulead ImagePals 2 Go and PhotoImpact SE	Caere OmniPage LE, Ulead ImagePals 2 Go and PhotoImpact SE	Visioneer PaperPort	Caere OmniPage (OCR) and PageKeeper (document management), HP ScanJet Copy Utility, Adobe PhotoDeluxe 2.0	Ulead PhotoImpact SE and ImagePals 2 Go, Caere OmniPage LE (OCR)
Warranty	no details	no details	no details	1 year Express Exchange	1 year Express Exchange	no details
Price	$299 list	no details	no details	$249 - $299 Cdn street	$399 Cdn "estimated retail"	$149 US list
Contact	Agfa Canada	Adara Technologies	Adara Technologies	HP Canada	HP Canada	Microtek USA
Phone	800-268-6270	310-956-4000 (no toll-free number)		800-387-3867		800-654-4160
Web site: http://www.	agfa.ca	adara.com		hp.com		mtek-lab.com

Low-Cost Scanners cont'd

Company	Microtek		Mustek		Plustek	
Model	ScanMaker E6	Colour PageWiz	Plug-n-Scan 600 II EP plus	Plug-n-Scan 1200 III EP	OpticPro 600P	OpticPro 4830P
Type	Flatbed	Sheet-fed	Flatbed	Flatbed	Flatbed	Flatbed
Interface	SCSI	SCSI	EPP (parallel)	EPP	EPP	EP
Platform supported	PC/Mac	PC/Mac	PC	PC	PC	PC
Ships with adapter/cable	Yes/No	No/Yes	n/a / Yes	n/a / n/a	n/a	n/a
Alternate Interface(s)	none	Parallel for PC only	none	none	AAF sets parallel port to EPP regardless of user settings to ensure quality	AAF sets parallel port to EPP regardless of user settings to ensure quality
Footprint (L x W x H)	19.1" x 14" x 4.7"	10.25" x 4.75" x 5"	17.3" x 11.8" x 3.4"	17.3" x 11.8" x 3.4"	16.5" x 11.7" x 4"	16.5" x 11.7" x 2.75"
Weight lbs/kg	16.5 / 7.5	3.3 / 1.5	no details	no details	2.8 / 1.7	11 / 4.9
Image sensor	Linear CCD with daylight fluorescent lamp	Linear CCD with daylight fluorescent lamp	CCD/cold cathode	CCD/cold cathode	not specified	not specified
Optical resolution	600 x 1200	300 x 600	300 x 600	600 x 1200	300 x 600	300 x 600
Interpolated resolution	4,800 x 4,800	1,200 x 1,200	4,800 x 4,800	9,600 x 9,600	4,800 x 4,800	4,800 x 4,800
Colour bit-depth	30-bit	24-bit	30-bit	36-bit	30-bit	30-bit
Greyscale bit-depth	10-bit	8-bit	10-bit	12-bit	10-bit	10-bit
Max scan size	8.5" x 13.5"	8.5" x 14"	8.5" x 11.7"	8.5" x 11.7"	8.5" x 12"	8.5" x 11.7"
Min object size	n/a	not specified	n/a	n/a	n/a	n/a
Doc feeder	optional	built-in	none	none	none	none
Transparency adapter	optional	n/a	none	none	none	none
Software bundle	Ulead PhotoImpact SE and ImagePals 2 Go, Caere OmniPage LE (OCR)	Xerox Pagis SE	Micrografx Picture Publisher 5.0 (full version), Xerox TextBridge Pro	Micrografx Picture Publisher 5.0 (full version), Xerox TextBridge Pro, Ulead PhotoPlus 4	Micrografx PhotoMagic, Expervision TypeReader	unspecified "OCR software, Image Editing Software" and Plustek Action Manager (scan, fax, copy)
Warranty	no details	no details	2 years	2 years	1 year parts & labour	1 year parts & labour
Price	$299 US list ($559 Pro version available with full Adobe Photoshop and Xerox TextBridge Pro)	$159 US list	$99 US street (about $200 Cdn)	$199 US street	$99 US street	$129 US street
Contact	Microtek USA		Mustek		Plustek Inc.	
Phone	800-654-4160		none except for tech support		408-453-5600 (no toll-free number)	
Web site: http://www.	mtek-lab.com		mustek.com		plustekusa.com	

Low-Cost Scanners cont'd

Company	Plustek	Polaroid		Storm Technologies		Visioneer
Model	OpticPro 9630PL	PhotoPad	EasyPhoto Reader !	EasyPhoto SmartPage Pro 220	EasyPhoto ImageWave	PaperPort 3000
Type	Flatbed	Photo scanner	photo scanner	Sheet-Fed	Flatbed	Flatbed
Interface	EPP	EPP	EPP	EPP	EPP	SPP/EPP
Platform supported	PC	PC/Mac	PC	PC	PC	PC
Ships with adapter/cable	n/a	n/a / Yes	n/a	n/a	USB requires separate upgrade kit	n/a / Yes
Alternate Interface(s)	AAF sets parallel port to EPP regardless of user settings to ensure quality	none	none	none (PageScan USB is separate model)	USB optional	USB is separate model (3100 USB)
Footprint (L x W x H)	19" x 11.7" x 3"	5.5" x 6.2" x 3.5"	5.5" x 6" x 3"	5.5" x 11.5" x 3.5"	15.75" x 10.5" x 3"	16" x 12" x 3"
Weight lbs/kg	12 / 5.5	350 g	not specified	not specified	not specified	8.3 / 3.9
Image sensor	not specified	Cold cathode fluorescent	CCD–cold cathode fluorescent	CCD–cold cathode fluorescent	CCD–cold cathode fluorescent	Linear CCD/cold cathode fluorescent
Optical resolution	600 x 1200	400	200	300 x 600	300 x 600	300 x 600
Interpolated resolution	9,600 x 9,600	n/a	1,200	5,000 x 5,000	5,000 x 5,000	2,400 x 2,400
Colour bit-depth	30-bit	24-bit	24-bit	30-bit	30-bit	30-bit
Greyscale bit-depth	10-bit	8-bit	8-bit	8-bit	8-bit	10-bit
Max scan size	8.5" x 14"	4.5" x 6"	5" x 7" (4" x 6" scan area)	8.5" x 14"	8.5" x 11.7"	8.5" x 11.7"
Min object size	n/a	1.5" x 2"	"Business card"	"Business card"	n/a	n/a
Doc feeder	none	one photo at a time	one photo at a time	one page at a time	none	none
Transparency adapter	none	n/a	n/a	none	none	none
Software bundle	Micrografx PhotoMagic, ExperVision TypeReader	"PhotoPad software"	EasyPhoto Image software, ClearScan	EasyPhoto software, Adobe Photo Deluxe, Xerox TextBridge, DocuMagix PaperMaster	EasyPhoto software, Adobe PhotoDeluxe 2.0, DocuMagix PaperMaster, Xerox TextBridge, ATT&T WorldNet, Netscape Communicator	"Visioneer PaperPort 1.5 and Web Publisher, PictureWorks PhotoEnhancer, Xerox TextBridge OCR, Corex CardScan SE, Quicken Expensable SE, Connectix QuickCards LE
Warranty	1 year parts & labour	1 year hardware, 90 days software	1 year parts & labour	1 year parts & labour	1 year parts & labour	"1 year"
Price	$249 US street	$199 Cdn "recommended retail price"	$139 Cdn suggested retail	$209 Cdn suggested retail	$139 Cdn suggested retail	$99 US list, $209.99 Cdn street
Contact	Plustek Inc.	Polaroid		Keating Technologies		Visioneer
Phone	408-453-5600 (no toll-free number)	800-268-6970		905-479-0230 or 800-565-3284		800-787-7007
Web site: http://www.	plustekusa.com	polaroid.com		stormtech.com		visioneer.com

Notes: Both Adara and Ulead are subsidiaries of Microtek International
! Storm Technologies' Easy Photo Drive has been discontinued.
* Small Computer Systems Interface requires a special adapter you must purchase if it's not supplied. If a cable is not supplied, check both adapter and device to make sure you get one with the right connectors.
** EPP: Enhanced Parallel Port, offering greater speed than the traditional version on many older systems. SPP: Standard Parallel Port. Check your BIOS setup to see which you have. USB: Universal Serial Bus, only available on newer systems and only after Windows 98 ships to provide the drivers.
*** If you can still see it, you can scan it on a flatbed; minimum size is only important on sheet-fed and photo scanners.

Digital Cameras

There is no way this section on digital cameras can cover all models that were on the market today. According to at least one source, the Digital Camera Resource Page (www.dcresource.com), there were at least ninety-two models available from twenty or more different companies.

Toronto-based Evans Research says that of units shipped in Canada in 1997 (total 37,000), 21 per cent were Kodak, 14 per cent Casio, 13.6 per cent Sony, and the rest were (in alphabetical order) AGFA, Apple, Canon, Epson, Fuji, HP, Konica, Minolta, Nikon, Olympus, Panasonic, Pentax, Polaroid, Ricoh, Sanyo, Vivitar, and Yashica. And therein lies the rub for consumers. It seems like everyone and her granny is in the digicam biz. I fully expect the market to shake out over time with only the fittest surviving.

I still have a comparison table, but instead of including all ninety-two models, I've enlisted the help of Evans to focus on the top ten brands currently available in Canada. That's going to be Kodak, Casio, Sony, Epson, Olympus, Ricoh, Panasonic, AGFA, Apple, and Canon (in that order). I'm also going to discuss price ranges and what you're likely to get at the top and bottom of the scale. More to the point, both here and in the "Spec tips," below, I'll try to outline the type of features available and indicate those I think are good – and not so good. Your homework assignment is to find the model that has more of the good features and the fewer of the drawbacks in your price range.

Reality 1, Hype 0

First, however, let's get some of the basic stuff out of the way. Despite the hype that surrounded digital cameras when they first began to appear in late 1995, I don't believe they are in any way going to replace conventional cameras. They can't produce the picture quality you can get even from a disposable camera, at a price that most consumers can afford to pay. Yes, there are professional models that can produce stunning pictures suitable for use in newspapers, but I suspect few ordinary folk will be shopping for one.

Even with a "photo-quality" inkjet printer on hand (see Chapter 12), you're still not going to get convenient photos for your wallet, for your albums, or to hand to friends and relatives around the dining-room table (at least not once you start figuring out the cost-per-print, you won't).

Forget the idea of digital cameras being less expensive than film. Start by adding the cost of the camera, extra memory for the camera to hold photographs (see below), and batteries. Then add the PC you need to store and process the pictures, the printer to put them on paper, and the hideously expensive "Photo Ink" cartridges required for the task. For that kind of money, you'll process a heck of a lot of film rolls and could put both prints and copies on either CD-ROM or diskette.

So, what is a consumer-level digital camera good for, then? Well, it still whips even one-hour photo shops for speed. Private investigators, insurance adjusters, real estate agents, some police agencies, and home-improvement estimators who want quick-and-dirty images love them. I use mine to take shots for a community newsletter I help produce. The chap who does our printing can't handle images with more than 65 dot-per-inch resolution. It's perfect and I can get and use my photos the same morning.

Images for Web pages don't need to exceed 75 dpi (the resolution of most monitors) and 24-bit colour is sometimes overkill, but there are other spot uses. For example, one day a new employee of the contractor who shovels snow off the parking lot of the hospital near my house piled snow on my sidewalk instead of where it should have gone. Four quick clicks, transferring the images to my PC, and integrating them into a letter to the hospital's engineering supervisor took twenty minutes. I had my complaint, documented with pictures, on his desk before the plough left the property. He was overwhelmed and the problem never reoccurred.

About to do some work inside your PC? Take a digital pic before you start and print it so you can get everything back the way it was. About to install some new software that may override some settings? Take a pic of the monitor with the appropriate settings dialogue on screen.

Tale of the tape

And how much is all this going to cost, you wonder? Well, again according to Evans Research, in 1997 it cost somewhere between just under $500 and over $1,500 Cdn. Evans's figures said the under-$500 figure covered about 16 per cent of total sales. Most consumers – 71 per cent of them in fact – spent between $500 and $999 for their digital camera. About 11 per cent spent between $1,000 and $1,499, while only 2 per cent spent $1,500 or more.

The sexy features you get that run the prices up include advanced storage options such as removable memory cards (think of them as the digital equivalent of reusable extra film rolls), LCD screens to preview and review your shots, in-camera editing, and voice or graphic annotation. Other features that can affect price include lens quality, range of focal length (from extreme close-up to wide angle), manual – as well as automatic – exposure and focus adjustments, and zoom lenses.

The quality and robustness of the software bundled with the camera can also affect cost. For example, a generic and rudimentary photo editor, "lite" or "special edition" software instead of the full product, or a lack of TWAIN driver to allow you to upload images directly to applications, are all fairly common ways of shaving price points. As with scanners, run – don't walk – away from any model that doesn't have a TWAIN driver.

More features

New features in today's digital cameras aren't available in all models, but here are some you may wish to seek, modified from a list published in the February 1998 edition of *Windows Magazine*:

Black and white: Most digital cameras capture images in glorious 24-bit colour, and the Epson PhotoPC 600 is no exception. But this camera also offers two black-and-white modes. At the opposite end, UMAX DMX-8000 images are captured in 30-bit colour. The extra six bits, representing ultra high and ultra low intensity values, are discarded, leaving a better image. This is also the concept used in 30-, 32-, and 36-bit scanners (see above).

Notes: If you need to take notes in the field, let the camera do it for you. The Canon PowerShot 600 and UMAX MDX-8000 are two of several, such as Kodak's recent DC-260, that include a built-in microphone. You can't record a speech, but you can say a few words that will help you recall the details later on. As another note-taking option, the Nikon Coolpix 300 features a large touch-sensitive rear-panel display. Using an accessory stylus, you can jot down an address, circle a dented fender or make any other kind of on-picture notation you need. Later, you can view the images with or without the notation.

Alternative picture sizes: If you need the big picture, the Epson PhotoPC 600 offers a setting for simulated panorama shots. The camera displays part of the last image on the LCD screen so you can properly align the next section of the picture. The Casio QV-700 permits continuous shooting as long as the shutter release is held down (think of virtual reality at your Web site).

In and *out*: For bi-directional photography, have a look at the Canon PowerShot 350, Casio QV-700, Epson PhotoPC 600, or Kodak DC-260, all of which allow you to transfer images from your PC into the camera. This can be handy for taking your presentation on the road. Take a few pictures, edit them on the PC, toss in a few charts or other printed material, then transfer the completed work back to the camera. Connect the camera to any convenient TV monitor with a video input feature and do your PowerPoint presentation without PowerPoint – and, better yet, without dragging along your laptop.

Using your digital camera in this manner does have its drawbacks, though. If you're using a camera with an excruciatingly slow refresh rate, you may have to wake your audience up from time to time. The LCD on the Agfa ePhoto 1280, for instance, takes a laborious nine to twelve seconds to refresh.

Squeeze: Because there's no such thing as a one-size-fits-all compression ratio (see the spec tips, below), the Wavelet compression system on the UMAX lets you decide. With the camera connected to the PC, use the accompanying software to set the image file size from 10 KB to more than 100 KB. Once set, you can disconnect the camera from the computer. But you won't be able to change the image size until you reconnect the camera to the PC.

Headed home

I've tested a number of digital cameras over the years, but not, I confess, all the models we're discussing here. I've watched them evolve from Kodak's DC-40, with its off-centre viewfinder and no LCD screen, to the over-$1,200 DC-260 that is the company's latest toy. Along the way I've also played with a couple of Epson models, again both with and without screen.

If I were to buy a camera today, I'd want the LCD screen as the least-advanced option. Although it's a battery-sucker, it's also a tremendous asset for checking your work before you leave a location, which can save a lot of time – particularly if the camera's optical viewfinder isn't adjusted to emulate viewing through the centre of the lens.

I'd also want a unit with zoom lens and variable focal lengths (plus a wide range of them). For example, the early DC-40 is pretty much useless any closer than three feet from a subject, and, because it has no zoom lens, you can't improve on it. Newer models let you get closer and, with a zoom lens, pull in objects farther away.

I'd also absolutely refuse to have a camera that didn't have a TWAIN driver so that I could view and transfer individual shots directly to my current application. While there arc times when you'll want to upload everything in the device to your PC (something TWAIN cannot do), the single-photo upload is still a timesaving option in most cases.

Digital camera spec tips

Uses AA batteries: Depending on the model, your new camera may use three, four, or six "AA" or even "AAA" batteries. By the time you power up a flash memory card and use the LCD screen to take – and then preview – your pictures, your shooting day may come to an abrupt early halt. Figure on adding the cost of either rechargeable NiMH (Nickel Metal-Hydride) or long-life Lithium batteries to your budget. Hint: A model that provides *both* an LCD preview screen and an optical viewfinder may make it less necessary to use the screen when battery supplies are low.

178 HOW TO BUY A COMPUTER

Flash memory cards: Using these cards for more pictures per session may sound like a good idea, but if the camera uses standard PC card memory, you may need a notebook computer to offload the images.

All CCDs aren't alike: The charge-coupled device (CCD) is the bauble that makes most digital cameras work. It forms a rectangular pixel matrix just behind the camera's focal plane, but the matrix dimensions aren't precisely what you want. For example, at 640 by 480, when you're expecting 307,200 pixels, the matrix may be 350,000 pixels. Cameras offering 1024 by 768 may provide around 800,000 pixels. The added scan can be used for housekeeping data such as artifact reduction or white balance adjustment.

These cameras have to work to deliver your image. On models where two resolution modes are offered, it may be using every other pixel for low resolution. Where things get funny is when colour fidelity is vital. If we look at your monitor, for example, we know that each pixel has at least three phosphors on the monitor face responding to red, green and blue (so we can change its colour). In CCD cameras, each pixel records only one colour. It, however, is made up of a guess. Adjacent pixels read the other two colours, then apply a complex 8- to 24-bit interpolation to arrive at an average. Getting this stuff right and completing the calculations before next Thursday is what you're paying for at the high end of the price scale.

Compression ratios: I'll try to keep this explanation as simple as accuracy allows. Let's say you can't afford a model that provides lots of pixels in its CCD to give you a range of resolutions. Still, you'd like to have high- and low-quality pictures – if for no other reason than to store more of them before you have to unload – and a less-expensive model that only offers 640 by 480 appears to offer quality adjustments, too. What's most likely happening is that it's achieving this by playing games with compression ratios.

I won't make you crazy by explaining how they're calculated, but the lower the ratio, the better the image. A practical example? Say your chosen model can store 30 images at 640 by 480. It would take roughly 26.4 MB of memory to do this uncompressed, but most of these cameras operate with 2 to 4 MB onboard. Something has to give.

A larger amount of memory in the camera allows for less compression and better quality for a larger number of images. It's an important factor because, unlike compression schemes, such as JPEG (Joint Photographic Experts Group), that attempt to restore data during decompression, anything lost in the camera's compression is gone forever.

And then . . .

Once you've filled the camera to overflowing with beautiful pictures, what do you do next? Unless you did your homework before you bought, that could be a problem. How many spare serial ports do you have on your PC (and what is currently using one or more of them)? Does the camera come with a serial port cable to offload images? SCSI? USB? Do you have the correct receiving port in your system (see "Flash memory cards," above)?

Digital Cameras

Company	Agfa	Canon	Casio		Epson	Kodak		Sony
Product	ePhoto 307	Powershot 600	QV-300	QV-10A	PhotoPC 500	DC50	DC120	DSC-F1
List price*	$299US	$999US	$900US	$399US	$699	$699	$1,399	$849US
Size	3" x 5.5" x 1.5"	6.25" x 3.6" x 2.3"	2.8" x 6.4" x 1.9"	2.6" x 5.1" x 1.6"	5.5" x 3.2" x 2.1"	6" x 4.7" x 2.5"	5.7" x 4.3" x 2.2"	4" x 3" x 1.6"
Weight w/battery	13 oz.	21.1 oz.	10.2 oz.	7 oz.	10.6 oz.	18.6 oz	18.4 oz.	10.6 oz.
Viewer	optical	optical	LCD	LCD	optical	optical	optical/LCD	LCD
LCD screen	none	none	2.5"	1.8"	1.8 optional	none	1.6"	1.8"
Photo info								
Internal memory	2MB	1MB	4MB	2MB	2MB	1MB	2 MB	4MB
Low resolution/images**	320 x 240/72	320 x 240/17	320 x 240/192	320 x 240/96	320 x 240/60	756 x 504/22	640 x 480/24	640 x 480/108
Medium resolution/ images*	n/a	640 x 480/6	n/a	n/a	n/a	756 x 504/11	640 x 480/7	640 x 480/58
High resolution/images**	640 x 480/36	832 x 608/4	640 x 480/64	n/a	640 x 480/30	756 x 504/7	640 x 480/2	640 x 480/30
Colour depth	10 bits/colour	24 bits	24 bits	24 bits	24 bits	24 bits	24 bits	24 bits
Black and white	no	8 bit	no	no	no	no	no	no
Autofocus	"focus free"	yes	no	no	no	yes	yes	no
Normal lens focal distance	24" to infinity	16" to infinity	12" to infinity	11" to infinity	8" to infinity	29" to infinity	29" to infinity	20" to infinity
Macro/Telephoto	no / no	no / no	yes / yes	yes / no	optional / optional	yes / yes	yes / yes	yes / no
Zoom	no	no	no	no	no	3x motorized	3x motorized	no
Automatic shutter speed	1/8 to 1/10,000	1/30 to 1/500	1/8 to 1/4000	1/8 to 1/4000	1/30 to 1/10000	1/16 to 1/500	1/500 to 16 sec	1/30 to 1/500
Manual shutter speed	no	1/30 to 1/500	no	no	no	1/16 to 1/500	no	1/7.5 to 1/1000
Exposure auto/manual	yes / no	yes / yes	yes / yes	yes / yes	yes / yes	yes / yes	yes / yes	yes / yes
Sensitivity (ASO/ ISO equivalent)	125	100	100 to 1600	100 to 1600	130	84	160	100
Aperture range	no info	f/2.5 to f/1	f/2.6 or f/8	f/2.8 or f/8	f/2.8 to f/8	f/2.5 to f/24	wide: f/2.5 x f/16 tele: f/3.8 to f/24	f/2 to f/22
Flash auto/manual	yes / no	yes / yes	yes / yes	yes / yes	yes / yes	yes / yes	yes / yes	yes / yes
Voice annotation	no	yes	no	no	no	no	no	no

Company	Agfa	Canon	Casio	Casio	Epson	Kodak	Kodak	Sony
Product	ePhoto 307	Powershot 600	QV-300	QV-10A	PhotoPC 500	DC50	DC120	DSC-F1
Add-ons								
Custom memory	no	n/a	no	no	2MB to 4MB	no	yes	no
Micro Card memory	no	n/a	no	no	no	no	no	no
PC Card memory	no	4MB	no	no	no	yes	no	no
PC Card hard disk	no	170MB	no	no	no	yes	no	no
Custom lens	no	wide angle	no	no	no	no		no
Download/output								
Serial/Parallel	yes / no	n/a / yes	yes / no	yes / no	115.2 Kbps / no	115.2 Kbps / no	115.2 Kbps / no	yes / no
IrDA	no	no	no	no	no	no	no	yes
Video output	no	no	yes	yes	no	no	no	yes
Twain drivers	yes	yes	yes	yes	yes	yes	yes	yes
Recording modes								
Single	yes	yes	yes	yes	yes	yes	yes	yes
Continuous	no	no	no	no	no	no	no	yes
Multiscreen	no	no	yes	yes	no	no	no	yes
Timer	no	yes	yes	yes	yes	yes	yes	yes
Power								
Batteries/rechargeable	4xAA / no	NiCad / yes	4xAA / no	4xAA / no	4xAA / optional	4xAA / no	4xAA Lithium / no	LIP-10 lithium / yes
Power adapter	optional	yes	optional	optional	optional	yes	optional	yes
Details								
Tripod screw mount	no info	yes	yes	yes	yes	yes	yes	yes
General lenses and filters	no	no	no	no	37 mm video-camcorder lenses and filters	no	37 mm video-camcorder lenses and filters	no
Phone	416-241-1110	714-438-3000	201-361-5400	201-361-5400	310-782-0770	800-465-6325 ext 3600)	800-465-6325 ext 3600)	800-326-9551
Web site: http://www.	afga.com or interlog.com/~agfator/	csis.canon.com	casio.com	casio.com	epson.com	kodak.com	kodak.com	sony.com

* Prices are for relative comparison only and will probably have changed by the time you read this.
** Where resolutions are the same, picture quality is affected by the amount of compression used to store the images in the camera.

12

Printers

A computer will help you to do your work more efficiently (and bring more enjoyment to your leisure), but without a printer, all you can do is invite folks over for dinner to show them what you've accomplished.

There are very few things you will do with a computer that you won't want to print. Of course, there are slide shows, demonstrations, and game playing – these activities rarely require printing – but word processing, spreadsheets, accounting programs, and databases are (in that order) the most common programs run on personal computers, and all of them require printing at one time or another.

If you're like the majority of computer purchasers in Canada (approximately 70 per cent), you won't buy your printer when you buy your computer, and a little time spent shopping will rapidly tell you why. Not only are the printers that are "bundled" with systems at the low end of the price and performance scale, but except for limited circumstances, they rarely fill the needs most people have. You'll often find that buying the printer separately gives you competitive pricing and a much wider range of choices.

Although there are still a variety of computer printer technologies available, including dot-matrix, inkjet, laser, thermal wax transfer, and dye sublimation, I'm going to focus on the types of units most consumers will consider. The dot-matrix printer is, to all intents and purposes, dead as a consumer item. It still has limited and diminishing use in some small businesses to print multi-part receipts, but smaller printers attached to point-of-sale systems are making them obsolete.

Advanced technologies such as thermal wax transfer and dye sublimation remain the preserve of commercial printers. Only in rare circumstance will you ever find them in a home or small business. I will discuss colour laser printers, but only to bring you up to date on the state of the market. These units are better than ever before, but still carry a price tag of over $5,000 Cdn, putting them well out of the consumer market.

Instead, we're going to focus on the three printer formats that are left: inkjet (including "photo" ink printers), "personal" laser and LED printers, and multifunction printers that can print, copy, fax, scan, and entertain the cat.

To simplify your choices somewhat, however, I'm going to venture these broad (and safe) observations:

(a) The quality of the print of dot-matrix printers is not suitable for business correspondence. They are only recommended if you need multiple-impact copies, if you're on an excruciatingly tight budget, or your ageing uncle gave one to you.

(b) Inkjet (or bubblejet) printers have an attractive purchase price and they can produce colour. This is the technology the majority of consumers will purchase, but they also have the highest cost-per-page for consumables of any printing technology except dye sublimation.

(c) Laser/LED printers (which print black and shades thereof) cost less than you think, and the cost-per-page is less than everything except dot-matrix models.

(d) Multifunction printers (combined fax/scanner/printer/copier), expected to be *the* hot products of the 1990s, didn't live up to their advanced billing, even though some now print colour.

Before we discuss each technology, there are a few things to note that apply to all kinds of printer. For example, we still need to discuss drivers. These are not the people you yelled at on the way to work yesterday. In the computer world, "drivers" are the interpreters between your software and many hardware devices, such as a printer. True, the problem of incompatible drivers is not as crucial under Windows and its successors as it was under DOS, but there are still some concerns.

In the section below, you may notice that I've used the words "driver" and "drivers" indiscriminately and interchangeably. I could just as easily have used the convention "driver(s)" because any given model of printer may have one driver, or more than one. For example, a printer that can accept multiple page description languages (e.g., PCL and PostScript) may have both choices bundled into one driver or it may supply two or more to be used depending on which page description language is used. In addition, a printer may use one software driver to print locally, another to accept instructions over a network, and yet another to report consumable status or error conditions.

Depending on the brand and model of printer you buy, it may use the Windows Graphics Device Interface (GDI) and rely on your system's memory to function well. If it does, or if it uses the bi-directional nature of modern parallel ports – particularly to feed messages back to your screen – you need stable drivers. If you plan to put a scanner, CD drive, or other removable storage device on your computer's parallel (i.e., printer) port, you'll need a printer driver that supports parallel port sharing. Ideally, the printer and its drivers will use advanced parallel port services such as EPP (enhanced parallel port) or ECP (enhanced capabilities port).

If the drivers for your printer don't come with Windows (95, 98, NT, or what have you), you'd best hope the printer manufacturer has a Web site with a driver library that is regularly updated. You won't have to worry about whether the other software applications running under some flavour of Windows can use your printer, because Windows is supposed to be a device independent operating system.

Device independence means that the operating system provides driver support for peripheral devices, theoretically making it unnecessary for each separate application to provide a suite of drivers for an infinite number of devices. In other words, it shouldn't matter which brand or version of a word processing program you buy, it should print from Windows, so long as Windows has the correct driver for the printer. This doesn't mean that Windows supports every printer there is. And, just because a printer has been on the market for a while it doesn't necessarily mean that the Windows driver for it will still be present in future releases. In fact the older the printer, the less likely the next revision of Windows will support it.

Even if a particular model is supported under Windows 9x, you cannot assume a printer will work if you use another operating system for some applications. You need to tell the vendor you're using MS-DOS, OS/2 (there still are some fans), UNIX (or a variant such as Linux or FreeBSD), Be Inc.'s BeOS, or that you own a PowerMac. If you don't discuss your needs with the vendor and get all assurances you receive that your chosen printer will work written on the sales agreement, you have no one to blame but yourself if you get the printer back to your computer and it doesn't print.

Windows 9x supports more printer models than any other operating system. However – and this is an item to note – simply because the printer is supported under Windows 9x does not mean it will be happy working with Windows NT. Talk to the vendor.

Many types and brands of printer within each type will seem like a really good deal when you first purchase them, right up until you have to buy more consumables – then the real headaches can start. It's a good idea to do some homework before you make your final decision. Check out your local vendors of business supplies. How easy is it to get brand-name ink cartridges, toner, or whatever? Do you have to get them from the original manufacturer (expensive) or are they widely available? Do third-party manufacturers have lower-priced alternatives (and do their products carry a warranty)? According to several printing industry executives I've interviewed, the main profits for printer manufacturers come from the sale of consumables, *not* from the sale of printers.

After you've read the material below, you may still be undecided about which printer you should buy. If all else fails, here are a few more pointers:

• Computer equipment generally has no trade-in value, and that includes printers. If you're uncertain about a printer, or any other piece of computer equipment, go to a rental agency and try it for a month. Then decide.
• A man who repairs broken computer equipment for a living offered this good advice about reliability: "Some models are more rugged

than others. You can't expect to run a $200 printer all day long, every day, and expect it to handle a lot of five-part forms or heavy stock without it sooner or later wanting to visit the doctor."

Inkjets

"Pssst . . . C'mere! Ya wanna see somethin' neat? No, don't look around. Come closer . . . closer . . ."

I don't know what it is about the inkjet printer market that reminds me of a street hustle. Maybe it's the emphasis the various manufacturers place on how close the quality is to what you might get from a laser and how expensive lasers are compared to how inexpensive the inkjet is. Maybe it's how they fudge the cost-per-page figures by using unreasonably low coverage rates to make it appear less expensive than it really is.

Inkjet printers (they are called "inkjet" by Hewlett-Packard and "bubblejet" by Canon, and both terms are used by other manufacturers) have become an important segment of the computer printer market. If you're planning to buy a colour inkjet printer, you're not alone. About 75 per cent of the total number of printers sold in Canada in 1997 were inkjets, according to a joint IDC Canada–ACNeilsen Canada study. That's up from around 67 per cent in 1996 and 47 per cent in 1995, making the colour inkjet market the fastest-growing segment of the computer printer industry. Total unit sales in 1997 rose by 30 per cent over 1996 to just over a million units say both IDC and Toronto-based Evans Research.

Canon was the sales leader, with 30 to 43 per cent of the market, followed by Hewlett-Packard with 28 to 30 per cent. Epson was a clear third with 16 to 20 per cent and Lexmark was next with 8 to 15 per cent (the range of figures reflects slight differences in how the two research agencies collect their statistics). The numbers were virtually identical from both sources for the two "name" brands at the bottom of the list: Apple with less than 2 per cent and NEC with less than 1 per cent.

That leaves the familiar "others" category, largely occupied by Citizen, Tektronix, and Okidata (totalling less than 1 per cent for all of them). However, it should be noted that Tektronix sells to the high-end professional market and Okidata was a complete newcomer to this market segment and had no inkjet products to sell in 1997.

There are a few other statistical bits and pieces you may find interesting. The price of printers has fallen steadily over the four-year period from 1994 through 1997. The average price for all types of printer was $850 in 1994 and $670 in 1997, says the IDC/ACNeilsen study. This is a good indicator of at least one reason the colour inkjet market has mushroomed. According to Evans Research, the average price of inkjet printers in the third quarter of 1997 was $220 (down from $257 at the beginning of the year).

I've cut the comparison table (below) off at the $500 Cdn (list) mark because over half of Canadians who purchased a printer in 1997 paid between $200 and $500 (ACNeilsen).

Common ground

While the average price of a colour inkjet printer may be just over $200, the mean price (the point where there is the largest concentration of purchases) is $420. You'll find that most of the models in the table are grouped at the higher end of the range.

While consumers have been purchasing more colour inkjets over the past few years, they've also become more sophisticated about the features demanded and the time spent shopping. The IDC/ACNeilsen study shows that around 75 per cent of people buying printers bought them within six months of buying their computer, instead of as part of a "bundle" with the computer.

The number of models available with only one ink cartridge has also fallen. It doesn't take long for people to understand that the vast majority of the printing they do is black. A single cartridge (either using three colours to make not-terribly-good black or with three colours plus black) either produces low-quality results or it runs out of black and has to be discarded while still full of colour.

Two innovations arrived around the end of 1997: photo colour and at least one low-cost unit with four separate cartridges (this option was formerly available only in high-end and high-cost units).

The arrival of "photo" colour inks is a direct result of the rising popularity of digital cameras (see Chapter 11). Using special paper, these printers generally produce high-quality colour, often by replacing the black cartridge in a dual-head printer with a special unit containing two pastel colours, plus black, to raise the total number of colours from four to six. While most photo-colour printers give reasonable reproduction (none are as good as a photograph printed the old-fashioned way), you'll pay heavily for it. Replacement cartridges cost as much as double the price of a standard colour replacement cartridge and produce far fewer "pages" before they're exhausted. See "Spec tips" (below) for a discussion of such issues as cost-per-page.

Some models, specifically aimed at the photo market (such as the Epson Stylus Photo), are not in our table because their cost was over $500.

Another item most models have in common is on-screen reporting of paper and/or ink status. The driver software, in addition to the printers themselves, will report at least this much by way of remote diagnosis, but keep in mind that you'll need a computer with at least a bi-directional parallel port (as well as a cable that supports bi-directional operation) for it to work.

Okidata's Okijet 2020 was worth a mention in 1998, partly because it was brand new – and the company's first inkjet product – and partly because it was one of the first low-cost colour inkjet to offer four separate ink cartridges. The only other unit with a similar feature was the Xerox HomeCentre (see "Multifunction printers," below). Xerox added several new inkjet models using a similar scheme later in the year.

The four-cartridge approach is good because you only replace empty cartridges instead of tossing one that's half full of two colours, but empty on the third. There are a couple of other issues, however, that make it slightly less attractive after a first glance. For one thing, the cartridges have to be small to fit, forcing lower ink capacity. It means you'll be pricing black cartridges in particular and in case lots.

Both the 2020 Okijet and Xerox models are single-head units. You have a choice of an optional high-capacity black printhead/cartridge unit or a colour printhead with four separate cartridges. The cartridges have a lifespan, but so does the head. You'll have to replace it about every 3,000 "pages" (see "Spec tips," below, to find out why "pages" is in quotes).

Another item about the Okijet: Everyone and his aunt wants to use the PC parallel port for their device, including scanners, external CD-ROM drives, removable cartridge drives (such as the Iomega Zip and Syquest SparQ), and direct cable networking. Most of these new parallel services demand high-speed ports in order to function properly. This means setting your system not only for bi-directional port operation, but also for either EPP (enhanced parallel port) or ECP (enhanced capabilities port). It also means that any printer you have on the same port has to support port sharing. The Okijet 2020 doesn't, though later models may.

Neither did Canon's BJC-4200 (not covered in our table because Canon has dropped the model), but Canon says its newer models have overcome this problem. The company has one other innovation worth noting. Along with a photo ink cartridge it also sells neon ink for some really wild results. Unfortunately, it is not available in Canada (check with Canon Canada to see if they've reversed this policy).

Port sharing is an issue that some printer manufacturers wish would go away, and as a result none of them mention it in their marketing material. Even when I asked, I got a lot of vague "We'll have to get back to you on that one" answers. Your best bet, if you can't get a straight answer when you ask – and even if you do get an "Oh, sure; it will do that" – is to have any assurances written on the invoice. Then it's the vendor's problem to get it right, not yours.

Yet another couple of innovations and cautions: I've faithfully reproduced the type of media each company says its printers support and followed up with queries to make sure the marketing material matches reality. You'll note that some printers support iron-on transfer paper, self-adhesive labels or continuous "banner" paper, while others don't mention these specialty media (and it should come as no surprise that the reason is often that the company doesn't make its own brand of the special media required). When the company quoted size and thickness restrictions, I've added those, too. If you want to use your printer for anything other than standard letter, legal, or transparency stock, pay close attention to these specifications – and ask the vendor to guarantee that the printer will handle the stock (yes, in writing on the invoice).

Thermal Bubblejet Technology

Commonly used by Hewlett-Packard, Canon, and everyone else, other than Epson. In this form of inkjet printing, the ink is heated instead of the nozzle.

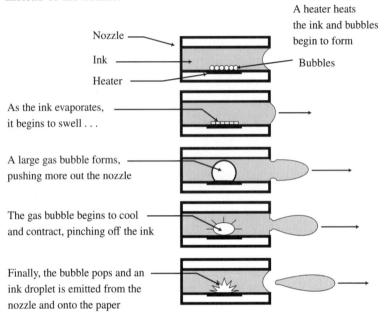

What's in a name?

When you go shopping, you'll find two different terms in use, depending on the manufacturer. There is no major technical difference between an "inkjet" and a "bubblejet" printer. Both use a method known as "thermal bubble" to apply ink. The printhead contains a small reservoir of ink which is heated to boiling. In effect, when you print, small bubbles of the ink are pushed out of nozzles in the head onto the paper (or whatever media you choose).

The only printers in our table that do not use this method are from Epson. Instead of thermal bubble technology, Epson uses a piezoelectric head that shakes ink onto the paper. Epson claims, with some justification, that the result produces smaller drops and less splatter, for a smoother result. Because there is no ink vapour to cool

Inkjet Piezoelectric
Drop-on-demand Print-head

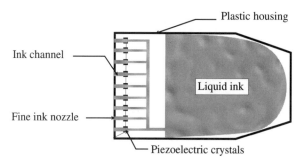

Fine droplets of ink are squeezed out of the nozzles when the crystals heat the nozzles. Because the ink isn't heated, it doesn't clog the heads when it dries. By 1998, Epson was the sole printer manufacturer using this method, in its "Stylus" family of printers.

and clog its heads, they last longer without blocking (although I've recently had to send a Stylus 500 back for repairs when one of its heads *did* clog and stop printing black – fortunately a free fix under warranty.)

Epson can also take a bow for being first off the mark with what I fully expect will be the future of computer printing. The Stylus 740 made its debut in late September 1998 and was to my knowledge the first printer to connect to a PC's Universal Serial Bus (USB) port instead of its parallel port. Unfortunately, it arrived too late to be included in our table. Next time!

Last, but not least (and, yes, I know I'm repeating myself, but dammit, this is *important*), please remember my warning about the cost of consumables. When compared to any other printing technology except dye sublimation, inkjets have the highest cost per page (by anywhere from 800 to 1,500 per cent). It's something to consider if colour isn't important in your day-to-day printing life, particularly with personal monochrome lasers selling in the same price range (starting at just over $300).

Spec tips

Laser quality output: I don't want to get drearily technical, but inkjet printers do not produce laser quality results, particularly when it comes to filling large areas with solid black or colours. Although modern inkjets do produce on-paper resolutions of 300 dots per inch or higher (just like a laser), the paper handling and printing mechanisms are quite different. In an inkjet, the image is laid down in strips. In a coloured area, there will be a separate head pass for each colour (and another for black). Then the paper is jerked forward, hopefully by so precise an amount that you won't see the seam where the bands meet. Good luck.

Head type: Even if the printer is advertised as shipping with both black and colour cartridges, that doesn't mean you get to load them at the same time. You'll waste a lot of time – and ink – if you have to remember to change cartridges depending on the operation. If all you get is a single, four-colour cartridge (three colours plus black), you'll be throwing a lot of them away with only the black empty. If all you get is a three-colour cartridge, with black produced by a combination of them, the quality won't live up to your expectations.

Head nozzles: Although some companies do a lot with their print drivers (such as HP's REt, or Resolution Enhancement technology, which varies dot size as well as playing games with overlapping to give smoother, less jaggy images), the number of nozzles in the head will also indicate how small the dots it produces will be. Keep in mind that the image you see on paper is made up of both the dots *and the spaces where their edges don't overlap*. The more nozzles, the smaller the dot, and the less jagged the result.

Max speed: As with the cartridge life and monthly duty-cycle figures quoted elsewhere in the table, this is a fudge figure. The printing industry uses an 8.5 x 11-inch sheet with about 5 per cent coverage of the page when calculating these specs. To say your results may vary from the manufacturer's claim is the understatement of the year.

Inkjets are slower than dot-matrix and laser printers. Colour printing is always slower than monochrome printing, and we often see speed quoted in minutes per page, not pages per minute. But if most of the printing you'll be doing will be black-and-white, here's where the real differences lie. It's not unusual for "personal" lasers to print four to eight pages per minute (ppm), and there are 10 to 12 ppm models available for under $1,500. If you can find an inkjet that will do better than five pages per minute in letter-quality mode (about 150 characters per second), I'd like to see it.

Resolution: I made several companies crazy asking them whether the dot-per-inch resolution figure they quoted represented horizontal by vertical or vertical by horizontal. Most replied, "Huh?" as though it didn't matter. (The horizontal figure represents how many dots the heads produce across the page. The vertical figure is a combined factor of both head density and how often the page is moved). Only Canon admitted that its high resolution (720 x 360) was the result of "smoothing" applied by the software driver to overlap dots.

Maximum printable area: I chose this figure for the table instead of a "minimum margin." (No printer in our price bracket will print to the edge of the page – i.e., a "full bleed.") It's based on a legal-sized page.

Print colours: Aside from the banding noted above, another funny thing will happen to your colour documents when you print them. Your monitor represents colour using a combination of red, green, and blue – RGB. Colour printers use cyan, magenta, yellow, and sometimes black – CMY(K). The translation between colour schemes is often not exact. Computer users also expect to be able to see 24-bit colour (16.7 million values) on screen, so printer manufacturers quite naturally claim they reproduce this many. But this isn't a function of the hardware; it's a function of the software print driver. You also won't see pure colours. Most printers produce only six: red, green, blue, cyan, magenta, and yellow (plus, of course, black). So the remainder will be approximated using techniques known as "dithering" or "error diffusion." Trying to get the companies to specify what method is used to get the colours was an impossible task. If you do need to reproduce 16.7 million pure colours, you're not going to get them with this technology. You're looking at a dye sublimation printer and a second mortgage on your house.

Print cartridge life: This is another fudge figure most companies are reluctant to discuss in detail. Hewlett-Packard, for example, refused to quote me a figure for the number of pages to expect from a print cartridge until I nagged. Most of the rest, while admitting the figure is usually based on an unrealistically low 5 per cent coverage for black and 15 per cent for colour (5 per cent for each colour), are less forthcoming when you ask what resolution was used for the test and whether the figure includes both text *and* graphics or whether it's for text only. Once again, your results will vary from their claims.

Languages, optional languages, and operating systems supported: If you have a specific task in mind that requires the use of anything other than Windows 3.1x or Windows 9x and you don't tell the person who sells you the printer, you have no one but yourself to blame if the printer doesn't work properly. We've included the one Apple Stylewriter that made it under the price cutoff, but only a few models listed work on both PCs and Macs. An equally small number ship with either OS/2 or Windows NT drivers in the box (or have them available at all).

Monthly duty cycle: Monthly duty cycle is the number of pages you can logically expect to print in a month without damaging the printer through overuse. It's a figure of more interest to small businesses, but as with print speed and cartridge life, it's also a largely mythical and variable figure – and for the same reasons. Nevertheless, it's some type of yardstick. Note that some companies couldn't or wouldn't answer the question.

Media types: It's not so much what's in this list as what is missing from it that should grab your attention. If you want to print adhesive labels, iron-on transfers, small cards, thick stock, or continuous-sheet banners, be aware that some models don't support these media, or don't recommend them, or (and possibly more to the point) don't sell their own brand.

Memory: Inkjets traditionally don't come with a lot of on-board memory. Too little memory and you'll notice that your whole system is slower, longer, while you're trying to print. The print driver is slowing down the amount of data being sent to the printer so it doesn't spill over the printer's meagre memory buffer.

Say what? You can transmit approximately 1.25 MB of data per second from a PC parallel port set to one of the high-speed modes (ECP or EPP, see above). Your printer doesn't work that quickly. It needs time to process the data before it can act upon it. When data arrives at the printer, it is stored in memory in the printer to wait its turn for processing. If you're sending a 2 MB document to a printer with a 512 KB buffer, it's like pouring a two-gallon pail into an eight-ounce glass. Something has to give. In this case, the driver slows the output to keep the buffer from filling up. Note that none of these printers has a memory upgrade option.

Interfaces: Most companies quote something called the IEEE 1284 "standard." It simply means the printer wants a bi-directional parallel port and cable with a Centronics connector at the printer end. It does not indicate whether the printer supports parallel port sharing or high-speed ports.

Parallel port type: Some printers get cranky when asked to use a parallel port set in EPP (enhanced parallel port) or ECP (enhanced capabilities port) modes, primarily because the higher speed produced by these port settings overwhelms them. Note from the blanks in the table which companies were reluctant to discuss the issue or unable to answer the question.

Optional interfaces and automatic I/O switching: A printer that offers parallel, serial, network, Universal Serial Bus (USB), and/or Mac LocalTalk or EtherTalk interfaces is very flexible. If the printer can also be hooked up to more than one of these simultaneously and can figure out which one to use without the operator having to tell it, it will probably cost more than the models featured here.

Carriage width: Wide-carriage models cost extra and none are on the table below, but they are worth the expense if you have to print on surfaces wider than 8.5 inches. While here, ask about how envelopes are handled.

Check the output: Print samples produced for promotional purposes always look great (you never get to see the rejects). If you can't see the printer make a page with graphics in the shop, make sure you can take it back if you're not satisfied once you get home. Please note that returning the printer if it's broken is a warranty issue. Taking it back because it doesn't give you the quality you wanted is very different – and unless this is discussed ahead of time and *written on the sales agreement* you will be stuck with it without recourse.

Inkjet Printers

Company	Canon		Epson		Hewlett-Packard	
Model	**BJC-250**	**BJC-4300**	**Stylus 600**	**Stylus 800**	**DeskJet 692C**	**DeskJet 722C**
Head type	single head thermal bubble	dual head thermal bubble	dual head Piezoelectric	dual head Piezoelectric	dual head thermal bubble	dual head thermal bubble
Head nozzles	Colour: 48 (16 each); optional Black (BC-02): 64	Black: 64; Colour: 72 (24 per colour) – optional BC-20 black cart has 128	Black: 64; Colour: 96 (32 per colour)	Black: 128; Colour: 192 (64 per colour)	Black: 50; Colour: not quoted	Black: 300; Colour: 192 (64 each)
Resolution*, Black (dpi)	720 x 360 with smoothing, BC-02 cartridge only	720 x 360 with smoothing	econo 180 x 180, mid 360 x 360, better 720 x 720, best 1440 x 720	econo 180 x 180, mid 360 x 360, better 720 x 720, best 1440 x 720	econo 300 x 300, normal 600 x 300, best 600 x 600	econo 300 x 300, normal 600 x 300, best 600 x 600
Resolution*, Colour (dpi)	360 x 360	720 x 360 on plain paper	econo 180 x 180, mid 360 x 360, better 720 x 720, best 1440 x 720	econo 180 x 180, mid 360 x 360, better 720 x 720, best 1440 x 720	300 x 300 on plain paper, 600 x 300 on transparency and glossy paper	300 x 300 on plain paper, 600 x 300 on transparency and glossy paper
Resolution*, Photo (dpi)	360 x 360	720 x 360	n/a	n/a	600 x 300 with 6 inks on all paper types	600 x 300 with 6 inks on all paper types
Margins (minimum – top, bottom, sides; inches)	no info	no info	0.12, 0.54, 0.12	0.12, 0.54, 0.12 (left), 0.35 (right)	Not quoted	Not quoted
Max printable area (inches)	8 x 13.6	8.24 x 13.61	8.26 x 13.34	8.03 x 13.34	Not quoted	Not quoted
Print Colours	up to 16.7 million	up to 16.7 million	up to 16.7 million	up to 16.7 million	up to 16.7 million	up to 16.7 million
Max Speed, Black (ppm = pages per minute; mpp = minutes per page)	4 ppm (optional BC-02 cartridge) @ 360 x 360	5 ppm with optional BC-20 black cartridge @ 360 x 360	6 ppm @ 180 dpi	8 ppm @ 180 dpi	Econo 5 ppm, normal 3 ppm, best 1.7 ppm	Econo 8 ppm, normal 5 ppm, best 4 ppm
Max Speed, Colour (ppm = pages per minute; mpp = minutes per page)	0.27 ppm (about 3.5 mpp) @ 10 characters per inch (cpi). Graphics speed not quoted.	2 ppm @ 10 cpi using resident fonts. No graphics speeds quoted.	4 ppm @ 180 dpi	7 ppm @ 180 dpi	Econo 1.7 ppm, normal 0.8 ppm, best 3 mpp, photo up to 4 mpp (5x7)	Econo 7 ppm (1) / 4 ppm (2), normal 4 ppm (1) / 1.5 ppm (2), best 4 ppm (1) / 2 mpp (2), photo up to 3 mpp (5x7)
Print Cartridges	1 colour (cyan, magenta, yellow); optional photo and black (BC-02) cartridges available	BCI-21 head contains separate black and 1 x 3-colour tank. Optional 1 black and one 3-colour (cyan, magenta, yellow, or black or photo	1 black and 1 colour (cyan, magenta, and yellow)	1 black and 1 colour (cyan, magenta, and yellow)	1 black, 1 colour (cyan, magenta, and yellow), and 1 photo color	1 black, 1 colour (cyan, magenta, and yellow)
Cartridge life rating (8.5" x 11" letter with 5% black coverage or 15% colour coverage (5% per colour) except where noted)	Black (BC-02); 930 pgs @ 5%; Colour: 200 pgs @ 7.5% per colour; Photo 90 pgs @ 7.5% per colour	Black (BC-20): 1600 pgs @ 5%; BCI-21 black: 300 pgs@5%; Colour (BCI-21): 200 pgs @ 7.5% per colour; Photo: 100 pgs @ 7.5% per colour	Black: 540 pgs @ 360 dpi, Colour: 300 pgs @ 360 dpi	Black: 900 pgs @ 360 dpi, Colour: 300 pgs @360 dpi	Black: 650 pgs.; Colour: 313 pgs	Black: 840 pgs; Colour 422 pgs

Company	Canon		Epson		Hewlett-Packard	
Model	BJC-250	BJC-4300	Stylus 600	Stylus 800	DeskJet 692C	DeskJet 722C
Replacement cost*	Black: (BC-02): $39.50 (srp); Colour: $59.00 (srp); photo: $59.99 (srp)	Black (BC-20): $52.50 (srp); BCI-21 black: $12.50; BCI-21 head with colour and black tanks: $84.25; photo: $69.99	black: $28.99, colour: $32.99 (mlp)	black: $32.99, colour $32.99 (mlp)	Black: $34.99 (street); Colour: $34.99 (street); Photo: $49.99 (street)	Black: $45.99 (esp); Colour: $49.99 (esp)
On-screen paper out/ ink low or out reporting **	no / no	no / no	yes / yes	yes / yes	yes/no	yes/no
Languages, Standard	IBM x24E; emulation: Epson LQ 510, Canon extended mode	IBM x24E; emulation: Epson LQ 2550, Canon extended mode	ESC/P 2 (Windows & DOS)	ESC/P 2 (Windows & DOS), IBM x24E	HP PCL 3	Printing Performance Architecture
Languages, Optional	none	none	none	Poscript level 2 w/Pantone Calibrated approved colours	none	none
Automatic Language Switching	Yes	Yes	No	No	No	n/a
Monthly Duty Cycle	Not quoted	Not quoted	Epson will not quote	Epson will not quote	1,000 pages black	1,000 pages black
Paper Trays, Std.	1	1	1	1	1	1
Media Capacity	100	100	100	100	100 sheets	100 sheets
Envelopes Input	15	15	10	10	20	15
Media Types	Plain Paper, Greeting Cards, Back Print Film, High Gloss Film, Transparency film, Fabric Sheets, High Resolution Paper, T-Shirt Transfers, Bubble Jet Paper (water resistant), labels; Envelopes; letter, legal, A4, #10 or "European" envelopes	Plain Paper, Continous banner paper, Greeting Cards, Back Print Film, High Gloss Film, Transparency film, Fabric Sheets, High Resolution Paper, T-Shirt Transfers, Bubble Jet Paper (water resistant), labels; Envelopes; Paper sizes: letter, legal, A4, A5, B5; #10 or "European" envelopes	thickness: .003" to .004" weight: 17 to 24 lb - plain, bond, Epson premium, transparencies, iron-on transfers, #10, DL & C6 envelopes	thickness: .003" to .004" weight: 17 to 24 lb - plain, bond, Epson premium papers and photo quality glossy paper and film, transparency, iron-on transfers, self-adhesive labels, #10, DL & C5 envelopes	Plain and special paper, continuous-feed banner paper, envelopes, transparencies, labels, iron-on transfer paper	Plain and premium papers, photo papers, transparencies, cards, envelopes, labels, and iron-on transfers

Company	Canon		Epson		Hewlett-Packard	
Model	BJC-250	BJC-4300	Stylus 600	Stylus 800	DeskJet 692C	DeskJet 722C
Memory, Std.	40 KB buffer	26 KB buffer	32 KB buffer	32 KB buffer	512 KB; 32 KB buffer	256 KB
Memory, Max.	Not upgradeable	Not upgradeable	Not upgradeable	Not upgradeable	Not upgradeable	Not upgradeable
Scaleable Typefaces	True Type support through Windows, 7 resident bitmap fonts	True Type support through Windows, 7 resident bitmap fonts	Roman, SanSerif (from DOS, full True Type support from Windows)	Roman, SanSerif (from DOS, full True Type support from Windows)	35 TrueType for Windows	None, font support via Windows
Interfaces, Standard	Bi-Centronics parallel	Bi-Centronics parallel	parallel (IEEE 1284, "nibble mode"), serial (RS-422, up to 900 KB/sec)	parallel (IEEE 1284, "nibble mode"), serial (RS-422, up to 1.8 MB/sec)	Centronics parallel, IEEE-1284 compliant with 1284-B receptacle	Centronics parallel, IEEE 1284-compliant with 1284-B receptacle
Parallel port type	SPP, EPP, ECP	SPP, EPP, ECP	SPP, EPP – ECP with Win95B or better	SPP, EPP – ECP with Win95B or better	Not quoted	Not quoted
Interfaces, Optional	none	none	None	Ethernet, Local Talk, serial, buffered parallel, coax, twinax	None	None
Automatic Interface Switching	n/a	n/a	n/a	No	n/a	n/a
Platform / operating system compatibility	Windows 3.1x, 95 (NT drivers must be down-loaded, OS/2 available but doesn't provide full functionality)	Windows 3.1x, 95 (NT drivers must be down-loaded, OS/2 available but doesn't provide full functionality)	Windows 95, 3.1x / MacOS 7.x or higher (single user)	Windows NT 3.51 or higher, 95, 3.1x / Mac OS 7.x or higher (single user)	Windows 3.1x, 95, DOS	Windows 3.1x, 95, DOS
Size (in) WxHxD	14.2 x 6.8 x 8.5	15.1 x 9.1 x 8	16.9 x 6.1 x 9.1	18.7 x 6.97 x 10.78	17.2 x 7.9 x 16	17.5 x 7.3 x 14
Weight (lbs / kg)	5.5 / 2.5	7.7 / 3.5	11.5 / 5.27	14.3 / 6.5	11.6 / 5.3	12 / 5.5
Warranty	1 year InstantExchange (some restrictions)	1 year InstantExchange (some restrictions)	2 year	2 year	1 year	1 year
Price (Cdn funds)*	$274 (srp)	$329 (srp)	$369 (mlp)	$499 (mlp)	$329 (esp)	$449 (esp)
Contact	Canon	Canon	Epson Canada	Epson Canada	HP Canada	HP Canada
Toll free	800-263-1121	800-263-1121	800-463-7766	800-463-7766	800-387-3867	800-387-3867
Web site: http://www.	ccsi.canon.com	ccsi.canon.com	epson.com	epson.com	hp.com	hp.com

Inkjet Printers cont'd

Company	Lexmark		NEC Technologies		Okidata
Model	**3000 Color Jetprinter**	**5700 Color Jetprinter**	**Superscript 150c**	**Superscript 750c**	**Okijet 2020**
Head type	dual head thermal bubble	dual head thermal bubble	single head thermal bubble	dual head thermal bubble	single head thermal bubble
Head nozzles	Black: 56; Colour: 48	Black: 208; Colour: 192	Black: 50; Colour: 27 each (71)	Black: 64; Colour: "67" (whether per Colour or total not indicated)	High-capacity Black: 128; Colour: 24 each cyan, yellow, magenta, 48 Black
Resolution*, Black (dpi)	Win95/3.1x: 600 x 300; OS/2, WinNT or DOS: 300 x 300	1200 x 1200	600 x 300	600 x 600	600 x 600
Resolution*, Colour (dpi)	Win95/3.1x: 600 x 300; OS/2, WinNT or DOS: 300 x 300	1200 x 1200	600 x 300	600 x 600	600 x 600
Resolution*, Photo (dpi)	n/a (there's no software driver for photos)	1200 x 1200 (adds 2 pastels & black for 6 colours)	n/a	600 x 600	n/a
Margins (minimum – top, bottom, sides; inches)	"maximum print line 8 inches (portrait)"	no info	.5" top, 1" bottom margin	.5" top and bottom margin	no info
Max printable area (inches)	8 x 13.43	8 x 13.43	.5" top, 1" bottom margin	.5" top and bottom margin	8.1" x 13.6"
Print Colours	up to 16.7 million	up to 16.7 million	up to 16.7 million	up to 16.7 million	up to 16.7 million
Max Speed, Black (ppm = pages per minute; mpp = minutes per page)	Win95/3.1x or OS/2: 5 ppm; WinNT: 4 ppm (all draft)	draft: 6 ppm higher res figures not given	3 ppm	6 ppm	4 ppm @ 300 x 300- optional high capacity black printhead up to 6 ppm
Max Speed, Colour (ppm = pages per minute; mpp = minutes per page)	OS/2, WinNT: 1 ppm; Win95/3.1x: 1.5 ppm (all draft)	draft: 4 ppm higher res figures not given	3 mpp	2 ppm	1 ppm @ 300 x 300
Print Cartridges	1 black and 1 x 3 colour (cyan, magenta, yellow)	1 black and 1 x 3 colour - or optional photo ink cartridge and 3-colour cartridge	1 colour (cyan, magenta, yellow). Optional black cartridge sold separately	1 "Midnight" black and 1 x 4-colour (cyan, magenta, yellow, black)	1 colour head with 4 separate cartridges, black, cyan, magenta, yellow; optional high-capacity black cartridge also available replaces colour cartridge
Cartridge life rating (8.5" x 11" letter with 5% black coverage or 15% colour coverage (5% per colour) except where noted)	Black: high yield 1300, std yield 600; Colour: high yield 240, std yield, 200	Black: 600; Colour: 200	Black: 545; Colour: 275	Black: 650; Colour: 325	High-capacity black: 1460 pages; Colour: 275 (black), 295 colour (each)
Replacement cost*	Black: $51.99 (mlp); Colour: $56.99 (mlp)	Black: $44.99 (mlp); Colour: $53.99 (mlp)	Black: $35.99 (mlp); Colour: $47.99 (mlp)	Midnight Black: $29.99 (mlp); Colour: $33.99 (mlp); Photo Kit (once) $82.99 (mlp); Photo ink: $68.99 (mlp)	Black: $15.39, Colours: $16.79; Optional high-capacity black: $64.39. Colour print head $69.99 for 3000 pages
On-screen paper out / ink low or out reporting **	yes / yes	yes / yes	yes / no	yes / no	yes/yes
Languages, Standard	Windows printing system, PCL 3 (Deskjet 500)	Windows printing system	HP PCL 3+, IBM Proprinter	HP PCL 3+	HP PCL 3c emulation
Languages, Optional	none	none	none	none	none

Company	Lexmark		NEC Technologies		Okidata
Model	3000 Color Jetprinter	5700 Color Jetprinter	Superscript 150c	Superscript 750c	Okijet 2020
Automatic Language Switching	No	n/a	No	No	n/a
Monthly Duty Cycle	500 pages	1000 pages	200 pages	200 pages	1000 pages
Paper Trays, Std.	1	1	1	1	1
Media Capacity	100	100	40	120	150
Envelopes Input	1	10	1	25	10
Media Types	plain or coated (high res., premium or glossy, photo) paper, Iron-on transfers, greeting card stock, labels, transparency film, index cards, post cards, letter, legal, A4, B5, A5	plain or coated (high res., premium or glossy, photo) premium, Iron-on transfers, greet-ing card stock, labels, trans-parancy film, index cards, post cards, letter, legal. A4, B5	plain, bond, premium, ultra glossy paper, transparency film, iron-on transfer; Paper: Letter, legal, executive, A4, B5 Envelopes: Commercial 10 and International 10, DL, C5, C6	plain, bond, premium, ultra glossy paper, transparency film, iron-on transfer; Photo and snapshot photo. Paper sizes: Letter, legal, exec-utive, A4, A5, A6, 4" x 6" or 5" 8" notecard, Envelopes: Commercial 10 and International 10, DL, C5, C6	plain, coated, or glossy paper, index cards, transparency film, card stock up to 110 lb, labels, envelopes; Paper sizes 3.9" x 3.9" to 8.5" x 14" (16 to 36 lb)
Memory, Std.	75 KB	512 KB	128 KB	1 MB, 32 KB buffer	512 KB, 64 KB buffer
Memory, Max.	Not upgradeable	Not upgradeable	Not upgradeable	Not upgradeable	Not upgradeable
Scaleable Typefaces	Font support (True Type) through Windows	Font support (True Type) through Windows	Font support (True Type) through Windows, 5 PCL fonts	Font support (True Type) through Windows, 42 PCL fonts	Font support (True Type) through Windows
Interfaces, Standard	Parallel IEEE 1284	Parallel IEEE 1284	Parallel IEEE 1284	Parallel IEEE 1284	Bi-directional parallel, IEEE 1284
Parallel port type	SPP, EPP, ECP	SPP, EPP, ECP	SPP "nibble-mode" only. EPP/ECP not supported	SPP "nibble-mode" only. EPP/ECP not supported	SPP only. EPP/ECP not supported; port sharing not recommended
Interfaces, Optional	none	none	none	none	none
Automatic Interface Switching	n/a	n/a	n/a	n/a	n/a
Platform / operating system compatibility	Windows 95, 3.1x, NT; OS/2, DOS	Windows 95, 3.1x, NT	Windows 95, 3.1x	Windows 95, 3.1x	Windows 3.1x, 95, DOS
Size (in) WxHxD	17.9 x 7.7 x 8.4	17 x 6 x 8	14.8 x 14.2 x 7.9	18.1 x 9.3 x 18.3	14.4 x 7.6 x 11.8
Weight (lbs / kg)	9.5 / 4.32	6 / 2.7	4.84 / 2.2	9.9 / 4.5	10.1 / 4.6
Warranty	1 year LexExpress or customer carry-in	1 year, next biz day exchange	1 year overnight replacement (some restrictions)	1 year overnight replacement (some restrictions)	2 year limited with Overnight Exchange (Canada and US only)
Price (Cdn funds)*	$349 (mlp)	$439 (mlp)	$175 (esp)	$255 (esp)	$349 (mlp)
Contact	Lexmark Canada	Lexmark Canada	NEC Technologies	NEC Technologies	Okidata
Toll free	888-453-9226	888-453-9226	800-NEC-INFO (800-632-4636)	800-NEC-INFO (800-632-4636)	800 OKIDATA (800-654-3282)
Web site: http://www.	lexmark.com	lexmark.com	nec.com	nec.com	okidata.com

(1) black text with colour highlights, (2) mixed text and graphics, REt = Resolution Enhancement technology ™
* esp = estimated street price; mlp = manufacturer's list price; srp = suggested retail price; street = at least one quoted retail price -- may vary by vendor and region
** requires bi-directional parallel port
Notes: Epson does make a photo printer, the Stylus Photo, but at $699 Cdn, it fell beyond our price limit.
As a policy, Hewlett-Packard normally doesn't quote cartridge life, however, the company made an exception for us.
Xerox has a line of inkjet printers that were new in mid-1998, but information about them was so minimal that most categories on this chart would have read "no info."
Hopefully, the company will have revised its Web site by the time you read this

Lasers and LED Page Printers

If you have no pressing need for colour, and particularly if you have a lot of business correspondence, there has never been a better time to think about buying a personal laser printer. If you have the idea that laser printers are $2,000 products, think again. The crop we're going to discuss started at $299 and all cost less than $1,000 Cdn in 1998. If you think you'll have to shore up the floor to take the weight or move everything out of the room except the printer, you're in for a second pleasant surprise. "Personal" lasers have become as small as a breadbox and lightweight (the range in the table is from 8.4 to 21.2 lbs.).

You also don't have to give up much in the way of quality. Most models produced 600 dot-per-inch (dpi) quality – and at respectable speeds. At the low end of the scale, 4 page-per-minute (ppm) models are getting scarce; 6 and 8 ppm have become the norm (one promises 12 ppm) – much faster than any inkjet you'll find.

You'll also be pleasantly surprised by their cost-per-page figure.

What are the choices? You'll find personal lasers under $1,000 Cdn from the regular gang: Brother, Hewlett-Packard, Lexmark, NEC, Okidata, Panasonic, and Xerox. Missing, however, are both Canon and Epson. Although both companies were once in the personal laser market, both appear to have dropped out (although you may still find some discontinued models here and there) and all reference to personal lasers has been excluded from the respective companies' Web sites.

Laser printers all work the same way. Once the instructions from your software leave the computer and arrive at the printer, a laser is directed through a series of lenses and mirrors onto a photosensitive drum. The drum acquires an electrostatic charge on its surface, which attracts black dust from a toner container. The toner is transferred to the paper and heat-fused to its surface. (In a colour laser, the same thing happens, but the page is passed over four separate toner cartridges, one each for cyan, magenta, yellow, and black).

Early laser printers used helium/neon gas lasers (HeNe). While you may still find one or two gas laser models in larger industrial, high-speed units, it is far more common today to use a light emitting diode (LED) laser. Yet another method, popularized by Okidata in its

Configuration of a Laser Printer
(flow chart)

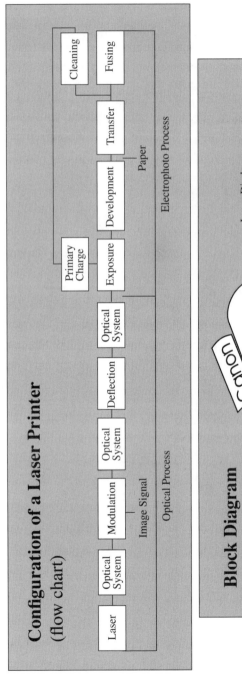

Block Diagram
(Canon LPB)

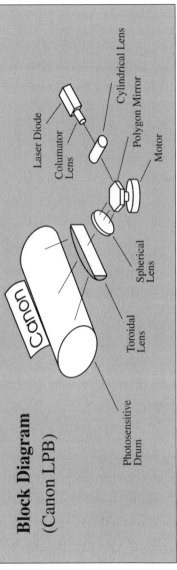

"LED page printers," has liquid crystal shutter arrays arranged in line just before the drum. In early test models the shutters were opened or closed to form a latent image, but Okidata's commercial models "have no moving parts." They use a series of LEDs (2600 or more of them) in line, which are turned on and off as appropriate.

How all this takes place, the speed with which it happens, and how the printer figures out how to get onto paper an image that more or less resembles what you sent it is what costs you money. Together with the various paper-handling mechanics, it makes laser printers wonderfully complicated machines.

Picking a personal laser printer

There are enough differences among laser printer models that the answers to the following questions may help you sort out a few from a fairly large list. Answering the questions before you shop may also save you headaches later.

Just which model is this, really? Many manufacturers create similar, but not identical, models of their products for sale in electronics/furniture/office supply superstores. This can happen to full computer systems, but seems to be endemic with products such as printers, scanners, digital cameras, and other external peripheral devices. These special models may not have exactly the same features, software bundle, warranty, or options as the model the manufacturer highlights in its advertising. In other words, it may be very similar, but is downgraded a bit to allow it to be sold at a low, low price. The full model designation (the name, all the numbers, and any letters in the model designation) is important and any differences you detect aren't necessarily because you wrote it down incorrectly or a product of your faulty memory. (Gotcha!)

What types and sizes of media can the printer accept? If you need to print business cards, legal-sized documents, transparencies or envelopes, make sure the printer can deal with them. While you're at it, check to see specifically what type of transparency stock the printer requires. Some want the type with attached paper backing and some will jam if you use that kind.

Does it have a single-sheet bypass? Bypass paper paths come in two flavours: one that requires you first to unload the paper in the main tray or to remove the whole tray, and one that actually bypasses the tray altogether and ignores it. A separate manual feeder is desirable option.

Does the printer have a straight paper path? If the printer doesn't have a straight-through path for handling thick stock, you may not be able to print envelopes, heavy paper or card stock. (The normal paper path from input tray to output bin requires pages to turn some fairly tight corners. A straight-through path normally dumps the output from the back of the unit. Will you have enough space behind the printer to accommodate this feature, even if you get it?)

Does it have a dual-tray option or at least does it have a second tray available? If not, you may be spending more time on your feet loading and unloading paper and shuffling trays than you do printing. If you need to switch constantly between two different stock sizes, or between letterhead and bond paper, a unit with two input trays (at least as an option) is what you want.

How does the printer handle envelopes? Can you load multiple envelopes into the standard input tray, through a special (and probably expensive optional) tray or must you feed them one at a time? If you do a lot of mailings and plan to use the laser to print the envelopes (instead of printing labels), a model that allows you to load multiple envelopes is a good idea. Otherwise the straight paper path noted above may have to suffice as a minimum. Most laser printers will *not* take a 9 x 12-inch, full-sized business envelope (models from Brother appear to be the single exception in the "personal laser" category).

Does it have a special way of handling stick-on labels and are there restrictions on the brand or type of label sheet it can use? Can the labels be loaded into the standard input bin/tray?

What's the capacity of the input tray? If you print high volumes and don't want to spend half your time reloading the printer, you'd be better off with a printer whose input tray can hold 200 to 250 sheets or more instead of 50.

What's the rated duty cycle? "Personal" lasers are just that. They're not really robust enough to handle extremely large loads hour after hour and day after day. It may be less expensive in the long run to buy a more robust printer than to have to replace a lighter variety every year or two. The duty cycle is the number of pages you can logically expect to print each month without damaging the unit through overuse.

Is there an output tray? Many smaller, less costly personal lasers have scrapped the separate output tray. They either deliver output to a small bin on the top of the unit or to a small piece of plastic that protrudes like a tongue from the front. Other models may simply drop printed pages onto your desk or the floor.

Will multipage print jobs be collated with pages in the proper order? While we're on the topic, you may often have to run multiple copies of a multipage document. If either your software application (e.g., your word processor) or your printer's driver(s) will collate the results, that's good. Hint: If the pages don't come out face down or if your software won't allow you to print a document in reverse order, you'll spend hours reshuffling pages.

Where do you load the paper? Depending on the model, you may load the paper from the front, from the back, or from the top (where it can curl if left there too long). If easy access is important, a top- or front-loader may be for you.

What size is it, really? When all the input and output trays are closed, personal lasers aren't much larger than a breadbox, but will often occupy more real estate when the input/output/bypass/straight path trays, tongues and/or chutes are fully deployed. Try to discover the dimensions when all options are open.

How often will you have to replace a toner cartridge? Toner cartridges are rated at *xxx* pages per cartridge. This page count is based on an industry standard of 8.5 x 11-inch letter with 5 per cent page coverage and varies from brand to brand and model to model. Your count may vary quite a bit.

How easy are cartridges to find? Drop into a few of your local business supply stores and superstores. Ask whether they stock both brand-name and third-party replacement cartridges for the brands *and models* you're considering. You might also pick up the Yellow Pages and pick a few toner cartridge recyclers to see if less-expensive, recycled cartridges are available for your unit (hint – find out if use of a third-party or recycled cartridge voids the manufacturer's warranty).

How much does a replacement toner cartridge cost? The cost per page for a laser printer is in the one- to two-cent-per-page range, but the expense comes in one lump each time you need to replace the toner cartridge. Keep in mind that a model with a high rating for toner cartridge capacity may give you a rude shock when you come to replace it. No matter how many pages the cartridge is supposed to print, your cost is still going to be one to two cents for each page. (Gotcha!)

How easy is it to replace a cartridge? Try before you buy or get a demonstration at the store; you'll find some systems are much simpler to service than others.

How often do you need to replace the drum? Toner cartridges aren't the only replaceable parts. There are more expensive parts, such as photoconductor drums, that have lifespans, too. A small percentage of the models we've considered provide a new drum with each cartridge (which jacks up the cost of one). See spec tips, below.

Are drivers for your software readily available? In order for what you see on paper to resemble even faintly what you saw on screen, you need software drivers for the printer that translate what the operating system or application is sending into codes the printer can understand. You *must* discuss which operating system, which applications, and which versions of them you are using with the vendor before you pay for the printer *and* get any assurances that it will work properly written on the sales agreement. Warning: if you're using OS/2, or you've moved up to Windows NT or still do a lot of work in MS-DOS programs, and particularly if it's a Mac that greets you in the morning, your choice of models will be much more limited than if you stick with Windows 9x.

How will you get technical assistance and updated drivers when the printer manufacturer either upgrades them to fix problems or there is a new version of your operating system or your application software? Does the manufacturer have a technical support phone number? BBS? Web site? How long is the warranty? Does the vendor offer overnight exchange or on-site service if your printer goes on the fritz?

The software is nice, but do you need it? Many printers come with oodles of software applications bundled with them. Are they of any use to you? Are they compatible with your operating system? Can you get a version of the printer for a lower cost if you don't want them?

The software may be nice, but is it useful? This is a different question. What you may really be offered is "lite" or "special edition" software (demoware that is time or function limited) designed to get you to buy the real thing.

Spec tips

n **pages per** *xxxx*: The page-per-minute figure, like the cost-per-page, toner-cartridge page count, and photoconductor-drum-life figures, is based upon an "industry standard," letter-sized page with 5 per cent page coverage or less. That's essentially a couple of small paragraphs using 12-point type. If you're printing legal-sized pages, pages covered with substantially more text, pages with graphics or large fonts, transparencies or labels, none of the advertised figures are even remotely accurate.

Pages per minute: The page-per-minute figure is based on copied pages (if, say, you're making ten copies of that brief letter). It doesn't reflect the time it takes to have the printer warm up (they all "go to sleep" now to save power) or to get the first page out of the printer even if it's already warm. It doesn't take graphics into account and it varies if there's lots of text/graphics/large fonts on the page. Figure about twenty to thirty seconds for the printer to wake up, then another twenty seconds or more for the first page to appear. All this is after your software does whatever it has to do to prepare the document for printing (which in turn will depend on the speed of your computer, the speed of your hard drive, and the amount of memory it has available for the Windows GDI heap to use).

Photoconductor-drum life: You'll note on the comparison table that Brother quotes two different figures for drum life, depending on whether the unit is used for one-page jobs or multiple-copy jobs. The figure seems low compared to the rest, but *it's also more honest*. The drum rotates once for each job, whether there is one copy or twenty copies, and while this doesn't affect how long it will last, it does affect how many printed pages you'll get before it needs changing. The few companies with models that replace the drum with each toner cartridge are defensive about the cost of their cartridges, which may make them appear to be overpriced compared to the competition. But it all comes out in the wash, because here you don't have to buy a separate photoconductor drum periodically.

Toner quality: Companies that use a fairly large toner particle don't want to talk much about toner quality. Hewlett-Packard and others stress their "microfine" toner to indicate that the smaller particles give smoother results, less banding in sold colours and denser blacks.

Memory: As noted above, typical PCL laser printers need 1.5 to 2 MB of internal memory before they can print full-page graphics or complex documents. PostScript needs even more (2 MB is a bare minimum and 4 MB is more common as a minimum). GDI printers don't need nearly as much memory. Nevertheless, embarrassment over the small amount of memory in Panasonic's KX-P6500 GDI model prompted the company to leave this information out of their spec sheets. I had to nag the company to get it.

Footprint: Brother is very clear to state, in its spec sheets, that the quoted size is with trays *closed*. Other manufacturers are not as specific. You will want to check the dimensions of the printer when it is fully deployed if space is a major concern for you.

List price, SRP (suggested retail price), estimated retail prices versus street prices: All manufacturers quote list prices that can vary significantly from what the units sell for at retail, and some vendors take a smaller markup than others. Once you've decided on the model you want, shopping around for price is a good idea.

Why didn't you report the number of on-board fonts? In the DOS days, the number of on-board fonts was an important deciding factor when choosing a laser printer. That was then; this is the era of Windows and True Type. All of these printers will allow you to download True Type fonts (i.e., to send a software description of the font to the printer at the time you print), so that what you see on screen is darn close to what you get on paper. The number of fonts you can have in any one document depends on the amount of memory you have in the printer – unless it's a GDI model.

In *White's Compubabble Dictionary* (http://web.idirect.com/~myles), "font" is defined as a description of a character of type that includes all of its characteristics, including shape, slant, weight and decoration. For instance, a **bold** character is a different font from an *italic* character, even if they are the same typeface. This is why most PostScript printers say they come with thirty-five built-in fonts, but in reality have only thirteen differently shaped typefaces. Times Roman is a typeface. Times Roman normal, **bold**, *italic*, and ***bold italic*** are four different fonts.

Resolution: You're unlikely to see any difference between a 300 dpi image and a 600 dpi image when you're looking at the middle of a black object. Where the differences appear are at the edges of curved or slanted objects, in fine curved lines, in halftone screens and gradual fills. You'll also see the difference in small type sizes.

Colour Lasers

I've confined my coverage of personal lasers to black and white printing, even though scads of readers are curious about colour laser printers. Why? The short answer is that colour lasers are alive and well and they still cost too much for the likes of you and me to afford. These are still professional machines for companies that need quality prepress samples. Nevertheless, I'm always curious about this segment of the laser printer industry, too, and never turn down an opportunity to play with a colour laser printer when I have a chance.

When I first wrote about colour laser printers in 1992, there were no models on the market for under $60,000 or that didn't weigh as much as a small car. By mid-1995, QMS, Hewlett-Packard, and Xerox all had models selling for as little as $8,500 (QMS) and ranging up to $12,000 (Xerox 4900).

By the end of 1997, prices had fallen to $5,000-$7,000. QMS had abandoned the market, but Panasonic, Lexmark, Tektronix and Okidata had jumped in, and Xerox, instead of producing the most expensive model in the pack, now had the least expensive. Instead of being restricted to 300 dpi and 11-inch page lengths, 600 and 1200 dpi

Personal Laser Printers

Company	Brother International				Hewlett-Packard	Lexmark
Model	HL-720	HL-730 DX+	HL-760+	HL-1060	6L	Optra E+
Cdn street or suggested retail prices	$499/$399	$599	$699	$1299/$999	$690/$549-$686	$700/$595-$699
Print technology	laser	laser	laser	laser	laser	laser
Print type	GDI	traditional	traditional	traditional	traditional	traditional
Size (W x D x H)	14.4" x 9.8" x 13.9"	14.4" x 9.8" x 13.9"	14.4" x 9.8" x 15.1"	15.8" x 17.3" x 10.8"	13.2" x 12.3" x 8.9"	13.7" x 9.7" x 8.6"
Weight	14.3 lbs.	14.3 lbs.	15.4 lbs.	21.2 lbs.	15.9 lbs.	13.2 lbs.
Pages per minute	6 ppm	6 ppm	6 ppm	10 ppm	6 ppm	6 ppm
Toner cartridge	Units ship with "starter cartridge" – 1,000 pgs @ 5%. Standard replacement cartridge rated at 2,200 pgs @ 5%			2,200 pgs @ 5%	2,500 pgs @ 5%	3,000 pgs @ 5%
Photoconductor drum	20,000 pgs			6,000 pages @ 1 page per job. 20,000 at 20 pages per job	replaced with each toner cartridge	20,000 pgs
Memory (std/max)	512 KB / 2 MB	1 MB / 2 MB	1 MB / 33 MB	2 MB / 33 MB	1 MB / 9 MB	2 MB / 6 MB
Stock	letter, legal, envl. (up to 9 x 12)), trans., labels, cardstock, postcard, organizer				letter, legal, envl., trans., labels, card stock	letter, legal, trans, envl., index cards, labels
Minimum margins (l, r, t, b)	no info	no info	no info	no info	.25", .25", .17", .17"	no info
Single-sheet bypass	Y	Y	Y	Y	Y	Y
Straight-through paper path	Y	Y	Y	Y	Y	N
Capacity (input/output)	200/100	200/100	200/100	200/100	100/100	150/100

Company	Brother International				Hewlett-Packard	Lexmark
Model	HL-720	HL-730 DX+	HL-760+	HL-1060	6L	Optra E+
Optional second tray	N	N	N	Y	N	Y
Optional envelope tray	N	N	N	N	N	N
Page description language(s)	Proprietary "Brother Printing Solution for Windows 3.1x/95" (GDI)	PCL 4, software emulated PCL5e, IBM Proprinter XL Epson FX-850, includes NT drivers	Proprietary "Brother Printing Solution for Windows 3.1x/95" and PCL 4, PCL5e emulation, IBM Proprinter XL, Epson FX-850	PCL 5e, software PostScript emulation, IBM Proprinter XL, Epson FX-850	PCL 5	PCL 5
Postscript upgrade	N	N	N	n/a	Y	Y
Print resolution (dpi)	600 x 600	600 x 600	1200 x 600 (graphics), 600 x 600 (text)	1200 x 600 (graphics), 600 x 600 (text)	600 x 600	600 x 600
Tech support options	Toll-free phone, auto fax back, BBS, Web				phone, BBS, toll-free fax back, CIS, AOL, Web (limited, no direct interaction)	toll free phone, ftp, Web (software updates and e-mail)
Warranty	"1 yr Limited"	"2 yr Limited"	"1 yr Limited"	"1 yr Limited"	1 yr carry in	1 yr LexExpress or carry in (customer's choice)
Company	Brother Canada				HP Canada	Lexmark Canada
Phone	800-361-6466				800-387-3867	888-453-9226
Web site: http://www.	brother.com/E-product/e-prodca.html				canada.hp.com	lexmark.com/canada

Personal Laser Printers cont'd

Company	NEC		Okidata			Panasonic	Xerox
Model	SuperScript 660+	SuperScript 860	Okipage 4W	Okipage 6E	Okipage 6EX	KX-P6500	Docuprint 4508
Cdn street or suggested retail prices	$499/$395-$445	$565/$569-$599	$369/$299	$559/$459	$799/$625-$695	$650/$649	$999/$999
Print technology	laser	laser	LED page printer	LED page printer	LED page printer	laser	laser
Print type	GDI	PrintGear	GDI	traditional	traditional	GDI	traditional
Size (W x D x H)	13.8" x 9.5" x 9.9"	14.6" x 16.9" x 9.1"	12.2" x 7.5" x 5.9"	12.6" x 14.2" x 6.9"	12.6" x 14.2" x 6.9"	5.2" x 14.9" x 11.3"	14.2" x 14.4" x 7.2"
Weight	16.5 lbs.	20.28 lbs.	8.4 lbs.	17 lbs.	17 lbs.	14.4 lbs.	17 lbs.
Pages per minute	6 ppm	8 ppm	4 ppm	6 ppm	6 ppm	6 ppm	8 ppm
Toner cartridge	3,000 pgs @ 5%	5,000 pgs @ 5%	1,000 pgs @ 5%	2,000 pgs @ 5%		1,000 pgs @ 4% shipped with unit. Std. Cartridge: 2,000 @ 4%	4,000 @ 5%
Photoconductor drum	20,000 pgs	replaced with each toner cartridge	"1 year limited warranty" (to 10,000 pgs)	"1 year limited warranty" (to 20,000 pgs)		15,000 pgs	replaced with each toner cartridge
Memory (std/max)	256 KB / 4MB	1 MB / 5 MB	128 KB / 128 KB	1 MB / 18 MB	2 MB / 35 MB	512 KB / 4.5 MB	2 MB / 34 MB
Stock	letter, legal, heavy paper up to 28 lb., labels, envl., trans.	letter, legal, heavy paper up to 28 lb., labels, envl., trans.	Letter, legal, heavy paper up to 32 lb., labels, envl., trans.			letter, legal, heavy paper up to 32 lb., labels, envl., trans.	letter, legal, heavy paper up to 36 lb., labels, envl., trans.
Minimum margins (l, r, t, b)	no info	no info	no info	no info	no info	no info	no info
Single-sheet bypass	N needs tray removed	Y	Y	Y	Y	N	Y
Straight-through paper path	N	Y	Y	Y	Y	N	Y
Capacity (input/output)	150/100	200/50 face up, 35 face down	100/30 (face up)	100/50 face up, 100 face down	100/30 (face up)	100/50	250/125 face down

Company	NEC		Okidata			Panasonic	Xerox
Model	SuperScript 660+	SuperScript 860	Okipage 4W	Okipage 6E	Okipage 6EX	KX-P6500	Docuprint 4508
Optional second tray	Y	N	Y	Y	Y	N	Y
Optional envelope tray	N	N	N	Y	Y	N	N
Page description language(s)	GDI / PCL 5 (DOS)	Adobe PrintGear, PCL 4.5	PCL 4.5 emulation	PCL 5e emulation, Epson FX, IBM Proprinter III XL, HiPer print (GDI)	PCL 5e emulation, Epson FX, IBM Proprinter III XL, HiPer print (GDI)	GDI or "HP LaserJet lip" (PCL 4.5)	PCL 5e emulation
Postscript upgrade	N	N	N	N	N	N	N
Print resolution (dpi)	600 x 600	600 x 600	600 dpi interpolated (300 x 1200)	600 dpi interpolated (300 x 1200)	600 dpi (text), 600 x 1200 (graphics)	1200 dpi interpolated (2400 x 600 in GDI mode)	600 x 600 dpi
Tech support options	toll-free phone, AOL, CIS, MSN, Web, toll-free fax back		toll-free phone, automated FAQ, fax-back, BBS, Web			toll-free phone	toll-free phone
Warranty	2 yr "limited overnight replacement"		1 yr limited, overnight exchange, 5 yrs on LED head			1 yr exchange, "other details from dealer"	3 yrs, plus overnight exchange
Company	NEC Technologies Canada		Okidata Canada			Panasonic Canada	Xerox Canada
Phone	800-NEC info (632-4636)		905-238-4250 or 800-654-8326 ext. 9			800-742-8086	800-ASK XERO
Web site: http://www.	nec.com		okidata.com			panasonic.ca	xerox.com

Prices are for relative comparison only and will certainly have changed by the time you read this. If a rebate is offered, ask whether it is in US or Canadian funds.
No info: this information is not commonly available in the company's published specifications. You'll have to ask if it's important.

resolutions are available and all models currently print to 14-inch (legal) stock. Cost per page has dropped in some models from an average of 32 cents for 30 per cent coverage to less than 15 cents.

All currently available models use four toner cartridges (cyan, magenta, yellow, and black) and pass the paper three or four times (you can generally select whether to use three or four colours) through the system, but otherwise they behave just like a standard laser printer. Once all four colours are laid down, a voltage drop releases a dry toner, which is fused on in a single pass through another part of the mechanism.

The advantage of colour lasers is that they use plain paper and a familiar technology. You generally get a choice of page description language that will include PostScript (but may cost extra).

If this is the printer for you, then watch out for the following items while shopping:

(a) The base price quoted often doesn't include enough memory to reach the highest resolution stated in the advertising. PostScript and network connectivity may also be extra. Figure around $1,500 on top of the base price to get everything.

(b) Check on toner availability – this is new stuff and it may not be widely available in your area without ordering from the manufacturer.

(c) Get a friend to help you move one – these units are smaller than a car, but still weigh as much as a small refrigerator.

Here's a quick overview of the models available in early 1998. Lexmark (Optra SC1275), Panasonic (KX-P8475), Tektronix (Phaser 560), and Xerox (C55) all released new colour laser printers in early 1998. Okidata's colour laser didn't arrive until later in the year. I was able to play with the Lexmark, Tektronix, and Xerox.

First the bad news: Although the street price for the least-equipped version of the C55 (standard memory, no PostScript) was about $4,900 Cdn ($5,900 list), that's as low as we go. The KX-P8475 had a suggested retail price of $6,000, while the base model of the Phaser 560 carried a $5,436-$5,755 price tag ($6,395 list).

Now the good news. The colour output is not only gorgeous, but you also get to see it far faster (the Lexmark was the quickest of the three I tested), on more paper types (including legal) and in more ways than ever before.

All four models can come equipped with a network interface card (NIC), and if you're buying one for an office, it's probably one of the options your company will want right away. Trust me; in an office and at this price, you're going to be sharing one of these. All of them support IPX/SPX network protocols, as well as TCP/IP (see above). Only Xerox, however, has tried to put the C55 as a stand-alone node on a Windows NetBEUI/NetBIOS peer-to-peer network. This is a task that not even Microsoft recommends, and unfortunately, while Xerox made a game effort, at least for the machine I tested, the performance wasn't good.

NetBEUI, particularly when run over Ethernet, spends a lot of time talking to itself. The Xerox NetBEUI print spooler/redirector appears to keep poking its head out to the net – either to see if the printer is still there or to chat with the neighbours – with the result that my 200 MHz Pentium behaved like a 386 when it was invoked. However, it worked fine after I gave up and simply plugged the printer into the parallel port of one of the computers in the network and did peer peripheral sharing the traditional way.

Two other networking issues merit mention. You'll want to be running Windows 9x or NT if you plan to use TCP/IP to connect to these printers – and in the case of both C55 and Phaser 560, it's worthwhile because each printer has a built-in "Web page" that provides monitoring and remote setup. I've left Windows for Workgroups 3.11 off the list, because it has no TCP/IP stack of its own, and TCP/IP drivers for anything other than accessing the Internet are hard to find.

The other issue is minor and confined to the Lexmark Optra 1275. Lexmark uses a proprietary NIC in the unit that comes only with an RJ-45 jack (the special connector used for two-wire network cables) – no BNC connector (the special connector for those using coaxial network cabling).

Multifunction printers

They slice; they dice; they make beautiful radish rosettes! Uh-oh, wrong commercial; but it's easy to get carried away over machines that will send and receive faxes, make copies, print from your computer, and scan images back into it. In the first edition of *How to Buy a Computer*, I called these machines "offices in a box," and during their early days on the market, they were given several different names (including Swiss army knife fax machines and multifunction fax machines) until one name stuck. Today, they're mostly called multifunction printers. And your first of the homework assignment is to discover precisely which functions each provides.

The basic functions include printing, copying and scanning, but some also have fax send/receive, and others, notably Brother and Sharp, have added another function – phone answering – to the mix. The task isn't only to find models with features added to their multiple functions. You'll also want to look out for some that have reduced functionality. For example, you'll find a couple of models that copy, but don't scan back to a PC. You'll find others that have no built-in fax modem.

You'll also see full-function devices advertised as five- or six-function machines and that can be confusing. Count with me on your fingers. Print, scan, copy, and fax appear to be four and, even if you add phone answering, that's only five. So, what gives? Simple: if the unit will send and receive faxes by itself, *plus* allowing you to send and receive faxes through software on your PC, too, that's counted as two functions, not one.

A couple of companies (Hewlett-Packard and Xerox) dropped fax from their units and gave the same excuse. Said one Xerox executive, "Most people with a PC already have a fax/modem they'll use to send and receive faxes; they don't need one in their printer, too." Don't argue with me; write to Hewlett-Packard and Xerox. Taking this a step farther, Xerox unveiled four new products in late 1998: WorkCentre XE80, XE82, XD100, XD102. These are technically multifunction lasers, but they only print and make photocopies – there are no fax, scanning, or any other services. The company may add scanning back into the mix in units scheduled for release in 1999.

One other "new" feature has hit this market: colour. In 1995, there was only one unit, from Lexmark (which has since dropped out of the market), that would do anything in colour. And at that, it would only print in colour, not scan or copy. Today, there are a couple of models that do everything in colour except fax. By the way, the long-awaited colour fax standard never arrived, and Internet e-mail will probably kill fax as a technology long before it ever does.

When the multifunction devices began to arrive in 1995, they represented technology I'd been waiting years for the computer industry to introduce. Everyone, me included, thought these products would take the world by storm. Guess again. After an initial flurry of "Gee whiz, lookkidit do *that*," people went back to buying separate inkjets and scanners. The market didn't dry up entirely, but its not nearly as large as some people though it would be. Industry folk I've discussed this with are as puzzled as I am (although they still think these machines are a *great* idea), but most of their explanation amounts to a suspicion that people don't trust them (see disadvantages, below). Nevertheless, they do fill a niche.

If you've recently decided to set up a home office, you'll soon realize that the services you're used to having in a corporate environment are right where you left them – back at the corporation. I'm not just talking about people such as a secretary, receptionist, or shipper. I'm talking about machines – a computer, a printer, a fax machine, a scanner, and a photocopier. If you were to buy (and could afford to buy) each one separately, just out of sheer curiosity, where would you put them all? Most home offices I've ever used or visited do not have enough available flat space on which to put stuff. And that's where the multifunction printer shines by providing these services in one small footprint.

The market offers a range of models and prices. At the low end of the price scale are units by Xerox and Sharp. Xerox has the WorkCentre 450c and the HomeCentre. Sharp's FO-1850 is also known as the UX-1400, a model that is nearly identical except that you can't add memory to it. Both sell at places such as Business Depot for between $500 and $600. In the middle of the range, starting at close to $1,000 and rising to nearly $3,000, are a number of companies and choices. Xerox (WorkCentre Pro 610 and 535 – both lasers – and its inkjet-based 3000 series) and Sharp (FO-2770) are in this market, too, as are Brother (MFC series), Canon (Multipass C2500), Hewlett-Packard (OfficeJet series), Toshiba (TF421), and Panasonic (KX-PS600).

I'm not going to venture into the high, corporate end of the scale, but if that's the market that interests you, Canon, HP, Xerox, Mita, JetFax, Ricoh, and Konica all have products designed for high throughput and multiple functions at prices that will make your hair turn green.

The market is divided along technological lines. At the high end of the middle price range are the multifunction laser printers. At the lower end of the mid-range, as well as in the low range itself, you'll find inkjets. At the lowest end, there are still units using thermal-transfer technology. Within each category, there are going to be choices, and how you see yourself using the device will determine which ones you make.

For example, although the current top speed for fax transmission is 14.4 kilobits per second (Kbps), you'll find that some units only have slower 9.6 Kbps modems.

There's no point sending faxes at a resolution higher than about 200 dpi, because that's the top of the fax standard, and it's okay for most optical character recognition, too, but if you're planning to scan images into your PC for further processing, 200 dpi probably isn't high enough. However, not all of the scanners achieve 300 dpi or higher. If you do plan to make use of the scanner, even if only once in a while, find out if it is TWAIN compatible. If it's not, you don't want it (see the TWAIN section in Chapter 11).

Your printing won't look that good at less than 300 dpi – particularly in the inkjet and thermal models. If the "photocopies" you make are just for you, and the quality isn't important, 200 dpi and 64 or fewer shades of grey might be okay. It probably won't be okay if you're giving the copies to others – particularly if they contain any halftone images. For this, you'll want 256 shades of grey and 300 dpi.

Then we come to sending and receiving faxes. Most of those I send are one-offs. I have nowhere I need to send faxes repeatedly, I don't often have to send the same fax to lots of locations, nor do I have any need to respond to fax-on-demand. If you do any of these, then the number of stored fax numbers, whether the system can handle broadcast faxes and whether it can do polling will be important.

Is your fax traffic, both coming and going, so high that you need two phone lines to handle it? If so, you're looking for a machine that can handle outgoing and incoming lines simultaneously. The number of pages it will hold in memory are important, too – you don't want to miss incoming faxes while replacing the ink or toner – but almost as important is what the machine will do with faxes held in memory. For example, can you ask it to hold them overnight and move them to your PC in the morning, or do you have to print them immediately, then scan them into the PC?

Last, but not least, have a close look at the warranty. While multifunction devices take up little space, cost less than the separate components they replace, and use less power, they have one major disadvantage. If something goes wrong with part of the system, the whole thing – and all of those services – are out of action until you get it fixed. Not a big concern, you say? Well, I had one stop printing in the middle of a long document recently and nothing I could do brought it back to life (it was not out of ink). The replacement unit the company sent me also stopped printing two days after it arrived. Fortunately, I have more than one computer equipped with a modem and fax software; otherwise, I'd be stuck.

Another feature to seek is tight integration between the software driver and the machine. At least one model (the HP OfficeJet LX) allows you to enter group dial and delayed transmission information (which means, send this lot after midnight when I'm asleep and the rates are less expensive) into the fax software, then have it stored in the device. You can turn the computer off and still have your instructions carried out.

None of the systems listed in the table below promise to be able to handle corporate office-level copying. Think of these as more along the lines of a personal copier where you don't need to make more than ninety-nine copies and have all day to do it. Most of the models will copy up to three pages per minute, and may take nearly a minute (or more) to produce an original page. Features to check here are the ability to reduce or enlarge (and the subtlety of the degree of zoom) and the number of shades of grey that the system can both see and reproduce.

One last observation, which may justify dropping fax from these devices and may also, along with the one-fault-kills-all problem, account for lacklustre sales: E-mail. For the monthly fee you pay an

Internet Service Provider, you get unlimited access to e-mail from your computer. Receiving a fax costs money for ink and for paper and; unless you scan the document into your computer or have it sent there in the first place, then subject it to optical character recognition, you'll have to retype any information you want to use in a word processing document. A waste of time.

I use fax only when I want something in a hurry that isn't already in digital format. My multifunction printer/scanner isn't even hooked to my PC. I have the room, and the need, for separate products that provide better quality than it can. When it's working, I use it primarily as a copier. Think about it.

Multifunction printer spec tips

Multifunction: Good. Which functions? Simply because it says "multifunction" doesn't mean it provides them all. Some models don't scan, some don't connect to a PC for faxing, and some don't fax. Only a few models do all that and offer a phone answering system as well.

Fax at *nn* seconds per page: There are two common speeds for modems to have in multifunction devices, 14.4 Kbps and 9.6 Kbps. The companies who make these things know that you're keenly aware that 14.4 is faster than 9.6. So, to confuse you, they've started quoting seconds per page instead, a figure that will change depending on how densely the page is covered. The equivalents? Nine seconds per page equals 9.6 Kbps. Six seconds per page equals 14.4 Kbps. Keep in mind that some companies shoot themselves in the foot by being too honest here and include the time it takes to scan in images with the transmission time.

Scan/copy/print at *nn* pages per minute: "Personal" laser printers (see above) typically print at 4 to 6 ppm. Faster home/office lasers print at 8 to 12 ppm. However, the specs are often stated in such a way that makes you think you can fax and scan at these speeds instead.

***nn*-page memory**: Higher is better. Remember that it takes about 1 MB for a typical laser to print a full-page graphic. This figure doesn't help you determine how much memory the printer actually has. A rough estimate: 58 pages equals 730 KB, but again, the number of pages you can store depends on how much information there is on each page. These figures, as well as those for transmission and scan speeds, are based on an "industry standard" letter-sized sheet with 5 per cent page coverage.

nn **levels of grey**: The unit may scan and print at 64 levels of grey or more, but it most likely sends faxes in black and white. Look for ones that will actually fax halftones.

Print in colour: Wonderful. To my knowledge, the HP 1150C and Xerox HomeCentre are the only two units that will also scan and copy in colour. Neither unit faxes at all. In fact no multifunction unit will fax in colour because no one could receive the results.

Missing specs: It's amazing what some companies consider to be full disclosure in the specifications they provide for the public. I found several that didn't mention memory, print method, speed of transmission or speed of scan, levels of grey, TWAIN compatibility and a whole bunch of other useful bits of information. In my experience, companies brag about what they have and go mysteriously quiet about things they lack. Keep that in mind.

Multifunction Printers

Consumer Multifunction Printers	Canon MultiPass C2500*	Canon MultiPass C3000	Canon MultiPass C5000	Canon MultiPass L600	Brother MFC-390MC
Suggested Retail Price	$975 Cdn list	$349 US street	$395 US street	$599 US street	$679
Width x depth x height (inches)	19x19x14	15.8x14.2x7.8	15.8x14.4x8.1	14.4x14.4x9.5	9.4x11.8x5.3
Weight (pounds)	17	13.2	12.3	18.9	6.2
Capacity for paper/transparencies/envelopes	150/50/20	100/50/10	100/50/10	100/na/7	paper roll
Functions					
Fax	Y	Y	Y	Y	Y
Fax to/from PC	Y	Y	Y	Y	Y
Scan to PC	Y	Y	Y	Y	Y
Copier	Y	Y	Y	Y	Y
Print from PC	Y	Y	Y	Y	Y
Print/copy/scan in colour	Y / Y / Y	Y / Y / Y	Y / Y / Y	n/a	n/a
Answering machine	N	hookup only[2]	hookup only	hookup only	voice and fax
Printer					
Printer type	colour ink jet	colour ink jet	colour ink jet	monochrome laser	thermal transfer
Standard/maximum RAM	32K/32K	no info	no info	no info	512K/512K
Rated engine speed in black/colour (ppm)	5/>1	5 / 2	5 / 2	6 / na	2 / na
Maximum resolution with standard RAM (dpi)	720 x 360	720 x 360	720 x 360	600	200 x 400
Copier					
Makes multiple copies/collates	Y/N	Y / N	Y / N	Y / N	Y/Y
Enlarges/reduces	N/N	N / Y (mono only)	N / Y (mono only)	N / Y	N/N
Max copies	99	99	99	99	99

Consumer Multifunction Printers	Canon MultiPass C2500*	Canon MultiPass C3000	Canon MultiPass C5000	Canon MultiPass L600	Brother MFC-390MC
Fax and Scanner					
Scanner is TWAIN compliant	Y	Y	Y	Y	Y
Optical resolution fax/scanner (dpi)	203 x 196	200	300	360	200 x 400
Fax-modem speed (Kbps)	14.4	14.4	14.4	14.4	14.4
Scanner speed (seconds per page)	30	23	9 - 78 (mono), 39 - 274 (colour)[4]	9 - 20[4]	10
Black-and-white or grey-scale scanning	grey scale (64)	64 shades of grey or 24-bit colour	64 shades of grey or 24-bit colour	grey scale (256)	grey scale (64)
Document feeder capacity (pages)	20	20 (20 lb stock)	20 (20 lb stock)	20 (20 lb stock)	10
Fax document memory		672 KB (42 "pages"[3])	672 KB (42 "pages"[3])	"122 pages"[3]	15 min of voice or 20 pages (512 KB)
Telephone handset	Y[1]	N	N	N	Y
Number of pass-through telephony ports	2	2	2	2	2
Misc.					
Battery backup	1 hour	no mention	no mention	no mention	N
Warranty	1 year	1 year limited with InstantExchange (subject to restrictions)	1 year limited with InstantExchange (subject to restrictions)	1 year limited with InstantExchange (subject to restrictions)	1 year
Online support	BBS, WWW	BBS, WWW	BBS, WWW	BBS, WWW	WWW or e-mail
More info:	800-263-1121 or 905-795-1111	800-263-1121 or 905-795-1111	800-263-1121 or 905-795-1111	800-263-1121 or 905-795-1111	800-853-6660
Web site: http://www.	usa.canon.com	usa.canon.com	usa.canon.com	usa.canon.com	brother.com

Multifunction Printers cont'd

Consumer Multifunction Printers	Brother MFC 1950MC plus	Brother MFC 4550 plus	HP OfficeJet 350	HP OfficeJet 1150C Pro	Xerox Document WorkCentre 450C
Suggested Retail Price	$1,199	$1,999	$839	$1,329 Cdn List	<$700 street
Width x depth x height (inches)	14.8x15.9x8.4	15.1x17.8x9.9	17x16x11	21.3x17.7x12.8	no info
Weight (pounds)	13.2	18.8	20	32.2	no info
Capacity for paper/transparencies/envelopes	200/1/1	200/1/1	100/20/20	150/40/15	150/150/10
Functions					
Fax	Y	Y	Y	N	Y
Fax to/from PC	Y	Y	Y	N	Y
Scan to PC	Y	Y	Y	Y	Y
Copier	Y	Y	Y	Y	Y
Print from PC	Y	Y	Y	Y	Y
Print/copy/scan in colour	n/a	n/a	n/a	Y / Y / Y	Y/N/N
Answering machine	voice and fax	N	N	N	N
Printer					
Printer type	thermal transfer	monochrome laser	monochrome inkjet	colour inkjet	colour inkjet
Standard/maximum RAM	512K/1MB	512 K / 2.5 MB	256K/256K	1.5MB/1.5MB	no info
Rated engine speed in black/colour (ppm)	2 / na	6/-	3/-	8/4	6 or 4 / 15
Maximum resolution with standard RAM (dpi)	200 x 400	600 x 600	600 x 300	600 x 600 bw / 600 x 300 c	600 x 600 (mono) 300 x 300 (colour)
Copier					
Makes multiple copies/collates	Y/Y	Y/N	Y/N	Y/N	Y/Y
Enlarges/reduces	Y/Y	Y/Y	N/Y	Y/Y	Y/Y
Max copies	99	99	99	50	99

Consumer Multifunction Printers	Brother MFC 1950MC plus	Brother MFC 4550 plus	HP OfficeJet 350	HP OfficeJet 1150C Pro	Xerox Document WorkCenter 450C
Fax and Scanner					
Scanner is TWAIN compliant	Y	Y	Y	Y	Y
Optical resolution fax/scanner (dpi)	200 x 400	200 x 400	300 x 300	300 x 300	300 x 300
Fax-modem speed (Kbps)	14.4	14.4	9.6	n/a	14.4
Scanner speed (seconds per page)	10	7	50	varies	10
Black-and-white or grey-scale scanning	grey scale (64)	grey scale (64)	black and white	grey (256) and colour (16.7 m)	grey scale (64)
Document feeder capacity (pages)	20	30	20	1	20
Fax document memory	20 pages (512 KB up to 1 MB)	"up to 60 pages"	24 pages	n/a	"23 pages"[3]
Telephone handset	Y	Y	N	n/a	N
Number of pass-through telephony ports	2	2	1	n/a	2
Misc.					
Battery backup	N	N	N	N	N
Warranty	1 year	1 year	1 year	1 year	1 year
Online support	WWW or e-mail	WWW or e-mail	AOL, BBS, CIS, WWW	AOL, BBS, CIS, WWW	CIS, WWW
More info:	800-853-6660	800-853-6660	800-387-3867 or 905-206-4383	800-387-3863	800-ASK XEROX
Web site: http://www.	brother.com	brother.com	hp.com	hp.com	xerox.com

1 Extra-cost option
2 One phone jack is intended to be connected to an answering machine
3 Based on industry standard letter with 5% coverage
4 Depends on resolution and amount of data on each letter-sized page
5 6 ppm with optional high-capacity black cartridge, 4 with colour printhead
*Canon MultiPass 2500 may be discontinued when you read this

13

Graphics

Here, we're going to look at three product classes: video graphics controllers, monitors, and products designed to get television video into and out of your computer. None of them will have an accompanying product comparison table. My reason is quite simple: this segment of the industry changes so quickly that any product I list now will almost certainly be gone and replaced by something newer before this book gets off the presses. Just to give you one example, in 1997, the average speed for video graphics controllers increased seven different times (yep, just under every two months).

The technological bases for both the software and hardware for these products are also changing rapidly, although I'll make some safe predictions about where they'll go. For example, video graphics controllers are leaving the PCI bus in favour of the new Accelerated Graphics Port. Changes in Windows 98 affect how we use graphics and television input. Emergence of the Universal Serial Bus (USB) will affect TV image-grabber products and monitors. Monitor purchasers are moving away from 14- and 15-inch models to 17-inch and bigger, and flat panel, TFT monitors and wide-screen models are appearing in droves.

New players also keep getting into the act. In late 1997, for example, I did a roundup of TV products for *We Compute*. It was very thorough and covered every product including combination units (tuner, input, output, and grabber), those that only grabbed stills, and those that provided output only. Four months later, the number of products in some of the categories had increased six-fold.

In short, all three are rapidly shifting markets. So, instead of telling you what you could have bought way back then, I'll give you some information you can use in your homework on future purchases.

Video Controllers

This is not the section on television-related products. Here is where we'll talk about the devices used to get the video your computer produces on screen where anyone looking over your shoulder can see it. I'll use the generic term "controller" instead of circuit board or expansion card (or some variation of the two). Although a separate circuit card or expansion board may indeed provide these functions, the video controller could also be located directly on the system's motherboard or a multimedia chip could provide the functions.

There are some other bits of jargon associated with video graphics that we may as well deal with now. To begin to understand the issues involved in choosing a graphics controller you need to be familiar with pixels, resolution, colours, palettes, and acceleration.

A *pixel* (short for picture element) is the smallest unit on the screen that can be addressed by computer memory. In other words, it's the smallest portion of the picture that the computer can change. Think of the screen being divided into points similar to the dots that make up a newspaper photograph.

Resolution is the term used to describe how many pixels can be displayed on the screen at one time. A resolution of 640 by 480, for example, means 640 pixels horizontally and 480 rows of pixels vertically (for a total of 307,200). Doing the math here isn't simply an exercise; it will help you to understand why a graphics controller requires more memory to provide additional colours at higher resolutions and why your system will slow to a crawl if you don't have it.

For instance, at 1024 x 768, there are 786,432 pixels. If each pixel at that resolution is called upon to be any one of 16 colours, we're dealing with 12,582,912 choices. At 256 colours, the controller has to deal with 201,326,592 factors. At 65,536 or 16.7 million colours, my calculator gives up.

Colours refers to the number of colours that can be displayed on screen at any one time, while the *palette* is the total number of colours the system can generate.

To put more colour into your system as you increase resolution, the controller must be able to do two things. It must have the ability to assign more bits of data to colour rendering and it has to have enough memory to produce the results. Basic PC colour requires only 4 bits of data to produce 16 shades and very little memory is needed. Better PC colour requires 8 bits of data producing 256 shades simultaneously. You'll need at least 256 KB to get this many at 640 by 480. To get 65,536 shades requires 16 bits of data and 512 KB of memory at 640 by 480. You'll need 1 MB to generate 24-bit, 16.7 million shade colour at 640 by 480, 2 MB to get it at 800 by 600 and 4 MB to render it at 1024 by 768.

Why do we stop at 24-bit colour? Medical and optical research has shown that in the "best" of human eyes, each of the three colour receptors is capable of distinguishing up to 256 shades of colour (256 shades each of red, green, and blue). That's a total of about 16.7 million colours. For a graphics controller to produce these colours, it assigns 8 bits to each colour channel.

Whether you'll need 16.7 million colours at 1024 by 768 is a different story. Artists, desktop publishers, and designers may. Most of you won't. There are a few games and pictures from the Internet, but little else that uses more than 65,536.

Standards: Most of the early standards, such as VGA (video graphics array) and SVGA (super video graphics array) have fallen by the wayside. What you'll want to know is how fast the controller is when it produces the two-dimensional graphics common to most computer applications as well when it's rendering the three-dimensional images common to high-end games. You'll want to know how much video memory the controller has, of what kind, and what that will do in your system. You may care about how high a resolution the controller can produce, but as you'll see when we discuss monitors, the concern may be less than you imagine. You'll definitely care what kind of slot you need in order to plug the controller into your computer, if it isn't already on the system's motherboard (and if it is on the motherboard, you'll also want to know how to turn it off so it won't interfere with your plans if you wish to upgrade your video in the future).

MPEG: One standard, however, is worth mentioning. Motion Picture Experts Group (MPEG) is a method of encoding (compressing) and decoding (decompressing) motion video. MPEG video may come from the Internet or, more likely, from digital video/versatile disc (DVD). If a product mentions MPEG, that's good, but start asking questions. Does it support MPEG-1 or the newer – and better – MPEG-2? Is the MPEG decoding handled in hardware on the controller (good) or is it merely a software emulation in the controller's driver (not as good)? To get MPEG hardware, do you have to add what is known as a daughter-board or a whole new circuit board (and do you have either enough space or extra slots to accommodate it)? How much does that cost?

Acceleration: Modern graphics controllers use a variety of ways of producing images quickly. The speed with which you can move windows full of information around on screen, or redraw a page, or get those space boogers lined up for another shot, is a function of the computer's central processor (CPU) and the video controller working together. When the software asks the CPU to change a point on screen (e.g., make this pixel colour 102,987), the CPU does the calculation and passes the instruction to the video controller, which in turn passes its command to your monitor. Anything that speeds the process up will be welcome.

Four of the more popular ways to do this are to increase the internal bandwidth the video controller uses to do its work; to add special, fast forms of memory to the video controller's input/output buffers, and more of it; to add a video coprocessor to the controller, which

.

relieves the CPU of some of its duties while providing special rendering techniques; and to use the relatively new AGP technology to "borrow" additional memory from the main system pool.

More bandwidth: In a Pentium or Pentium II-based PC, the external system bus uses 64 bits at a time to transfer data among components. This allows the system to move some very large numbers. Modern graphics controllers can't receive any more than 64 bits in any one cycle, but those at the high end use 128-bit internal buses to give them lots of room to chew on the numbers they do get.

Memory: Several memory schemes are employed. Instead of using slower DRAM (dynamic RAM), for example, many low- and mid-range controllers use faster EDO (extended data out) or even faster SGRAM (synchronous graphics RAM). Others use what is known as dual port memory, memory that can simultaneously receive data from the CPU and write it to the output buffer. Two of the best known variations are VRAM (video RAM) and WRAM (Window RAM). (See Chapter 8 for detailed definitions.) Adding memory to the controller not only allows it to display more colours at higher resolutions, but also aids in 3-D rendering and animation.

Special graphics coprocessors are a high art form. The engineering that goes into the controller's chipset and its coprocessor (also known as a digital signal processor) determine a lot of its characteristics. The same chipsets are often used by multiple brands, and which is the best, fastest, and so on, is the subject of hot debate. Your best sources of information will be magazines and USENET newsgroups devoted to computer gaming.

Accelerated Graphics Port (AGP): Developed by Intel and embraced by the graphics controller industry, AGP arrived with the introduction of the Pentium II with a 440LX chipset in mid-1997. It requires a special slot on the motherboard to add a controller later, but an embedded controller can also employ AGP, so long as it's accompanied by a motherboard chipset that supports it. You can't employ AGP if you don't have a chipset that explicitly supports AGP, or if the slot isn't present on your motherboard.

AGP is similar to MMX (the multimedia instruction set in the later-generation Pentium and Pentium II processors and their equivalents), the Katmai new instructions coming in early 1999, and AMD's

3D-NOW instructions in its K6-2 processor. They all need driver support from the operating system (not available until Windows 98) *and* they require special coding in software applications to wake them up. For example, when the first AGP controllers appeared and were tested against PCI models of *the same generation*, using standard non-AGP-optimized software, the only difference anyone could detect was price.

This is no longer true. Even without specific AGP software, these boards are now faster than a PCI-based equivalent. All the current research is going into AGP products, not PCI, because that's what the industry wants you to get. They find PCI too restrictive (you can't get at main system memory directly from the PCI bus, for example), and the sooner the last PCI-based graphics controller is off the market, the better they'll like it.

Summing up

Okay, if you're confused, let's make it simple. You want a graphics controller that will give you the best bang for the buck and suits what you want to do. If you plan to use your system primarily for business applications, 3-D game acceleration isn't going to be a big consideration. If you're planning to turn your system into a home entertainment system, then a controller that does everything including television (see below) is a good bet. If you're a gamer, you'll want to steep yourself in the acceleration/3-D chipset lore and pick a side in the game-speed debate. Artists, designers and desktop publishers will be looking for high resolution (for those 19- to 21-inch monitors) along with enough memory for 16.7 million colours at their chosen resolution.

Everyone, however, will benefit from a controller with respectable "2-D" acceleration features, whether it's to see a spread-sheet redrawn, to produce a "lost puppy" poster with a home desktop publishing program, or to use an interactive encyclopedia.

When you shop around for a graphics controller, you'll find some name brands repeated over and over: ATI Technologies (as of mid-1998, the company selling the largest number of controllers in the world), Matrox, Diamond Multimedia, Number Nine Corp., the Cirrus Logic division of Crystal Semiconductor, SiS (the same people who produce motherboard chipsets), and Trident are the most common (and popular in about that order). I'm sure it's just a coincidence that the two most popular are Canadian companies, ATI (Toronto) and Matrox (Montreal).

Before selecting the graphics controller for your system, see it in operation, using the software you want to run, on a monitor you can afford. And make no mistake, affordability is a major issue here. It is not only possible, but quite likely, that you will spend as much or more on the graphics controller/monitor combination for your computer as you paid for the computer itself. But we haven't even talked about monitors yet. They're next.

Monitors

Whether you're evaluating the monitor that's supposed to come with your new computer or you're shopping for a new monitor, your choices have never been more widely varied, nor have you ever been able to get so much for so little. The number and variation of models available are high, and prices keep falling.

If you have an unlimited budget, the size of your screen can be as much as 42 inches (but be prepared to shell out over $8,000). In the more sensible segment of the market in mid-1998, prices were under $1,000 Cdn (or $820 US). One American online discount dealer presented me with a list of 625 different models in the 14-, 15-, 17-, 19-, and 20-inch ranges. In fact, the availability of 20-inch models from manufacturers such as Sampo Corp., Viewsonic, and a few others at close to $1,000 was one of the computer market stories of 1997.

There are so many issues to discuss that I've broken this section down into three main topics: basic monitor technology (call it Monitors 101), a section covering jargon, and tips on reading specifications. I've also included some shopping hints as well as some pointers on how to get better use of your monitor (with less strain on you and your eyes). I'll start with a broad overview of the market as it existed while I was writing.

Overview

Computer monitors continue to be grouped in price depending on their size, but there are now two generic types. As a class, monitors using a cathode ray tube (CRT) are less expensive than the newer "flat" models using the same thin film transistor (TFT) screens as notebook computers. As a general rule for both classes, the larger the screen, the more you'll pay. For CRT models, individual monitors within each price group can be divided into "value" and "professional" models, and both types can now be found with built-in speakers. TFT monitors are priced at a point where none of them fit the definition of "value" products.

You should try to find a monitor with USB connectors and they should do double-duty. In theory, you can hook together a chain of 127 USB devices at any one time (e.g., connecting a keyboard, mouse, scanner, external storage device(s), digital camera and so on). The reality is quite different. Many USB devices not only pass and receive data over the connection, they also get their power that way, too. And, after every four or so devices, there usually needs to be a booster, known as a powered hub. If the monitor does have USB, one of the first things you should check is whether it also functions as a powered hub. Expect to be grateful if it does, and to pay for the privilege.

Your first assignment is to decide what screen size you want. Fifteen inches is by far the most popular size for home and small business users (over 40 per cent), with 17-inch closing the gap – particularly for those using any kind of desktop publishing application or drawing program. The 14-inch model is being forced out of the market by aggressive pricing and lack of consumer demand. In the professional/power user/workstation market, 20- and 21-inch monitors account for half the sales, with 17-inch units taking 35 per cent. According to Stanford Resources Inc., display technology analysts, the average price of a 15-inch monitor with .25 mm dot pitch and aperture grille (see below) in 1998 was about $400 Cdn.

Keep in mind that although computer monitor sizes are based on the diagonal measurement of the screen, the mask around the monitor face is *not* deducted from the figure. The viewable area may be anywhere from one to one and a half inches less than the quoted screen size, depending on the brand and model.

Screen technology is the next biggest factor in price. We've already noted that TFT screens – almost always called LCD Flat Panel Displays – will be the most expensive relative to size. Of the CRT models, shadow mask screens (with round dots forming the image) are less expensive than (and not as sharp as) the rectangular mask found in aperture-grille models (see "Monitors 101," below). Since Sony's patent on the Trinitron tube expired, several manufacturers have introduced aperture-mask screens (and the prices have also fallen). Note, however, that Sony still owns the rights to the name "Trinitron," so you'll still see it.

How quickly the monitor repaints its screen – its vertical refresh rate – will determine whether it flickers. If the refresh rate is less than 72 times per second (72 Hz), you may see a flicker. Below 60 Hz, you'll definitely see it. A good quality monitor will produce a refresh rate of 72 to 85 Hz or higher *at the resolution you intend to use* (see "Spec tips," below).

The minimum upper resolution for today's 15-inch monitors is 1024 by 768, while some models at the top of the price range can go higher. (See "Spec tips" and the pictures that accompany them to find out why this might not be such a big deal.) Nevertheless, the higher the resolution a monitor can reach, the more it will cost.

Dot- and stripe-pitch are perhaps the least understood of the specifications for monitors and, wouldn't you know it, some low-end manufacturers are fudging the results. In general terms, when everyone plays by the standard rules, the lower the dot- or stripe-pitch number, the sharper the picture and the more expensive the monitor. (See "Monitors 101" and "Spec tips.")

The more things you can change about your monitor and the more convenient it is to change them, the more it will cost. If you can adjust a long list of characteristics, if the controls are in front and easy to understand and if there is an on-screen menu with instructions covering how to use them, you'll pay extra.

Other special features add to price, but some don't. For instance, all monitors available in Canada are also sold on the US market, where you can't sell one any more if it isn't "Energy Star" compliant. Anything you find here will be, too.

Concerns over low-level radiation emanating from monitors have led to two international standards. The Swedish MPR-II standard is fairly strict, regulates electromagnetic, magnetic, and electric field emissions, and has recently been renamed SWEDAC). The TCO '92 or TCO '95 standards, also from Sweden but used throughout Europe, are even stricter and regulate electromagnetic field emissions as well as power and energy conservation standards. Any Canadian or American standards relating to low-level radiation are less than both Swedish standards. Monitors may come with none, one, or both emission standards, and this can affect price. If this is important to you, find out whether either the MPR-II or TCO '95 standards have been revised since this book was written.

Whether the monitor is "plug 'n' play" compatible with Windows doesn't make a whole lot of difference so far as I can tell. At the least, however, it *may* allow you, if your graphics controller's driver cooperates, to change resolutions and colour depth on the fly without rebooting. Windows doesn't need to know what kind of monitor you have, but your graphics controller definitely does. Find out what monitors your graphics controller supports before you go shopping, or have a look at its manual at least to see what values it needs. Then check the monitor manual to see how many of them you can force it to comply with. (Of course, a nice long conversation with the vendor and a written guarantee on the sales agreement that the two will work together wouldn't hurt, either).

Last, but not least, you may care whether the monitor is multi-synchronous, but most people don't need this and don't need to pay extra to get it. "MultiSync" is an NEC brand name. Multisynchronous means the monitor is equally happy to be used on a PC, a Power-Thingy, or a SunSPARC workstation. Most of us have only one type of computer and don't need to rotate monitors among different types for maintenance reasons. Hint: If you *do* own a Mac, you'll find that multisynchronous monitors sold in PC stores are just a bit (and sometimes a bunch) less expensive than those sold at Mac outlets.

More hints: If, when you go looking for specifications, the actual viewable area of the screen isn't one of the figures provided, start wondering what else the manufacturer isn't telling you. (Gotcha!)

One company can manufacture monitors for another, acting as the OEM (original equipment manufacturer) supplier. It isn't unusual, for example, for IBM, Compaq, Dell, and others to have theirs manufactured by a mainstream monitor maker, then to put their own name on the result.

Monitor jargon

Barrel: The (annoying) appearance of convex edges to the display image. (See Pincushion, below.)

Composite video input: The monitor receives only one signal – a composite signal – from the computer. The monitor must then decode the signal to determine and separate red, green, blue, and sync signals that can then be processed by the monitor.

Convergence: The colour monitor's ability to scan the three electron beams onto a single point to produce white. When convergence is misaligned (misconvergence), you get letters with ghosting images in one or more of the colours. May be corrected by degaussing or you may need a monitor doctor.

CRT: Cathode ray tube.

Dot or stripe pitch: The picture on your monitor is composed of glowing phosphor dots *and the space between them*. The less space there is, the more dots there are and the sharper the image is. The phosphors are grouped by threes (red, green and blue) so that areas of the screen can change colour.

The diagonal distance between phosphors of the same colour is the dot or stripe pitch. It's easy to measure on a shadow mask because the dots are distinct, but much harder to measure on an aperture grille, which uses rectangular areas, not dots.

The smaller the dot pitch number, the sharper the image, and a pitch of about .31 mm is as high as you'd want to go. Today's median in .28 mm, while you'll pay extra for .26 mm or less.

ELF: Extremely low frequency. For magnetic fields and alternating electric fields, the ELF fields range from 5 Hz to 2 KHz.

Full-scan: The capability to enlarge the image to the edge of the screen. Not all models can do this at all resolutions (only the expensive ones).

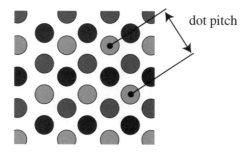
dot pitch

Shadow Mask

stripe pitch

Aperture-grille Mask

MPR: The Swedish National Board of Measurement and Testing. This council produces the recommendations for the magnetic and electrical field emissions guidelines. The council's name has been changed to SWEDAC and so will the name of the "standard."

Non-interlaced: You can't get interlaced monitors any more, thank goodness. They used to flicker. Today's non-interlaced monitor refreshes itself quickly enough that it can paint all lines, in one pass (no flicker), before the phosphors at the top of the screen go dim. The minimum refresh rate (see below) to achieve this is 60 times per second (60 Hz), but you'll still see a flicker unless yours does so at 72 Hz or higher at the resolution you most want to use.

Pincushion: The appearance of concave edges on the display image. (See Barrel, above.)

pixel pitch

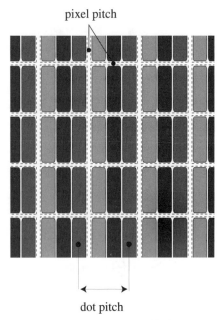

dot pitch

Pixel and dot pitch for an LCD/TFT screen.

Each LCD pixel (picture element) is composed of three crystal cells, each powered by one or two transistors (the extra is a backup in case the primary transistor dies, but is activated at the factory during quality control testing, not when you're using it). The transistors may be located in such a way that they block some light, or may be on the cell walls to produce a brighter display. The three cells represent red, green, and blue. Typical pixel pitches (the distance between pixels) is from 0.2 mm (200 microns) to 0.02 mm (20 microns). Typical dot pitch varies between 0.26 mm and 0.30 mm.

Pixel: Literally, picture element – the smallest area on the screen the computer's graphics controller can change.

Plug 'n' play: Allows devices, including monitors, to send information about their capabilities – screen size, resolutions supported, and refresh rates – automatically back to the system. Allows you to change these factors interactively without a system reset through Windows 98 or later.

Raster: The overall area that is scanned by the electron guns.

Refresh Rate: The image on the monitor is not static. It is constantly redrawn. The *horizontal scan rate*, expressed in kilohertz

(KHz), is the number of pixels that can be painted horizontally in one second. As the resolution increases, so must the horizontal scan rate. A monitor's upper horizontal scan rate will determine the high end of its resolution range.

The number of times the monitor can redraw the screen per second is determined by its *vertical refresh rate* (or simply, refresh rate). Monitors that don't redraw the image at high speed flicker or jitter. The absence of jitter is one key measure of how good that monitor is. Flicker can cause eyestrain and headaches, and can be especially pronounced under fluorescent light. The vertical refresh rate will also change depending on resolution, with the more expensive monitors being able to achieve a consistently high rate regardless of resolution. Consider a refresh rate of 72 Hz (72 times per second) at the resolution you plan to use most often as the minimum for rock-steady display and comfortable use.

Resolution: Typical (and comfortable – see "Spec tips," below) resolutions include 640 by 480 for a 14-inch screen, 800 by 600 for a 15-inch screen, and 1024 by 768 for a 17-inch monitor. Many monitors and graphics adapters are capable of higher resolutions such as 1280 by 1024 and 1600 by 1200. Some manufacturers will give suggestions for resolution on their monitors instead of telling a consumer the maximum the monitor can display.

RGB video input: The monitor receives red, green, and blue signals separately from the computer. These signals are sent directly to the electron guns for processing. You need a special set of RGB connectors on both graphics controller and monitor to use RGB, and most low- and medium-priced monitors don't have them. Most monitor/graphic card combinations use composite video instead (see above). Only rare, and more expensive, components use RGB and have the requisite connectors to do so. It's more common to see RGB used to connect to expensive data projectors or to high-end TV monitors for presentations.

Shadow mask: See "Monitors 101."

Super VGA: Technically, the SVGA (super video graphics array) "standard" calls for an interlaced signal at a resolution up to 800 by 600. A later, unofficial, addition to the "standard" raised the upper resolution to 1024 by 768. A monitor advertised as an "SVGA monitor" only has to provide the minimum 800 by 600 resolution to fit the description. It says nothing about dot pitch, vertical refresh rate, resolution range, controls or any of the other factors discussed above or below. (Gotcha!)

SWEDAC: Swedish Board for Technical Accreditation. This council produces the recommendations for the Swedish magnetic field emissions guidelines. Its previous name was MPR.

TCO: Swedish Confederation of Professional Employees. Developed the TCO '92 and '95 standards for low electric and magnetic emissions.

VLF: Very low frequency. For magnetic fields and alternating electric fields, the VLF fields on monitors range from 2 KHz to 400 KHz.

VLMF: Very low magnetic field, or same as VLF but only for magnetic field emissions that are more commonly accepted in Europe than the MPR/SWEDAC standards, which are less stringent.

VGA: IBM's video graphics array "standard" that includes the following resolutions: 320x200, 640x200, 640x480; 320x400, 640x350, 720x350; and 360x400, 640x400, 720x400.

Monitors 101

How a colour monitor works

(For details of how a TFT screen works, please see Chapter 9. For CRT models, read on.)

Inside a CRT colour monitor is a cathode ray tube, also called a picture tube. It has electron guns, a mask, and a glass screen coated on the inside with colour phosphors. When activated, the electron guns fire beams that are moved around the screen. They are tightly focused (or converged) and, from your point of view, start scanning in the upper left corner, move across to the right side, drop down a line, then start again. (See Refresh Rate, above.)

The mask shields and directs beams to specific phosphors. The phosphors illuminate or glow as the beam strikes them but only for a brief time.

Masks

After you've decided on the size of your monitor, the next factor that most heavily affects its price is the technology involved in displaying its picture. The CRT mask is a major component of the picture tube. There are two major types of CRT masks, the shadow mask and the aperture grille – also called a stripe mask. Both types can produce excellent image quality.

An aperture-grille monitor employs rectangular holes and displays images with rich, saturated colours that are brighter than shadow-mask colours. Despite producing sharp images, however, an optical illusion makes it appear that the image is slightly bowed at the outside edges. There is also an ultra-thin wire (on 14- or 15-inch models, with two of them at 17 inches or above) visible across the screen, holding the mask in place. (Although within a *very* short period of time you don't see it any more.) Popular aperture-grille technologies include SonicTron from ViewSonic, DiamondTron from Mitsubishi, and Trinitron from Sony.

The shadow mask is the technology used in most monitors and it's the least expensive to produce. A shadow mask uses round holes and appears to offer more precise images than the aperture grille. The best shadow masks are made of INVAR, an alloy that has high heat resistance to withstand prolonged usage without distortion. NEC's "CromaClear" tubes, while advertising a small dot pitch and using marketing jargon that may lead you to believe it uses an aperture grille, actually uses a shadow mask with oval instead of round holes.

Selecting between shadow mask and aperture-grille monitors is a matter of user preference and applications. For colour graphics applications such as electronic desktop publishing, the aperture grille is often preferred for its ability to display colours more vividly. However, engineers doing CAD/CAM (computer aided design/computer aided manufacturing) and other technical illustrators may prefer shadow-mask technology for precision drawings and the better representation of flat displays.

How colour monitors display colours

Three primary-coloured phosphors coat the inside of a CRT: red, green, and blue. These three colours are combined in different intensities to produce all the colours available. For example, if all three colour phosphors are activated, they produce white.

Note that red, green, and blue – or RGB – is the colour scheme used in monitor technology, while the vast majority of colour printers use cyan, magenta, yellow, and sometimes black – or CMY(K). That's why good monitors and colour devices such as scanners and printers come with calibration software to help you minimize the difference between what you see on screen and what is finally printed.

Controls

Any monitor you buy will have brightness/contrast, vertical height/position and horizontal width/position controls. However (trust me on this), digital controls that also affect geometric parameters – tilt (the picture's rotation), keystone and trapezoidal skew (the ability to make the corners 90 degrees), and barrel/pincushion (the ability to make the vertical edges straight, not bowed in or out) – will come in handy. Whether the monitor has on-screen representations of the controls is entirely your choice, but you'll pay extra if it does.

You'll also want the monitor to be able to "remember" the settings you make regardless of the resolution you use and have internal circuitry to make the picture fill the full screen regardless of resolution (many low-end models still don't do this).

Last, but not least, you'll want a button you can push to *degauss*, or demagnetize, the screen. You'll know it's time to utilize this control when you begin to see blobs of ill-defined colour gathering in the corners of your screen or when characters appear to get blurry (i.e., misconvergence).

Static and screen-dust bunnies

Yup, between you and your monitor there will be static. It's not dangerous, but if you place your hand near the screen surface and feel a tingle, that's static electricity representing the low voltage in your body compared to the high voltage inside the monitor. If you can feel the static on the screen, so can the dust in the air around you – and it must *like* it, because it will rush to collect on the screen's surface. Mid- to high-end monitors have better shielding to bleed this static discharge away from the screen so that they're dust-free. Low-end monitors may only paint the screen surface with an anti-static coating.

Spec tips

0.xx **mm dot pitch (or stripe pitch)**: Determines how many phosphor dots are on the inside of the monitor screen. Smaller numbers are better. A few naughty manufacturers at the low end of the market have started to measure the distance between the edge of the dots instead of from the centre, or to measure the horizontal distance (whichever is less) instead of the diagonal distance. It's hard to tell whether this has been done until you see two monitors side by side. The one with the grainy picture has had its numbers fudged.

Companies without aperture-grille models will claim that the rectangular mask rated at 0.25 mm is actually closer to a shadow mask at 0.27 mm (and I begin to smell male bovine excrement). I have both a 0.26 mm shadow mask monitor and two others with a 0.25 mm aperture grille. The picture on the aperture-grille models is sharper. Ads for monitors – or for really cheap (er . . . inexpensive) systems with monitors included – that don't mention the dot pitch are suspect. They may be offering monitors with a dot pitch of 0.35 mm, 0.39 mm or even as high as 0.43 mm – big enough to see the spaces, cheap to produce, and lousy to use.

xx **Hz refresh rate**: Quoting a refresh rate without also quoting the resolution in use tells you nothing. The maximum rate quoted may only be available at the monitor's lowest resolution. You want to know its maximum rate at all resolutions you're likely to use.

Anti-glare: The monitor face may have been treated to reduce glare, but that won't do you nearly as much good as if it has been shielded against static (see above). Otherwise, you'll constantly be cleaning dust off the surface.

Anti-radiation: Without stating whether the "standard" is MPR-I, MPR-II, TCO '92 or TCO '95 terms such as "anti-radiation," "MPR" (or its replacement, "SWEDAC"), or "PCO" don't tell you anything.

Colours: Your graphics controller and the amount of memory it has determine the number of colours you can see on screen, *not* your monitor. The only exception here is if you're buying a used system that is so old it has either a CGA or EGA monitor attached. Don't. It is even more difficult to find a monochrome monitor anywhere.

Energy-saving, "Green," or Energy Star compliant: Virtually all monitors shipped into Canada are also sold in the U.S. where they *must* be Energy Star compliant. Only worry if it isn't mentioned. Note that if DPMS (desktop power management system) isn't mentioned, the monitor may not power down automatically after a period of inactivity.

Flat-panel display: If you opt for one of the expensive flat-panel TFT displays, note that many of them require a special video connector at the computer. Unless you purchase a new computer that already has both standard and flat-panel connectors on it (such as some Compaq Presario models), then you'll want to make sure the special conversion adapter you'll need comes with the monitor, even if you have to pay extra to get one. As with TFT screens on notebooks (see Chapter 9), the warranty conditions covering dead transistors need to be spelled out clearly.

Resolution: As you increase resolution, more pixels are displayed on the screen and more objects become visible. However, the screen *size* doesn't change. The average icon on the desktop in Windows 9x will be about three-quarters of an inch wide at 640 by 480 on a 15-inch monitor, it will be less than half an inch wide at 800 by 600, and closer to a quarter-inch wide at 1024 by 768. At some point, text on screen or lines in a drawing will become too small to use effectively.

Comfortable resolutions, depending on monitor size are 640 by 480 on a 14-inch monitor, 800 by 600 on a 15-inch model, 1024 by 768 on a 17-inch screen and 1280 by 1024 on a 20-inch display. While you *can* run higher resolutions (if your graphics controller supports them) than those listed here, you may not be comfortable doing so. It helps to keep in mind that most multimedia CDs (games, encyclopedias, etc.) are optimized for 640 by 480.

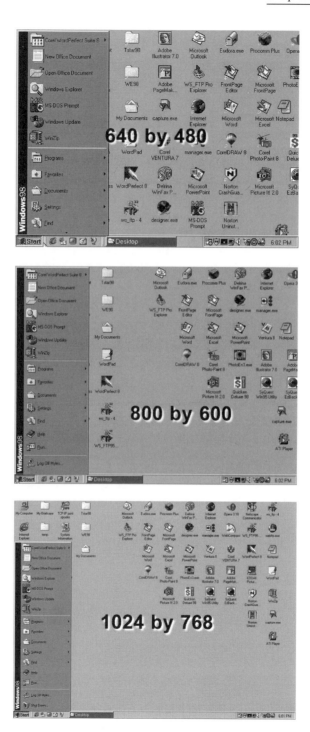

How to Pick a CRT Monitor

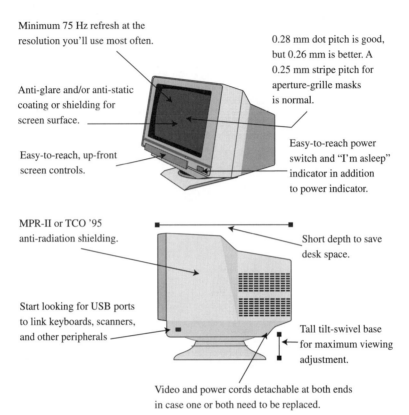

Minimum 75 Hz refresh at the resolution you'll use most often.

0.28 mm dot pitch is good, but 0.26 mm is better. A 0.25 mm stripe pitch for aperture-grille masks is normal.

Anti-glare and/or anti-static coating or shielding for screen surface.

Easy-to-reach, up-front screen controls.

Easy-to-reach power switch and "I'm asleep" indicator in addition to power indicator.

MPR-II or TCO '95 anti-radiation shielding.

Short depth to save desk space.

Start looking for USB ports to link keyboards, scanners, and other peripherals

Tall tilt-swivel base for maximum viewing adjustment.

Video and power cords detachable at both ends in case one or both need to be replaced.

SVGA monitor: With this vague description in hand, you don't know anything about the monitor you're being offered. Although it is probably non-interlaced (see under "Monitor jargon," above), at least at resolutions up to 800 by 600, there is no guarantee it will be non-interlaced at higher resolutions – you don't want to work at an interlaced display (flicker, headaches, bad karma) – or that it will reach higher resolutions at all.

Television Video Products

When I did a survey of the TV/PC market in 1994, everyone was still wondering when the two technologies were going to come together in any meaningful way at a price that most consumers could afford. By the spring of 1998, most of the questions had been answered, although Windows 98, with its built-in penchant for television and its ability to run up to nine simultaneously attached graphics controllers and monitors, was posing more.

One of the more recent developments – and one that was long overdue – was the emergence of all-in-one graphics boards that provide accelerated two-dimensional and three-dimensional SVGA graphics, a TV-tuner for pulling in signals from cable or myriad other video devices, a still-frame grabber, MPEG (Motion Picture Experts Group) video playback and, just for the heck of it, SVGA to TV output. In 1998, there were only two on the market (although in multiple models). Toronto-based ATI Technologies led with its All-in-Wonder Pro board (both AGP and PCI versions). The second was the Stealth 64v-2001 TV from Diamond Multimedia. Not a lot of choices, but two more than were available previously.

Having all these services in a single graphics controller may seem like a lavish choice, but ponder this: If you're buying a system for your away-from-home student, a computer with one of these controllers in it makes it unnecessary to also provide a TV set. If the system also has a DVD-ROM drive and stereo speakers, it doubles as an entertainment centre. All in one, small, compact area; just the thing for cramped student apartments.

Another item to emerge recently uses the high bandwidth IEEE 1394 connection standard, also known as FireWire. Again, there were two products, one by Miro Video, the Video DV-100 (which captures motion and stills), and one by Sony, the DBVK-1000 (stills only). Both units were intended as video capture boards for the Sony Digital Handicam, but you can expect to see both additional video output devices and computer components designed to interact with them appearing soon.

And that leaves us with the remainder of the products. They can be categorized into two main groups: those that will get a TV signal into the computer and those that will take the computer video out to a television device. By far the largest number of devices are those designed to get TV video into a computer, and this group can also be broken down into several sub-categories.

Some of the input boards or devices include a tuner that can use either an antenna or cable (or both) to pull broadcast channels directly into the computer. Tuner boards may provide full-screen TV-video, TV in a window on the screen, or both. Devices with a tuner may also have the ability to grab still frames, to capture full-motion video (with or without audio), to display and even to record closed-captioning, to allow scheduled events, to give multi-channel previews and to do video conferencing. *But few of them can do all of these tricks.*

If a board has a tuner, it will most likely also allow video to come from other television video playback devices, such as a video camera, VCR, or laser disc. If it has no tuner, the only way to see broadcast channels will be if the external playback device has its own tuner.

Did I mention that most consumer devices in this genre, especially the entire class of products that only grab stills, have no tuner at all?

Computer-to-TV output devices have a range of prices – including the multi-thousand-dollar units for broadcast-quality output. Most consumer units tend to be external scan converters, which take the computer's video signal and pass it through some technomagic on its way to a television set or recording device. While the external nature of these devices makes setting them up relatively simple, you'll want to note any that either severely limit the resolution of the picture or the number of colours you'll be able to see.

Compatible?

I don't want to get too technical about the ways that television and computer video are different. I'll just say that television is produced by an analog, interlaced signal with specific synchronization requirements, horizontal and vertical refresh rates, vertical line depth and methods of producing either monochrome or full colour and that computers don't do things the same way. Television specifications change depending on whether we're discussing the North American television standard (NTSC), the PAL standard used in the UK and parts of Europe, Africa, and the Middle East, or the SECAM standard used in the rest of Europe and much of the Far East. When the United States moves exclusively to High Definition Television (HDTV) in 2006, all the bets will be off and everything will change again.

In the meantime, none of the current broadcast standards have much in common with modern computer video standards, and things get even stranger when we start talking about the difference in sync formats between PC and Mac. To top it all off, most people who want to mix PC and TV video also want to see both simultaneously with the TV in a window.

It makes engineers glassy-eyed. Bringing the two video formats together technically requires some nifty engineering. This is why, when you're considering one of the tuner/grabber products, you need to pay close attention to any special requirements the device may demand. Even if there isn't a specific caution in the marketing material, you'll never want to buy one of these without telling the vendor what type of computer you have (PC or Mac), which operating system you're using, and which version of it. Explain which brand and specific model of computer video graphics controller you have, the brand and model of your monitor (it can make a difference) and any other quirky software or hardware you'll be running at the same time. If there's a doubt at all, get a guarantee of compatibility written into the sales agreement. Check the manufacturers' Web sites for lists of compatible and *incompatible* products. And if you want to be *really* thorough, a call to the tech support departments of both the TV device and your existing video controller – before you make your purchase – might save you headaches later.

It starts to make the all-in-one products sound better, doesn't it?

TV/PC spec tips

All-in-one products:

nn MB Memory: This can only affect the number of colours seen at high resolutions in standard computer video operations. It has no effect on TV functions.

SVGA chipset: Although you could buy one to get TV signals into your computer without having to sacrifice an additional expansion slot, you probably won't want to watch TV on your computer all the time. Pay more attention to the board's 2-D and 3-D acceleration features and other standard graphics controller functions – you'll use them more often.

Price: There was a significant price difference between the two products mentioned above – and in this case, you got what you paid for . . .

Grabber/Tuner/Motion capture products:

Type: Some of these products do all of the above and some even add FM radio (not difficult because TV sound *is* an FM signal) and video conferencing. Others, however, have more limited functions. Not all products do all things, and you may see this reflected in the price.

Bus/connector type: Some of these products will use an expansion slot. Some will use a parallel port, USB (Universal Serial Bus) connector or IEEE 1394 (FireWire) port. What does the device need, and do you have any of that type available? If the device is designed to use your parallel port and you're not sure whether your parallel port is bi-directional and high-speed ECP (enhanced capabilities port) or EPP (enhanced parallel port), if you don't know whether your printer supports port sharing, or if you have another device already using the port along with your printer, you need to check a lot of things before you go to the store.

Special requirements: Because getting TV into a computer is a technical hassle, some companies are quite specific about which SVGA graphics controllers, software applications, and/or operating systems are compatible or *incompatible* with their products. If you can't visit the company's Web site or can't phone them, you must discuss what you already have and plan to do with the device with the retailer before you bring it home. Get guarantees of compatibility written on the sales agreement, or ask the vendor to install the product and to make it work – otherwise problems you encounter later are *your* fault.

TV sources: Having an idea of what you plan to attach to your new TV gizmo helps here. While some provide a full spectrum of sources, including cable, broadcast antenna, S-Video (Y/C) connector,

RCA composite connector, and Hi-8 connector (and in some cases, FireWire), some are more limited. Check the output connectors from your camera, VCR, video laser disc player, satellite hookup or whatever, before you go to the store.

Tuner: Not all products allow you to select broadcast channels on them, and instead rely on your video sources (such as a VCR with its own tuner). Not much fun if you hoped to get your signal from cable.

TV channel preview: This is a nice feature to have if you're simply browsing for something to watch; otherwise plan to keep your TV guide handy or have an Internet connection to download your local broadcast schedule from Microsoft's special Web site for Windows 98 users.

Saves stills/motion: If you're planning to edit motion video, hardware and software that uses Motion Picture Experts Group (MPEG) encoding will save you oodles of disk space. The Windows .AVI (Audio Video Interface) format is a space hog. It's also nice to have a choice of still-frame save formats (such as .WMF, .BMP, .JPG, .TIF, .EPS, .PNG, .GIF, and .TGA, to name the most prevalent) so that you don't have to reprocess images before using them in different applications. Okay, okay, here's what the alphabet soup means:

.WMF – Windows MetaFile
.BMP – Bit-mapped graphic
.JPG – Joint Photographic Experts Group (JPEG)
.TIF – Tagged image file format
.EPS – Encapsulated PostScript
.PNG – Portable Network Graphic
.GIF – Graphic Interchange Format
.TGA – Targa format, a way of saving the video still in video format rather than converting it to a more common PC graphic format.

Max motion capture frame rate: Most manufacturers advertise that their product will capture television's thirty-frame-per-second rate without dropping frames. You may, however, be disappointed when you find there's a screen or window size or colour value limit that comes along with it. Only those companies that are really forthcoming about their product's strengths *and* limitations seem to publish the details.

Broadcast standards: If you never deal with any other video format other than the North American NTSC standard, you won't care about this. But if you're capturing images from PAL or SECAM sources, note that while some products handle all three, most have separate models that do one or another, but not all.

VGA to TV out: Normally a scan converter to deliver computer video to a TV is a separate product (see separate details below), but some of these models add this function to their bag of tricks.

TWAIN compliant: If you're buying this product primarily for its still capture features, get one that is TWAIN compliant. Only a limited number of tuner/grabber products have a software driver that is TWAIN compliant – but we can hope to see more in the future. If it is TWAIN compliant, you'll see it in the promotional material. If it isn't TWAIN won't be mentioned, and you don't want it (run away). (See Chapter 11 for a full discussion of TWAIN.)

VGA to TV scan converters:

These products are usually meant for corporate applications and are intended to allow computer video from an application such as a presentation program to be sent to an ordinary television set for sharing with a larger audience. Broadcast-quality models come in the multi-thousand dollar price range.

Because consumer models tend to limit either the size of the output picture or the maximum number of colours you can see on screen, few of them are suitable for doing things such as playing high-end games or surfing the Internet on a big screen. Look for those with high resolutions and 24-bit colour.

Only one manufacturer appears to make models in this category that are also full-fledged SVGA controllers (ATI), and only one explicitly outputs computer audio as well as video (Digital Vision TelevEyes/SC). Some don't mention audio, which generally means that there is no audio.

Complaints about these products focus on their tendency to flicker or to cut off portions of the screen. Ask to see a demonstration in the store, or get a guarantee written on the sales agreement saying that whether it works or not, you can take it back if the picture quality isn't up to your expectations.

14

Things That Click When They Move, Bop When They Stop, and Whirr When They Stand Still

It's time to look at cases, pointing devices (such as a mouse), keyboards, uninterruptible power supplies, and some related odds and ends.

Down to Cases

We take computer cases for granted, but there are a few things you should make sure your case has that will help you enjoy your computer as time goes by. When we talk about the system's case, we're referring to the tin box in which all the other internal parts are stored. For some people, the computer is only two or three parts: the monitor, keyboard, mouse, and "CPU" (in other words, the box in which are located the motherboard, hard drive(s), floppy drive, CD-ROM, etc.). I don't like the term CPU applied to this collection of components because it confuses people. I reserve "CPU" as applicable only to the central processor itself, not the case and everything in it.

If you're purchasing a name brand system, you won't get much choice over case configuration. You get what they sell, but if two such systems from different companies are equal in all other ways in your eyes, then it may be a deciding factor. Of course if you're building your own system, you can purchase the case separately from among myriad choices. If you're having a local retailer custom-assemble a system for you, then you can also discuss the type of case you'd like.

You must pick a case that matches your motherboard. The different form factors used in the older AT-style, Socket 7 motherboards and the newer ATX-style boards for Pentium II processors and their variations (see Chapter 7) means that each fits a different style of case. If you think you may change motherboards in the future, you may have to change the case, too.

There is no way to determine whether a case is a desktop or a tower other than from the way the label is attached and the orientation of the drive bays – but in most instances, it really doesn't matter. Floppy and hard disk drives don't care whether they lie flat or on their sides (but they do care about being upside-down or at an angle). So, if those are all the drives you have, you can turn your desktop case on its side anytime, just as you can lay a tower case flat. Some people insist that your hard drive should be formatted in the orientation in which it is going to operate, but I haven't had any bad experiences that lead me to worry about this. Most vendors will sell you an inexpensive plastic stand if you're nervous about a tower tipping over, but you likely won't need this unless you live with a large, boisterous dog or small kids.

About the only component that may not thank you for altering its orientation is a CD-ROM or DVD drive. If it's mounted vertically (i.e., on its side), the disc tray must have special clips to hold discs at the proper distance between the laser reader and the underside of the disc surface and to make sure it remains constant. If the tray on your CD-ROM drive doesn't have these clips, then it must be installed horizontally (instead of being mounted on its side). And, no, to my knowledge, you can't add the clips later.

If you want a tower case, there is no scale used to determine whether it's a full, "server-sized" tower, a mid-sized tower, or a minitower. All sizes are in the eye of the beholder.

The larger the case you get, the more it will cost – simply for the materials – but the more room you'll have to work inside it when upgrading components later. You'll have less of a chance of crimping a device cable when you put it back together. You'll have room to attach additional cooling fans. Depending on where you put it, you'll also have a greater chance of it taking a chunk out of your shins.

If you know, or even suspect, you'll be opening the case frequently to upgrade parts or to clean it out (a good idea), then a case with snap-off sides or some other scheme that makes it easy to get inside is something you can get if you hunt for it.

It's what is sold with the case and should accompany it that's of greater concern. Most PC systems will be quite happy with a 200-watt power supply. That's sufficient for a hard drive, floppy drive, CD-ROM drive, and most components that come with the motherboard. If, on the other hand, you even suspect that in the future you'll want to add another hard drive, a tape drive, additional internal SCSI or IDE devices and so on, then look for 230 to 250 watts or more. Most cases are sold with the power supply as part of the package. If you've done research to indicate that some power supplies are better than others, you may wish to try purchasing them separately.

It's also worth noting again that the LED read-out numbers on some cases, which appear to be clocking the speed of either the motherboard or CPU, are purely cosmetic. They are almost invariably set with jumper blocks or switches on the inside of the case itself. The vendor sets them; you too can set them, to any number you fancy.

Of course, in order to do this, you'll need the manual that should come with the case. It's also going to be invaluable on the day you open the case to add a component or to gently run a vacuum cleaner brush around the inside of the computer to clean up the dust that makes the system run hotter than it should. When you accidentally knock a wire loose connecting the motherboard to the system speaker, keyboard lockout, power supply, drive or case lights, you'll be glad you have the manuals for both your motherboard *and* case.

Your computer's case will both provide you with room to expand your system and limit the amount of expansion you can do. Pay attention to the drive bays and the cage that forms them. Do you have to remove the cage to get at other components (not good)? Are there several free bays available once you install your original complement of components? Do you have a good mixture of 5.25- and 3.5-inch bays for devices? Most backup devices, floppy drives and hard drives are 3.5 inches wide, while CD- and DVD-ROM drives are 5.25 inches wide. You can get inexpensive cradles that will hold a 3.5-inch device in a wide bay, but there's no way to put a 5.25-inch device in a narrow bay. Hard drives don't need to be visible from outside the case, but all removable media devices do need a case-front opening.

Last, but by no means least, is the case uniquely coloured, stylishly shaped, or do the drive bays require proprietary connectors to allow you to install additional devices? This is one of the bugaboos you'll face with some nationally advertised brand models. You won't be happy to learn that you have to purchase all future additional components from the same manufacturer at inflated prices in order to have them look good or fit at all.

Mice and Other Pointers

A mouse is an electronic pointing device. It may be attached either to a serial port (serial mouse), to a circuit board inside the computer (bus mouse), to a small, round PS/2 port (PS/2 mouse), or to a Universal Serial Bus (USB) port on the computer, the keyboard, the monitor, or some other device. A pointing device allows the user to manipulate the on-screen pointer, select objects, and perform many other tasks. It's almost impossible to live without one in Windows or any other graphical operating environment.

The mouse was originally designed by Xerox at its Palo Alto Research Centre (PARC) for the first graphical user interface – which the company's researchers also designed, and its marketing geniuses then nixed, believing it wouldn't go anywhere. It was later adopted by Apple for use in their original Macintosh systems, and is now an indispensable component in the PC world.

Computer mice don't eat crumbs; they hate them. Dirt and grime kills mice – dead. The mechanics of both mice and their upside-down cousins – trackballs – are the same. A rolling ball moves against pressure-sensitive rollers (usually three, but sometimes four). From the movement of each roller, the mouse generates binary codes representing two-dimensional movement co-ordinates. Other mechanics in the device also generate signals to indicate when one of its buttons has been clicked and released. Designs that began appearing in early 1997 now also include a rotating wheel. The wheel also produces a button-click (particularly useful in Internet browsers and in most applications running under Windows 98, even if the application wasn't originally designed to respond to wheel motions).

When these signals reach your PC it hasn't the foggiest idea what to do with them. The computer's CPU knows what a keyboard is and has instructions in its system ROM that tell it what the various key-strokes represent and how it's supposed to respond. But the signals coming from the mouse or any other pointing device need a software driver to interpret their signals for the CPU.

As important as having a driver is the ability to get an updated version when other software (such as the operating system) changes. Nationally advertised brand names, with telephone numbers you can call easily, or with Internet Web sites from which you can download an updated driver, have a better record of providing this needed service. They also cost slightly more, but that doesn't make them last longer.

I've never found a successful method of keeping anything with a ball alive for any appreciable length of time. Neither their cost nor the recognizability of their brand name has anything to do with longevity. Mice and trackballs alike all die, sometimes within a weekend, soon after they reach me (and I have a box of dead ones in my office as a constant reminder. Carefully painted, they're now Christmas tree ornaments – just kidding).

As my editor and my publisher's art director have reminded me, "prolonged work with a mouse can result in terrible shoulder strain." I'll add wrist and hand pain to the list. If these are problems you've been facing, or if you're one who finds the use of a mouse awkward, a couple of alternative technologies for moving the pointer around in Windows deserve some mention. For example, graphics tablets. For a number of years now, I've been using one by Wacom, together with either pressure-sensitive and non-pressure styluses or its four-button cursor "puck." Tablets are very popular among the CAD (computer-aided design) crowd, and I find them valuable for the artwork I do for various publications (anything I can sketch with a pencil, I can do with a stylus because it handles the same way). It took me over three years to kill a stylus (a record), and the tablet itself shows no signs of wear aside from a slight abrasion of its surface. Tablets are available in a variety of sizes from a variety of manufacturers, but none of them are as inexpensive as a generic mouse and some cost several times more (look to Cross and Cal-Comp as two other suppliers).

A nifty device that arrived a few years ago is the "eraser head" pointer found embedded in the keyboard of various models of notebook computers. While they take some time to learn to use smoothly and can be awkward when attempting to do any kind of drawing, they have the advantage of also being hardier than any trackball or mouse I've ever tried.

Last but not least is the most innovative approach of all, and one I recommend trying if all else fails: the touchpad, originally developed as the GlidePoint "mouse" by Cirque Corporation in Salt Lake City. Touchpads are replacing trackballs on notebooks, being sold as alternatives to mice for desktops, and can also be found built in to some specialty keyboards. A touchpad looks like a miniature graphics tablet, but you don't use a stylus; you use your finger instead. As you move your finger over the surface, the cursor moves. Tap the surface and it's the same as clicking the primary mouse button; double-tap and it's the same as a double-click, or you can use buttons on the edge. The small size of the touchpads make them ideal for use with a notebook and, unlike both a mouse and graphics tablet, even the separate units don't require a lot of desk space (and there are few moving parts to gum up and expire). A special button-tap sequence allows you to make it behave as though you were holding the left button down continuously, so it is also suitable for drawing (although not if very fine resolution is needed). A neat product, but one that has a learning curve and also uses a different set of muscles than you may be accustomed to using – and I know some people who never get used to them.

For special needs, such as presentations, there are a variety of mouse-like devices that use an extremely long cable or an infrared beam, allowing you to control a notebook from a distance. I've tried several, but no particular brand or model has overly impressed me.

The Key's the Thing

Short of the Microsoft Natural Keyboard, there have been few major innovations in keyboard technology since someone finally figured out that having cursor controls integrated into numeric keypads or function keys available only on the left side was a bad idea.

Nevertheless, there are two worth mentioning. Keep in mind that a keyboard advertised as a "Windows 95" (or 98) keyboard is not necessarily a Microsoft board ("seldom" is the word that springs to mind). It does mean it has one or more keys with the Windows wavy-window logo on them, and that these keys have special functions. Aside from calling up the Start Menu, various other keystroke combinations can provide other shortcuts.

The second innovation is the arrival of Universal Serial Bus models. The important thing to understand about them is that in order to use one:

- you need at least one USB port on your computer;
- special settings may need to be made in the computer's BIOS/CMOS setup before you can use the keyboard outside Windows;
- Windows 95 doesn't officially support USB – the patch files for it are rudimentary at best – you need Windows 98 for full USB implementation.

By the way, I have no hesitation recommending the *original* Microsoft Natural Keyboard. I've used a lot of types and styles, and this one puts less strain on my wrists than any other. It's best for a full-hand typist and "hunt-and-peckers" may not have as much fun with the slightly odd key layout. I'm not as happy with the newer Microsoft Natural Keyboard Elite. It takes up less desk space (it's both narrower and shorter), but the factor that appears to have the most impact on wrist pain – that it tilts down and away from you – is missing from the Elite. You'll also want to beware of imitations that look similar to the MNK for the same reason (they don't tilt down and away from you).

If yours is a standard keyboard, you can buy a moulded pad for your wrists to rest on that sits at the front of the board. Even better, says my editor, "While you type, try to keep your wrists high – about level with your elbow – as if you were playing the piano. That's what typists were trained to do in olden days, and we didn't hear any complaints about carpal tunnel syndrome (wrist nerve damage) from them."

Virtually all PC keyboards now have roughly the same layout: Twelve function keys across the top, separate alphanumeric, cursor, and numeric keypads, and dual CTRL, SHIFT, and ALT keys on either side of the spacebar with the "WinKey" positioned near them. You seldom see this style advertised as "enhanced" any more. Another innovation has shown up from companies such as Compaq and Hewlett-Packard – keyboards with extra keys programmed to aid in surfing the Internet. Third-party keyboard manufacturers, such as Key Tronic, also offer keyboards with programmable keys you can customize to suit yourself (www.keytronic.com).

Early IBM keyboards had a spring in each key that clicked when the key was pressed far enough to send a signal to the computer. I've spoken to some touch typists who prefer clicking boards because they know the keys are working without having to look at the screen. Whether you want the keys to click or thud softly is largely a subjective choice. Most people tend to favour the style they used when they first started computing. The important thing is to try out the keyboard – if how it feels is important to you – before you leave the store.

Uninterruptible Power Supplies and Power Conditioners

Once upon a time, the uninterruptible power supply (UPS) was regarded as something only corporate systems would ever need. That was in the days when certain widely used database applications would trash their records if not shut down properly and a sudden loss of power could be a disaster. But it was difficult for home users to justify the $350 (and up) cost. After all, if the computer shuts down while you're playing Quest, who cares? (You do, if you haven't "saved" recently.)

If you plan to use any modern flavour of Windows you'll care. Windows 9x will yell at you and perform other kinds of mean tricks if not shut down properly (such as a full hard-drive scan before you can get started again). While protection against blackouts is primarily what an uninterruptible power supply does, there are other electrical phenomena your local power company will send you that can be worse.

Dirty power comes in a variety of flavours (all of them bad):

Sags: Also known as brownouts, sags are short-term decreases in voltage levels and the most common type of power problem. Sags can "starve" a computer of the steady power it needs to function, causing frozen keyboards and unexpected system crashes with the end result of lost data. For example, you may get a slight voltage drop that isn't enough to cause your computer to reset, but is just enough to corrupt your system's memory while data is being written to disk.

Sags are typically caused by the start-up of another electrical device (including motors, compressors – such as in refrigerators – elevators, shop tools, automatic washers and dryers, and so on). They are also the electrical utility's short-term solution for coping with extraordinary power demands (during the supper hour as people turn on electric ranges or on especially hot days when folk run their air conditioners). The local company may also decrease voltage to suburban neighbourhoods (where you may have your home office) during the day when other areas such as business or manufacturing districts power demands are at their peak.

Blackouts: A blackout is a total loss of utility power caused by excessive demand on the power grid, or some sort of disaster, such as the 1998 ice storm in Quebec and Ontario. Sudden blackouts can cause databases to scramble their files, will result in loss of any work currently in memory, may cause a hard disk crash and loss of the file allocation table (which scrambles all the data on the hard drive), and will give networks the screaming fits – particularly if it takes place during a system backup.

If you are using Windows 9x or NT, a blackout will also prevent the orderly shutdown that these operating systems require in order to keep their files straight. I had one while writing this book and lost half a day reconstructing a chapter. Fortunately, no other damage was done, but you can guess that a "UPS" is going to eat up part of the advance money, just as soon as I'm done.

Spikes: Also known as an impulse, a spike is an instantaneous, dramatic increase in voltage. Akin to the force of a tidal wave, a spike can enter electronic equipment and damage or completely destroy components. Typically caused by a nearby lightning strike, spikes can also occur if utility power lines are downed. Spikes can enter your system through power lines, obviously, but might also come to visit via printer cables, modem cables, or telephone lines. (A phone line spike once struck one of my modems dead). Spikes can also arrive via the data line and/or USB port connecting an external backup drive or scanner.

Surge: A short-term increase in voltage, typically lasting 1/120 of a second or longer (anything less is a spike), usually caused when electrical appliances switch off and the extra voltage is dissipated through the power lines – and into your system.

Computers and other devices (such as monitors, printers, modems, and so on) are designed to receive power within a certain voltage range. Anything outside of the range will stress the components. They may not fail immediately, but prolonged and multiple stressing can cause premature failure of such things as memory chips.

Noise: Although not in the same league as sags, surges, spikes, and blackouts, electromagnetic interference (EMI) and radio frequency interference (RFI) are still power problems. The effects are sometimes difficult to judge, but could result in programs executing improperly, premature discharge of memory contents, weird patterns on your monitor, and print jobs that suddenly produce gibberish.

How to tell if you have a power problem

Power problems may masquerade as other problems – no one knows how often flaky program execution is blamed on other software or hardware, or on a virus, when bad power was to blame. Bad data on your hard drive may have come from a sag instead of the Michelangelo virus.

(1) Flickering lights are easy to dismiss as a problem because they are often not noticed. They occur literally in the blink of an eye. They may be symptoms of temporary power sags or even very short power outages. It may take a power loss or sag of hundreds of milliseconds

to cause a fluorescent tube to flicker, but in the computer's terms that may as well be forever.

(2) Data transmission errors between network nodes are a common problem for local area networks (LANs) and can have a couple of different causes: EMI/RFI and ground loops. The latter can occur between any two devices linked by a data cable, especially if the two devices are a considerable distance apart. When a voltage difference develops between the two devices, the difference equalizes itself as an impulse travelling on the cable. The result will be scrambled data in the cable and, if the voltage difference is large enough, could result in fried circuit boards at either end.

EMI/RFI can also be a factor of distance. For instance, it is common practice to connect a printer to a computer by a parallel cable. Unless heavily shielded, parallel cable runs of more than ten feet are chancy because of a tendency for the cables to pick up both EMI and RFI noise. In essence, the cable acts as an antenna and pulls the noise out of the air. The same phenomenon can affect network cables.

(3) Unexplained system lockup and random system crashes may also be signs of flaky power quality. While this can also be caused by software that doesn't work well with other kinds of software, it's possible that a power sag has done funny things to your computer's memory.

(4) Hard drive crashes and mysterious data loss may also be caused by sags or short blackouts. Just about everyone using a DOS 5.0 or later, including modern versions of Windows, is using some form of disk caching software (or you may have a cache on the hard drive itself). In earlier versions of Windows this service was provided by a program called SmartDrive, but in later versions, it's integrated into the operating system where you don't normally see it.

One of the things disk caches do is hold the drive's file allocation table (FAT) in memory for faster access. If the power goes out before the cache updates the FAT, pieces of data will still be on the disk, but without an address in the FAT, they may as well be on the far side of the moon, because you won't be able to find them. If the power goes out while the cache is writing to the disk, the whole FAT could go missing.

As well, disk drives like to spin at a constant velocity. Just as having an audio tape running at a funny speed will distort the sound you hear, data written to a disk that is spinning too slowly will be distorted when you try to read it back later at the proper speed.

(5) Loss of data in the CMOS isn't solely caused by your battery dying (see *How to Avoid Buying a New Computer*). While the computer is turned on, the CMOS draws its power from the same supply as the rest of the system. Spikes, surges and static discharges can clean a CMOS out completely (a good reason why you should print the contents of the CMOS out tonight, write down the information on hard disk type, cylinders, heads, write pre-compensation, and sectors-per-track on a disk label and paste it under your keyboard for safekeeping).

By the way, the CMOS isn't the only memory in your system that is subject to this sort of damage. The EPROM (erasable programmable read only memory) chips that control your keyboard, serial ports, BIOS, and other vital components (they're in printers and modems, too) are equally susceptible to power glitchery. Got a flash BIOS? Get protected.

(6) A system device behaving erratically when too many are turned on is another sign of a power problem. Harmonics aren't just what you get in a choir. They'll also show up on an oscilloscope as current or voltage disturbances when too many connected devices are drawing fluctuating amounts of power.

LANs are prime victims of this sort of thing, particularly when too many workstations are powered from the same circuit, because computer power supplies don't draw power smoothly. They suck it up in big gulps, then use capacitors to feed it to the system until they need another gulp (once about every 1/120 of a second or so).

(7) Frequently aborted modem transfers are also a sign of power trouble. Nothing will twist your crank faster than losing a modem transmission in the middle (or just before the end). Spikes and surges and EMI/RFI are particular problems in telephone lines. They scramble data and cause excessive bad block errors that may end up terminating the transmission. A less catastrophic result is that two modems may step down their transmission rates in order to compensate for the line noise (annoying enough with a local call, but expensive if you're on long distance or logged into a system that charges for time online).

(8) If the display on your monitor wavers, flickers, dances, or

sparkles, it could be a sign that there is low voltage (the size of the image shrinks), or that there is strong EMI fields nearby. Move that telephone and those speakers – not to mention the power supply in your computer – away a few feet. The disturbance showing up on your monitor may be slowly turning your expensive RAM chips into nothing more than curious jewellery.

Power line conditioners

You may not, despite the warnings, decide on an uninterruptible power supply. But I've always believed that everyone who owns a computer should have *some* type of power line conditioner.

Power line conditioners come in a range of prices and with a range of features. Some offer limited protection from the worst spikes and surges, while others may also offer EMI and RFI protection. Power line conditioners do not protect against sags or blackouts.

One of the first things to understand is that the multiple-plug extensions sold at many stores for $9.95 or less and *called* power conditioners may only be expensive extension cords. They may carry certification by either, or both, the Canadian Standards Association (CSA) or U.S. Underwriter's Laboratory (UL), but that certification may come only under the extension cord section of both agencies. In order to qualify for surge and spike protection, conditioners must be able to withstand repeated 6,000-volt hits without passing them through. At least one consultant I spoke to says he advises his clients that if the power conditioner costs next to nothing, that's about what it will protect.

These are some of the gizmos you'll want to find inside the conditioner to protect your system:

- *metal oxide varistors* (or MOVs) act as shock absorbers, clipping the tops off spikes and surges (one is not much good; you want yours to have several.);
- *capacitors* act to back up the MOVs in toning down surges and are also used to filter out EMI/RFI line noise;
- *rod core inductors* are additional EMI/RFI filters (think of a metal core with wire wrapped around it acting like a sponge).

The more of these items the power conditioner has, the more expensive it will be. The cost will also go up if it has additional connectors to ground a telephone line, but you can purchase relatively inexpensive phone line grounders that plug into one of the extension sockets.

Uninterruptible power supplies

A good uninterruptible power supply (UPS) will protect against spikes, surges, and EMI/RFI as well as dealing with sags and blackouts.

Aside from considerations of capacity (we'll get to it in a moment), you're going to be faced with two basic flavours of UPS. Even though everything that supplies power when the main current goes away is *called* a UPS, some of them don't supply the power instantaneously. The industry calls these standby power supplies (SPS).

The UPS has a sensitive static transfer switch, used to detect the loss of power during a deep sag or blackout. When the AC power from the wall vanishes, it switches to the power available from the unit's battery/inverter so quickly that your PC never knows the difference. Typically, a UPS will provide enough battery power to allow for five to fifteen minutes of operation – just enough for you to shut the system down in an orderly fashion. The longer the battery lasts, the more you'll pay for the system.

In an *online UPS*, the primary power source is the battery/ inverter, and you only get AC power directly if the battery gives out. This type of system generally provides cleaner power more consistently. Because of the way it is configured, a loss of AC power doesn't affect output. Classic online UPS systems include some models from APC, Sola, and Toshiba. Online systems tend to cost more than standby (SPS) systems.

The transfer switch in an SPS unit doesn't instantly sense the loss of AC power from the wall. The pause may be measured only in milliseconds, but there still needs to be time for the transfer switch to operate and for the battery to come on line. SPS units tend to have smaller battery chargers than online UPS systems, and they tend to produce less heat. As a class, they are less expensive than the other systems.

There are four other methods of managing power supplies: "online without bypass" and "line interactive," which are both variations of an online UPS system, and "standby online hybrid" and "standby ferro," which are, as the names imply, standby types (although with the hybrid, the line gets fuzzy). Some of these – the line-interactive models in particular – can get very expensive. But check 'em out.

How large a UPS/SPS will you need?

This section can also be used to calculate the minimum power supply value for your computer (good luck).

If everyone measured everything in the same way, this would be a simple matter, but they don't. Electrical equipment power usage is measured by the voltage it requires and by the amperes (amps) it uses. "Watts" are what you get when you multiply volts by amps. If you look on the back (or bottom) of all of your pieces of equipment (or components in your computer), you may see the number of watts they use, or it may be expressed in volts and amps. For example, one of my old external CD-ROM drives uses 115 volts and 0.2 amps (for a total of 23 watts).

If I perform the same calculation for every piece of equipment I plan to plug into a UPS, I'll eventually find out how much power the system needs. For external equipment, I'll want to include the power supply in the computer itself, and any external peripheral devices (such as an external drive, modem, and so on). I'll definitely want to add my desk lamp, but I'll have to think about whether or not to add my laser printer. It can use over 600 watts if it happens to be heating up its fuser when the lights go out, so I may decide to leave it off the UPS. I'll probably want to add about 25 per cent to my calculations to allow for some future expansion. For internal components, I'd do the same. Then I'll know how large a power supply or UPS to get, right?

Not necessarily. There's a trap. Quite a few manufacturers have adopted a scheme of measurement called volt/amps. They say it is a more accurate measurement of the amount of current required to produce the necessary power. You may see volt/amps expressed as

V/A or V-A or simply VA (and of volt/amps in the thousands expressed as KVA). So, if you see VA after a number where you might have simply expected to see V, it's not necessarily a spelling mistake.

During my research I found several confusing ways of explaining the difference between VA and Watts. Several manufacturers suggest simply multiplying Watts by 1.4, while others go on for pages carefully explaining that there was no precise way to measure the difference except that the wattage for PC equipment was generally between 60 and 70 per cent of the VA rating. Sheesh!

To keep it as simple as possible, a 300 VA power supply is really only putting out somewhere around 180 to 200 watts.

Part 3

Nailing Down Your Decision

15

Nailing Down Your Decision

You are almost ready to buy your new computer. You've created your plan, done some homework, and you've learned what the jargon means. You've begun to fill in the blanks on the checklist on page 288. Eventually, you may wish to fax this list to several vendors, or take copies with you as you shop, to get competitive quotes.

In this section we're going to summarize some of the main points and talk about some final budgeting concerns (where in the computer to put the money and in what order). We're also going to talk about operating systems, dealer tricks and scams, warranty concerns, and about how to evaluate one component against another. But by now you should have narrowed down the processor and motherboard chipset you want and also some of the other individual components under the hood.

Once you've collected advertisements and flyers from a number of stores, and the faxed checklists with your specifications have come back, prepare to start comparing prices. Are you ready to buy? Not quite.

Budgeting

Okay, this is the last time I nag you about this. *No one makes a whole computer.* A computer is an assemblage of components designed to work together, and no matter what company's name is on the box, the components inside will come from a number of manufacturers. Each component has a brand name, a model designation, and a set of behavioural/performance characteristics you can check (the US glossy magazines and some Canadian sources are testing them all the time). All components do not have equal quality or reputations for reliability. The result is, for example, that two 233 MHz Pentium-based computer systems may have absolutely nothing in common with each other *except* the processor.

So, the first and most important thing to realize when assessing price quotes is that unless each component is listed and specified by manufacturer and model, you don't have enough information to make a valid price comparison. Identifying the components and assessing their position in the quality and performance pecking order will have occupied most of your homework.

Review the price grid on page 25. If one element of your buying strategy is the ability to upgrade the system over time to extend its useful life, a trailing-edge system will either limit the potential for upgrading or make it non-existent. If the system appears to be based on up-to-date base hardware, the advertised price may not include basics such as a monitor, operating system, or any additional software.

Where to put the money

You can get virtually anything you want if you have enough time or enough money, but unfortunately none of us has enough of either, so we have to make choices. Here is where I'd put my money and the order in which I'd allocate it:

Processor: This has the greatest effect on performance.

Motherboard/chipset: This has the greatest effect on current services and future expansion potential. A board with an old or non-standard chipset could not only affect today's performance, but also prevent tomorrow's upgrade.

Memory: This comprises both main system memory and cache memory and has a big effect on performance.

Hard drive: High RPM drives (such as the 10,000 RPM Seagate

Cheetah) can affect overall system performance, and high capacity gives you breathing room before you buy another.

Video graphics controller: The size of my monitor will impose a practical limit on the resolution the controller has to produce and my needs will determine the number of colours I'll want to see, so the amount of memory is not a huge factor here. Instead, I want it accelerated to the teeth with excellent 3-D abilities and that may require additional memory. Even if I have a fast processor and lots of main system memory, a slow graphics controller would make my system appear to be a dog.

Monitor: I spend hours in front of my computers. I prefer an aperture-grille model with .25 mm stripe pitch and a high vertical refresh rate (at least 72 to 75 Hz). I run my 17-inch monitors at 1024 by 768 and they produce sharp pictures and no flicker. Your expectations and needs may differ, but a low-end monitor with slow refresh and high dot pitch (over .28 mm) will make you crazy.

Audio controller: This includes a 16-bit audio board with wave table synthesis, speaker and line outputs, line and microphone inputs. I use sound in public presentations, to conduct Internet conferencing, to listen to music (so I have good speakers with a sub-woofer) and to watch television if there's an auto race running when I have to work. I don't do much gaming where sound is an issue or compose music with my computer. This setup works for me, but if you need good sound, you may want to add a MIDI music port. By the way, my current sound controller is a Creative Labs Sound Blaster AWE 32 board.

Modem: Check your Internet-using friends to find out which Internet service provider(s) they recommend, then call for prices and services. At minimum you'll want a V.90 compliant modem, while keeping mind that it's the speed of your modem that most affects your Internet experience, not the speed of your computer. See Chapter 11 for information on alternative transmission methods.

CD-ROM drive: 8X to 12X will work just fine for just about everything you'll want to do. To get any benefit from 16X, 20X, 24X drives or faster, the data has to be at the disc's outer edge, and that's seldom the case.

DVD-drive: Frankly, I'd wait until there are more titles, but there's no reason not to get a DVD drive because it will read older CDs, too. Just make sure that MPEG (Motion Picture Experts Group) video and Digital Dolby (formerly AC3) audio are handled somewhere in the hardware of your system. A software-only emulator won't provide the quality you're expecting.

Keyboard: Microsoft Natural Keyboard (the original, not the Elite) if you're a full-hand typist and if you can afford it. If not, then get something you find comfortable to use. Keyboards grunge up and die unless you work in a sterile room. Expect to replace it.

Pointer: Get a mouse with a wheel, either from Microsoft or someone else. The wheels are handy gadgets when surfing the Web or in applications that involve scrolling. Mice and anything else with a ball – such as a trackball – grunge up, too, regardless of brand or price. Alternatives include touchpads and digitizing tablets (see Chapter 9).

Extras: Leave room for extras, not the least of which in Canada are provincial (PST) and federal (GST) sales taxes. In the United States, add federal, state, and local taxes. Other extras to tack on include a printer ($250 to $450 for a basic colour inkjet model, $299 to $995 for a personal laser) and software. A full suite of office software (word processor, information/contact manager, spreadsheet, presentation software, database and extras), will have a list price in the $450 to $650 range. But you may find a full suite for much less (usually a lot less) if it's bundled with the system at the time of purchase. Make sure it's the full suite, not the "lite" version and that it comes with both manuals and registration. Games and "edutainment" titles such as multimedia encyclopedias seldom exceed $79. Stand-alone products such as system utility, contact manager, personal information manager and basic image enhancement products seldom exceed $129. For more specialized products, such as drawing/illustration suites, desktop publishing, multimedia authoring, continuous speech recognition dictation products and so on, the sky is the limit, and paying over $500 – at least for your first purchase (upgrades are always less) – isn't unusual.

So far, we've talked about basic system components. Another part of your research involves finding out not only how to upgrade existing parts, but also how to add others. For example, no matter how large your hard drive appears now, it's bound to fill up. Planning to get

a second drive in future is good. Checking to see if there
free drive bays to accommodate it is better. Making sure yo.
the whole industry for new parts is essential.

Over time, you can add a tape drive or alternative storage .
(see Chapter 10) to make backing up your data relatively pain. ..
The day your hard drive dies (it can), you won't panic. You'll simply
reach to a shelf for your backup. Ensuring ahead of time that there's
a free drive bay for the backup device that opens to the case front is
a good idea.

Other extras include scanners (Chapter 11), and power conditioners or uninterruptible power supplies (Chapter 14) to protect against
surges, spikes, and other interference.

Ripoffs, scams, traps, and tricks

There aren't more crooks in the computer business than there are in
any other, but there aren't fewer, either. Profit margins in the computer retail sector are brutally small and the average computer retailer
is in business in the Greater Toronto Area for just under two years
(according to the Canadian Computer Retailers' Association).

Those who try to make a business out of using shoddy components to keep prices artificially low and hope to sell large volumes
before creditors and unhappy customers catch up with them are too
common. If the price is really that much lower than all the competitors, keep some things in mind. The computer retail sector is highly
competitive, and retailers slash profits to a minimum to compete. If
one dealer's prices are much lower than everyone else, something isn't
right. For local assemblers, particularly on budget systems, the only
way they can meet that price is to use whatever is the least expensive
component on the market that week, quality be damned. At worst, the
components may have been stolen. You should also ask yourself how,
at that low, low price, the dealer could afford to pay well-trained staff.
Just who is going to fix your computer if it breaks down during the
warranty period? Who will have the time to answer your questions
when you have a problem?

Some shady operators are making illegal copies of software and
placing them on computers to give the impression of value. This may

not be apparent to you right up until you call for support, provide a serial number, and get asked in a gruff voice, "What are *you* doing with that number?" (The absence of software manuals or registration forms is your first clue). You should expect to be given the CDs holding the original software, or see a message when you first start the system suggesting that you make backup copies in case your hard drive goes south. No matter what the ad said, *the software isn't free.* Its cost has been added to the price; otherwise the dealer would go out of business. Watch out for "lite" versions of software. They're far from being the full thing. You'll have to buy the applications anyway.

"Compatible" is an overworked word, too. Claims that a product of lesser price (and quality) will perform just like the real thing should be taken with a grain of salt. And there's a related problem to consider. Many mainstream manufacturers use what are known as the Original Equipment Manufacturer (OEM) version of a component instead of the full commercial version. This allows the company to advertise a popular brand-name component in the system, and so long as it comes with the same software and the same hardware components as the full retail version, this isn't a problem. Often, however, it does neither. Ask.

"Compatible" and "Ready" don't necessarily mean compliant. IBM and Compaq, for example, have sold consumer systems advertised as "network compatible" that wouldn't work on a network. IBM released models that were "Year 2000 ready" that required an update to conform to the Year 2000 problem. When pressed, company spokespeople told me that "compatible" and "ready" don't necessarily mean "compliant." Go figure.

Finding used components from returned computers being sold as new in new systems can be frustrating and there's virtually no way for you to tell in advance. Some of the national name-brand companies do and some don't. Those who do are supposed to put a warning on the box (but you may never see the box on the showroom floor). Nevertheless, whether you're shopping for a name brand or a locally assembled system, it doesn't hurt to ask what the company's policy is toward returned components.

Let's say you've done your homework and have specified to the store exactly what you want and have made sure the complete list with brand and model designation appears on the sales agreement. When you get the computer home, don't go on vacation. Open it up. Check what you got against what you should have received. Understand that in the heat of the moment, almost always by accident (perhaps a new employee) and seldom deliberately (sure), a less expensive component than the model you paid for might have found its way into the system.

If an ad is vague about the name and model of the items on the component list, it could be because the dealer is shopping for the lowest price in that week's market. For the name brands, there is a different rationale: "We need to be assured of supply, so we'll source something such as a CD-ROM drive from more than one manufacturer so we can fill orders without constraint," one executive told me. Whether the component they use also happens to be the least expensive that week isn't relevant, they say. Nevertheless, you may find some more reluctant than others to discuss component brand specifications. For example, IBM's policy is not to discuss the issue and not to disclose the source of their components. Others, notably Dell, may provide a list, but caution that fulfilling your exact specifications may mean waiting longer for the system. Fair enough.

Finally, various segments of the computer industry play interesting games with numbers to make marketing more fun. For instance:

• The entire tape industry advertises the storage capacities of its products based on the assumption that you'll get 2:1 data compression when you archive material. Each company is afraid its products will appear overpriced if it advertises the real capacity of its tapes (usually less than half the advertised number).

• One audio board manufacturer taught buyers that a 16-bit sound card provided more sound variations than an 8-bit card, then went on to market "AWE-32" and "AWE-64" products, with numbers that refer to something else entirely. Both products are still 16-bit controllers.

• The CD-ROM industry created a steady progression of performance in drives up to 12X, then changed the rules for 16X, 20X, 24X and "faster" drives to measure their performance in a different way. The actual average performance of the newer drives is half the number advertised.

• Some manufacturers of computer monitors have started measuring the dot-pitch (the distance between colour phosphors of the same colour) from the edges of the dots instead of from the centre points. The only way to tell is to see two monitors from different manufacturers side by side. The grainier of the two has had its numbers fudged.

Whatever happened to . . .

In the first edition of *How to Buy a Computer*, I warned of several shoddy practices that were current at the time among some retailers. Some of them are still around.

At the time, memory was priced at around $50 per megabyte, and some retailers were placing used modules in new systems or procuring their supplies from suspect sources of memory cobbled together from discarded parts. Since then, the price for memory has plummeted. But some of the practices remain. I've seen quite a bit of "homemade" memory in the Toronto area, and it may be stable and last as long as the computer for which it was purchased. But some consumers have contacted me to complain that their so-called new memory modules were causing problems. The same people who make other computer-related products also make memory. An incomplete list includes LG Electronics (formerly Goldstar), Hitachi, Toshiba, Fujitsu, and NEC. By all means examine the individual chips on the module (where you'll find a name and serial number, including one that indicates speed), but also turn them over to see if the name is on the back, too. That way you can be reasonably sure the same company manufactured and assembled both main parts.

Asking what "burn in" really means is still a good idea. If it's advertised as part of the service the company provides, it is supposed to mean that your system is set up, turned on, then subjected to a battery of tests for two to three days before you take delivery. Any electronic component can fail within the first twenty-four to seventy-two hours (even from a brand-name supplier). In some cases, however, "burn in" is a euphemism for "We don't have the parts in stock and if we keep you waiting long enough maybe you'll agree to take something we'll tell you is just as good as what you wanted." This is a version of the old bait and switch tactic. The classic version is to be offered a pricier system because they just sold the last one of the system you wanted. It's just possible that the marvellous system advertised was so popular that they ran out the day the ad first appeared, but I'd hesitate to stick around after I heard this excuse.

If your computer is supposed to come already loaded with Windows 98 or its successor, you are likely to get the full software complete with manual and original CD-ROM disc. But until the dust dies down over Microsoft's inclusion of Internet Explorer (IE) with the base package (the court action hadn't ceased before press time), you may get one where the Internet browser is disabled or missing in action. If you want IE, you may have to specify it. Yes, you still want to see, at the very least, registration cards, full documentation, and licences for any software installed. Note also that there are two versions of Windows that Microsoft sells to vendors. The less expensive "OEM" version has all the functionality of the more expensive full retail package, but it's up to the vendor, not Microsoft, to supply software support if you need it.

Asking whether this is the first time that the software has been installed is a valid question. Some retailers accept returned software, reseal the package, and offer it for sale again. There's a chance that it's been corrupted by a virus, so it's a good idea to subject all software going into your system to an anti-virus scan, just in case.

Last but not least, there was a CPU remarking scam that hasn't entirely gone away. When Intel produces a processor chip, it tries to make all of them as fast as possible. Those that don't pass the test for its highest speed are tested again at a lower speed. Those that pass at the lower speed are conscientiously labelled as such on the top of the chip. Up until the release of the 75 MHz Pentium, however, it was possible for unscrupulous folks to rub the markings off, place the processors on higher-speed motherboards, then run the slower chips at speeds that exceeded their stability. Intel has taken a couple of steps to stop this, such as putting Pentium and Pentium II processors back into manufacture to "lock" them at their rated speed. To go one step further, the 440BX chipset, designed for 100 MHz Pentium II motherboards, will query the processor and "downclock" the board (Intel's phrase) to 66 MHz if that was the speed the processor was designed to operate at.

However (you knew this was coming, didn't you?), some computer hobbyists deliberately overclock their Pentium motherboards.

Some motherboard manufacturers also produce boards able to jump from 66 MHz to 75 and 83 MHz, and several Internet sources have documented that the processor's internal speed jumps accordingly. Intel and others warn that this may shorten the life of both the processor and any expansion boards attached to the system's PCI bus slots. The risks are real, but whether you find out how to do it and try it is entirely up to you. What you hope is not happening is that a retailer has done this in order to sell a less expensive system at a higher price and hopes that you won't notice.

In early 1998, shortly after the release of what were then the new 100 MHz motherboards and 440BX chipset, several sources told me that by making some physical alterations to the system (no, I'm *not* going to provide details), it was possible to force Pentium II processors, designed to run on 66 MHz motherboards, to run on a 100 MHz board, too. Your only protection is to ask around about a retailer's reputation for integrity.

If this wasn't bad enough, there's more. In the summer of 1998, I was visited by the RCMP and someone from Canada Customs who had intercepted more than one shipment of forged 300 MHz Pentium II cartridges. The components had been manufactured to run at 266 MHz, but had been illegally modified to run faster. They wanted to know if I could tell it was a forgery. I couldn't. Nor could any retailer. There would be no way to tell as benchmark tests wouldn't detect the difference. At the time, 300 MHz Pentium II processors were priced at over $300 wholesale. Apparently, the forgeries were being offered by the case-load at $100 or less each processor. This is all the more reason to deal only with reputable retailers and be very suspicious of ultra-low prices.

One other practice has also arisen. Given the fluctuations in the market price for processors, there have been times when the notebook version of a processor was less expensive than the desktop version. When this occurs, some assemblers make use of a third-party product to mount the notebook processor in a desktop socket (I haven't heard of it being done for Pentium II/Slot 1 products, but you can never tell). So long as the computer works well and at the speed intended, this shouldn't bother you. To quote an Intel spokesperson who was asked about it, "A Pentium is a Pentium, and it will work the same way." It's when the system starts behaving oddly or doesn't seem to be as fast as you think it should be that you should start to ask questions (or maybe even before you buy it).

The only real way you can protect yourself is to ask around about the reliability of the vendor. It is highly unlikely you'll find these practices being carried on by brand-name manufacturers – they have too much to lose if they're caught. And most local assemblers are honest, too. They don't want customers to lose their trust in local assembly because of a few crooks. But, if you have reason to be suspicious, you may want to check your CPU. If it is covered by a label that says something such as, "Warranty void if label removed," I'd really be curious about exactly what was under it, because this is not a label that Intel would put on the part.

Keep in mind that the retailer may have had what it believes to be a good reason to put this label here and elsewhere in the system. For example, Toronto-based 3D Micro (IPC and Bondwell brands) does so as a matter of policy. One company spokesman explained that it was to protect the company from overly curious but inexperienced consumers removing parts and either damaging them inadvertently, or replacing them with broken parts in the hope of getting an undeserved refund. Both had happened, I was told. When I pointed out that bigger manufacturers – such as IBM, Compaq, and Dell – keep a database of part serial numbers to prevent this, the conversation more or less wandered off in another direction.

Lies, damned lies, and benchmarks

I didn't quote performance figures in the Ad Primer (see Chapter 5), but one other item you'll often see is the vendor's claims for how fast various devices are.

Each of the components in a system, as well as the overall system itself, will have characteristics you can check. For example, in various sections throughout this book, I suggest you find out how fast a component is before you buy it (for example, the CPU, memory, video controller, hard drive, drive controller, CD-ROM drive).

There are a number of ways of testing a computer to assess the performance of its components individually and collectively. Intel uses its own "iCOMP" rating. There are industry engineering-level benchmark tests including SpecINT and Bapco. Publishers of various glossy computer magazines have created their own (such as the Ziff-Davis Winbench and Winstone tests and *Windows Magazine*'s WinTune). At the consumer level, there are Symantec's Norton Utilities (System Information or SI) or more specific testing utilities, such as TouchStone Software's Checkit.

I don't claim that this is the entire list of benchmark tests – they pop out of the woodwork with dizzying regularity. I've also not given you specific version numbers for each one, as they're constantly being upgraded, and by this time next week there's liable to be a different version. What is important to understand is that the results you get from one version of a test can't be compared to results from a prior version, nor can they be compared to the results of an entirely different test. How long is one piece of string compared to another? One hundred is a bigger number than sixty, but it isn't when you're comparing millimetres to inches. Unless you use the same ruler to do your measuring, it's easy to wind up comparing apples and blocks of wood.

Another problem you'll encounter is that vendors sometimes don't tell you how the performance of each part was measured. You can take two identical video controllers and wind up with entirely different results from the same test, simply by putting one in a Pentium and the other in a Pentium II system. You can also skew the results by starting with the same processor and adding additional external cache memory and faster system RAM to one of the two computers.

In essence, the testing standard you settle on doesn't matter. You'll need to compile your results from the same test, with the same version number – and make sure the vendor reveals the environment in which the test was run. If you want to be really thorough, compile results from two different tests. Then ignore the specific numbers and assess the results for each component in relation to the others in order to get a sense of what's slow, what's fast, and what's faster.

Warranties, guarantees, and promises

If it isn't written on the sales agreement or invoice, it never happened. It doesn't matter how many promises the nice salesperson makes to you. If they aren't in writing, they don't exist. (Gotcha!)

Telling the salesperson what you want to do with the computer, according to the IDC/Service Dimension secret shopper survey, is more than likely to fall on deaf ears, and the response "Oh sure. It will do that" may be more of a reflex than a considered opinion. Get it in writing.

In our earlier discussion of places to shop, I cautioned about the exact meaning of "money back guarantee" for mail order and Internet purchases. The same cautions may apply elsewhere. Ask what it means.

If you feel like you need to keep both hands on your wallet while you're in the store, that the salesperson is rushing or attempting to intimidate you, or there's just too much "nudge, nudge; wink, wink" in the sales pitch for your comfort, go somewhere else. There are lots of choices.

If I were about to make a $1,000 to $5,000 purchase and I was concerned that I might have to rely on the warranty offered (because I was afraid the product might break), I'd be tempted to find out if the local Better Business Bureau had any complaints about the vendor. At least I'd want to know how long the store had been in business and whether there were any other satisfied (or worse, dissatisfied) customers. Your best source of information here are your friends, local computer user groups, and Internet USENET newsgroups.

Get the manuals

When you make your purchase, make certain you get complete technical documentation on all components in the system or attached to it, including details on the case. I'm not talking about the no-brainer manual that shows where the on/off switch is located. You want the manual(s) to tell you:

- what type of memory it uses so you'll know what to buy when you want more;
- what the various wires inside are attached to, and how, so you can reconnect them if they ever work loose (they will);
- how to identify the characteristics of the hard drive if the system ever loses track (and it will when the on-board battery dies).

The manuals are yours by right and they're a basic protection for you, whether you ever want to open the system yourself or not. If the retailer goes belly up (they do), how else will you get someone to fix the system if it breaks?

Ask about the manuals. Look at a set. Smart vendors know you're entitled to these manuals. If the vendor doesn't have extra copies of the original manuals (some buy parts in bulk and only get one manual for their own use), then you can ask for a photocopy of the one their technician will use to repair your system if it ever develops a problem. If they don't have the original manual, start worrying about how they will service the system if something does break.

Don't leave the store without the manuals and greet all assurances that you'll be given them eventually with deep distrust. They don't have manuals, can't, or won't show them to you? See the tricks and traps section above with regard to your "free" software. The last resort, and the one you can feel perfectly justified in applying if the hardware manuals (or copies of them) and the registration and manuals for the software aren't made available to you, is to explain politely but firmly why you're leaving the store – then run away. Shop somewhere else.

Final thoughts

The detail in *How to Buy a Computer* isn't meant to intimidate you. Instead, it's meant to prevent you from being intimidated or misinformed by everyone from well-meaning friends to poorly trained or malicious salespeople. Shortly before beginning to write, I spotted a short news item on Canada's CTV network about buying computers. Among some of the other abuses they noted (all of which I've covered here), there was a hidden-camera recording of a saleschap carefully explaining to a customer that the expansion slots on the motherboard were where you put programs. Stories of salespeople telling customers they don't need a larger hard drive because they have enough memory (or the other way around) are legion.

I don't want these cautions or the others above and elsewhere to frighten you or necessarily to annoy retailers (although if some are feeling uneasy, that's good). However, I do believe that a well-informed consumer makes a good customer.

I do understand that the level of homework I've asked you to do is extensive, but I have reason. I ask people, through my column in the *Toronto Star*'s Fast Forward section, in *We Compute*, on Discovery Canada's EXN.TV, and during various radio phone-in shows all over Canada and the United States, to bring me their computer problems. I seldom get questions from those who did their homework. Lots of problems and even some tears come from people who never talked to anyone else, didn't do any research, and took the salesperson's word for everything. Sometimes it makes *me* want to weep.

Computers are supposed to help you make some part of your life better, and using them should be enjoyable. If you didn't agree with that, we probably wouldn't be meeting here. Buying one shouldn't instil terror, either.

Good luck.

Computer Buyer's Checklist

| Store Name: |
| Phone: |
| Fax: |
| Address: |
| Salesperson: |

Component, Brand and Model	**Detail**	
Processor:	Speed:	
Motherboard:	Chipset:	BIOS:
Cache Memory:	Amount:	Type:
Main Memory:	Amount:	Type:
Hard disk drive:	Size:	Type:
Floppy drive:	Alternative:	
CD-ROM drive:	Speed:	Type:
DVD-ROM drive:	Disc capacity:	
Video controller:	Memory:	Mem type:
Video Acceleration.3D Chipset:	Other features:	
MPEG decoder:	Hardware or software:	
Monitor:	Screen size:	Resolution limit:
Monitor refresh rate:	Dot or stripe pitch:	
Other monitor features:		
Audio controller:	Wave table or FM synthesis:	
Modem:	Speed:	Standard:
Ports (#): Game: Parallel:	Serial:	USB:
Keyboard:	Special keys:	
Mouse:	Special features:	
Software bundle:		
Warranty details:	Base Price:	
Salesperson's verbal assurances:		

Salesperson's signature or initials:

Extras

SCSI adapter:	Price:
Network adapter:	Price:
Tape or other external drive:	Price:
Power conditioner:	Price:
Uninterruptible power supply:	Price:
Printer:	Price:
Scanner:	Price:
Other software:	Price:
	subtotal:
	GST:
	PST:
	Total:

Notes:

SPECIALTY INDEX

Tables
PC Price Grid, 25
PC Motherboards, 82-85
PC Motherboard Chipsets, 86-87
Memory Types, 94-96
Budget Notebooks, 115-118
Removable External Storage, 137
Low-Cost Scanners, 170-172
Inkjet Printers, 196-200
Personal Laser Printers, 210-212
Multifunction Printers, 222-225
Computer Buyer's Checklist, 288

Illustrations
Aperture-grille Mask Stripe Pitch, 237
How to Pick a CRT Monitor, 246
Inkjet Piezoelectric Drop-on-demand Print-head, 191
Pixel and Dot Pitch for an LCD/TFT screen, 238
Resolution v/s Screen Size, 245
Shadow Mask Dot Pitch, 237
Thermal Bubblejet Technology, 190
What Does the CPU Do?, 58

Get it in Writing
"Oh, sure; it will do that", 23
Buyer's Bill of Rights, 28
Motherboard processor compatibility, 77
Notebook power supplies outside North America, 114
Printer will share parallel port with other devices, 189
Printer will work with non-Windows operating systems, 185, 206
Returning printer if quality not good enough, 195
Returning TV products if quality not good enough, 253
TV grabber/tuner compatibility with existing video, 250
Verbal assurances alone aren't good enough to protect you, 285

General Warnings
All components aren't the same, 35
If you choose not to get an uninterruptible power supply, 266
Ink-jet consumable costs, 191
Used parts in new systems, 278
Warn the vendor if you're using OS/2 or Windows NT, 206

Gotchas!
CD-ROM drive "capacity", 139
Get it in writing, (see above)
Laser printer running costs, 206
LED readouts on cases aren't speedometers, 19
Monitors – actual viewable size, 235
Monitors – vague descriptions, 240
Motherboard cache capacity, 43
Precise model designations on superstore bargains, 203
Recordable DVD compatibility, 136
Sound controllers, 148
Ultra DMA hard drive speed limit, 46, 127
Upgrading Celeron systems, 65

Hints
Actual viewable size, 235
Digital camera LCD sucks batteries, 177
Face-down printouts are good, 205
Get 100 MHz SDRAM now, 75
How to tell when V.90 is revised, 158
Monitor resolution v/s size, 47

Homework Assignments
Chipsets, 72, 81
Decide about future upgrading, 74
Digital cameras, 179
First step, 8-9
How much?, 287
Level 2 cache, 92
Modem standards, 158
Motherboards, 173
Notebook computers, 100
Printers – Multifunction, 216
Printers (general), 185
Processors, 62

Speakers, 151
TWAIN, 165
Where most of it goes, 274
Why you need to do it, 1-2, 24, 28

Run Away!
"You don't need . . .", 121
Motherboard batteries, 77
No software manuals with purchase,
    286
No system manuals, 77
No TWAIN driver, 162, 252
No USB connectors on motherboard,
    77

Spec Tips
Digital Cameras, 177
Inkjet Printers, 192
Monitors, 243
TV/PC products, 249

GENERAL INDEX

1

100 MHz, 24, 62, 66-69, 75, 76, 79,
  97, 104, 281, 282

3

386 27, 63, 66, 67, 79, 215
3-D sound, 149, 151, 155, 156

4

440BX, 41, 45, 46, 62, 75, 79, 97,
  104, 281, 282
440EX, 41, 45, 46, 75, 79
440LX, 41, 45, 46, 79, 124, 230
486, 27, 60, 62, 63, 66-68, 79, 93

5

586, 63, 67

6

64-bit, 25, 41, 48, 69, 142
66 MHz, 61, 62, 75, 79, 104, 281, 282
68000, 57
68020, 57, 59
68030, 57, 59
68040, 57, 59
686, 63, 67
6x86, 27, 63, 67, 68, 90
6x86MX, see M II

7

786, 109, 228

8

80286, 57
80386, 57, 59
80486, 57, 59
8080, 57
8086, 57
8088, 57

AC3, see Dolby Digital
Acer, 103
Acer Labs, 15, 42
ADC, 143
AdLib, 150
Adobe, 163, 164
ADPCM, 152
ADSL, 52, 161
Agfa, 164, 165, 169, 176
AMD, 14, 15, 27, 39, 41, 44, 54, 63, 64,
  66-69, 73, 74, 77, 78, 90, 100, 230
AMI, 14, 42, 43
Amiga, 140
amplitude envelope, 146, 147
analog-to-digital converter, 143
anticipation, 26, 27
anti-virus, 281
Apple, 13, 14, 33, 34, 100, 103, 140,
  173, 186, 194, 257
AST, 103
AT&T, 158
Atari, 140
ATI, 231, 232, 247, 252
Aureal, 152
average access time, 60
Award Software, 14, 42, 43

bait and switch, 280
banding, 193, 208
bandwidth, 142
banners, 194
Bapco, 284
BBS, 206
BIOS, 14, 15, 38, 42, 43, 52, 73, 88,
  112, 158, 260, 265
bit-depth, 144
blackouts, 128, 262-264, 266, 267
Blue Lightning, 67

Brother, 201, 204, 207, 208, 216, 217
brownouts, 128, 262
burn in, 280

cable, 14, 52, 53, 111, 114, 123, 160,
  161, 179, 188, 189, 195, 247, 248,
  250, 251, 256, 259, 264
CAD, 241, 258
Canon, 173, 176, 186, 189, 193, 201,
  217, 218
CD-R, 17, 50, 54, 120, 130, 132, 133,
  136, 139
CD-ROM, 12, 15, 17, 42, 50, 54, 55,
  77, 80, 102-106, 108, 119, 120, 123,
  124, 126, 130, 132, 133, 135, 136,
  138-140, 150, 156, 174, 189, 254-
  256, 268, 275, 279, 281, 283
Celeron, 16, 25, 39, 44, 45, 49, 57, 61-
  65, 67, 69, 74, 78, 79, 90, 91, 100,
  105
central processing unit, 14, 38, 57
CGA, 244
Checkit, 284
chipset, 9, 15, 22, 27, 38, 41, 42, 45,
  48, 62, 65, 67, 74, 75-80, 90, 92, 97,
  104, 112, 123, 124, 125, 127, 145,
  230, 231, 249, 273, 274, 281, 282
Cirque Corp, 259
Cirrus Logic, 147, 231
clock speed, 58, 75
clock/calendar, 77
CMOS, 77, 260, 265
Commodore, 140
Compaq, 34, 35, 44, 68, 99, 103, 114,
  131, 142, 155, 236, 244, 261, 278,
  283
Computer Fest, 10, 72
Computer Paper, 9
Computer Post, 9
Computer Shopper, 9
cooling, 256
Coppermine, 69
Corel, 163
cost-per-page, 183, 186, 188, 201, 207
Creative Labs, 51, 92, 146-149, 154,
  275
crooks, 277, 283

Cyrix, 14, 27, 39, 44, 48, 54, 63, 64,
  66-68, 73, 74, 77, 90, 100

DAC, 144
Dell, 34, 36, 37, 103, 114, 134, 236,
  279, 283
device independence, 153
Diamond Multimedia, 92, 146, 149,
  158, 159, 231, 247
digital signal processor, 147, 149, 230
digital-to-analog converter, 144
DIMM, 76
DirectX, 153
Dolby Digital 104, 148, 152, 276
DOS, 21, 34, 45, 51, 145, 149, 150,
  151, 153, 154, 184, 208, 264
DRAM, 45, 48, 49, 104, 230
drive bays, 54, 255-257, 277
drive controller, 16, 38, 91, 123, 283
drivers, 111, 150, 153, 163, 164, 168,
  183, 184, 192, 194, 206, 215
Dual Scan (DSTN), 109, 110
dye sublimation, 182, 183, 191, 193

EDO memory, 104
EGA, 244
EIDE, 16, 17, 22, 45, 77, 80, 122-127,
  130, 131, 134, 139
electronic crib-death, 35
E-mail, 219
EMI, 263-267
emulation, 14, 49, 229
Energy Star, 234, 244
Epson, 167, 173, 175-177, 186, 188,
  190, 191, 201
ESDI, 122
Ethernet, 112, 215
EXN.TV, 3, 287
expansion bus, 68, 154, 155
expansion slots, 15, 39, 44, 74, 77, 80,
  110, 142, 286
external cache memory, 62, 78, 284

fan, 76
FAT, 264
fax, 11, 158-161, 164, 166, 183, 216-
  221, 273

fax/modem, 216
FireWire, 19, 80, 154, 247, 250, 251
flicker, 47, 234, 237, 239, 246, 253,
    264, 275
floppy drive, 55, 77, 102, 105, 108,
    119, 129, 131, 135, 254, 256, 257
floptical, 119, 135
FM synthesis, 51, 145, 146, 149, 151
full duplex, 153

game port, 53, 145
gamers, 92, 145
Gates, 27
Gateway 2000, 37, 103
GDI, 184, 207, 208
GIF, 251
GlidePoint, 259
Gravis, 92, 146

H/PC, 13, 15, 89, 99, 100, 102
HDTV, 249
heat sink, 76
Hewlett-Packard (HP), 34, 36, 99,
    100, 103, 131-132, 136, 165, 173,
    186, 192-193, 201, 208, 209, 216-
    219, 221, 261
Hitachi, 45, 99, 103, 106, 280

I/O, 195
IBM, 1, 13, 14, 16, 34, 36, 37, 39, 63,
    67, 68, 73, 78, 100, 103, 105, 114,
    120, 122, 134, 140, 154, 167, 236,
    240, 261, 278, 279, 283
IBM compatible, 14, 34
iCOMP, 283
IDE, 120-123, 256
iMac, 129
Imation, 131-132
instruction set, 59, 66, 67, 69, 230
Intel, 14, 15, 22, 23, 34, 39, 41, 42,
    44, 46, 56, 57, 59-67, 69, 74-76, 79,
    80, 81, 90, 97, 100, 104, 105, 124,
    142, 152, 155, 230, 281-283,
Interlaced, 47
internal cache, 64
Internet, 2, 9-11, 13, 18, 33, 36, 37,
    42, 49, 51, 52, 73, 80, 111, 113,

140-142, 149, 154, 156-160, 215,
    217, 220, 228-229, 251, 252, 258,
    261, 275, 281-282, 285
Internet Service Provider (ISP), 52,
    159
Iomega, 130, 134, 189
IP, 215
IRQ, 142, 154
ISA, 26, 44, 48, 60, 76-77, 142, 148,
    153-155
ISDN, 52, 159-160

JPEG, 179, 251

K5, 27, 66
K6, 63, 66, 67, 69, 73, 77, 78, 90, 100
K7, 69
Katmai, 25, 65, 66, 230
keyboard, 9, 13, 19, 39, 53, 98-99,
    106, 111-112, 150, 233, 254-261,
    265
Kodak, 173, 176-177

L2 cache (see also, external cache),
    16, 43, 44, 65, 90-92, 105, 106
leading, 139
LED page printer, 203
Lexmark, 186, 201, 209, 214-216
lies, 35, 54, 173, 283
lithium, 105, 107, 177
local bus, 26, 205
locally assembled systems, 35
LocalTalk, 195
Logitech, 167
LS-120, 131-132

M II, 63, 67, 73, 77
Mac, 10, 13, 20-21, 33-34, 125, 129
    (iMac), 131, 167, 195, 206, 235,
    249
magneto-optical, 119, 129, 139
mail order, 11, 33, 285
manual, 77, 175, 204, 235, 256, 281,
    285, 286
Matrox, 231, 232
Maxtor, 122
meaningless, 22, 149

memory, 15, 17, 62, 88-89, 92, 94, 96, 110, 113, 194, 208, 230, 249, 274, 289, effect 106-107, slots 105, speed 75
Merced, 25, 41, 69, 74
MFM, 122
micron, 69
Microsoft, 13, 34-35, 44, 51, 53, 99, 130-131, 140-142, 148, 152-153, 155, 215, 251, 260, 276, 281
MIDI, 19, 145, 148, 150-151, 154-156, 275
mid-sized tower, 255
Minolta, 173
Mitsubishi, 106, 241
Mitsumi, 139
modem, 9, 24, 39, 51-52, 78, 89, 105-106, 112, 155, 158-162, 216, 219, 263, 265, 268, 275
monitors, 232, 234-235, 239-240
Motherboard World, 10
Motorola, 14, 57, 59, 158
MPEG, 48-50, 229, 247, 251, 276
multimedia, 24-25, 41, 65-68, 99, 103-104, 110, 130, 136, 140, 153, 227, 230, 244, 276
MultiRead, 134
MultiSync, 235
multisynchronous, 235

name brand, 7, 33-35, 231, 254, 278-279
National Semiconductor, 14, 66, 67, 73, 100
NEC, 36, 45, 99, 103, 106, 109, 114, 136, 139, 186, 201, 235, 241, 280
network, 159, 251
NIC, 215
noise, 263
non-Intel, 22-23, 41, 44, 66-67, 81, 124
non-interlaced, 47, 237, 246
Norton Utilities, 284
Notebooks, 97, 100-102, 115-118, 289
NTSC, 104, 110, 248, 252
Number Nine Corp., 231

obsolete, 122, 142, 183
OCR, 164
OfficeJet, 217, 219
Okidata, 186-188, 201, 203, 209, 214
open architecture, 26
operating system, 13, 23, 34
OS/2, 13, 23, 140, 185, 194, 206
Ottawa Monitor, 9

Packard Bell, 36, 103
palette, 228
Palm III, 89, 100
Palm PC, 13, 15, 89, 99, 100, 102
palmtop, 13, 99
Panasonic, 103, 106, 131-133, 135-136, 139, 173, 201, 208-209, 214, 217
parallel port, 53, 54, 77, 124, 126, 130, 131, 134, 167, 184, 188-189, 191, 194-195, 215, 250
PARC, 257
partition, 123
PC 98, 142, 155
PC Computing, 9
PC Magazine, 9
PC World, 9
PCI, 26, 43-44, 48-49, 60, 62, 68, 77, 80, 142, 148, 153-155, 226, 231, 247, 282
PCM, 155
PCMCIA, 110
PD drive, 132-133, 136
PDA, 100
Pentium, 16, 24, 26-27, 39, 41-42, 44-45, 49, 54, 57, 59-69, 73-91, 97, 103-106, 124, 215, 230, 255, 281-282, 284
Pentium II, 16, 24, 26, 39, 41, 44, 45, 49, 54, 57, 60-67, 69, 74-91, 97, 103, 104, 124, 230, 255, 281, 282, 284
Pentium Pro, 27, 57, 63, 89
performance, 65, 126
Phoenix Technologies, 14, 42, 43
phosphor dots, 236, 243
piezoelectric, 190
pitch, 147, 237, 238, 289

pitch shifting, 147
pixel, 108, 109, 178, 227-229
Plextor, 139
pointing device, 18, 19, 111, 254, 257, 258
portable, 113, 251
ports, 18-19, 26, 39, 53-54, 104-105, 108, 111-112, 189, 195
Positional audio, 155
PostScript, 164, 184, 208, 209, 214, 251
POTS, 156-162
power conditioners, 127, 266, 277
power problem, 262, 263, 265
power supply, 39, 54, 55, 131, 256, 261, 262, 266-269
powerful, 8, 23, 58, 97, 100, 152
PowerMac, 13-14, 23, 33, 57, 99, 185
PowerPC, 14
proprietary, 26, 99-102, 131, 152, 155, 215, 257
PS/2, 19, 77, 112, 257

QMS, 209
Quantum, 122
Québec Micro!, 9

RAM, 15-16, 38, 44, 45, 49, 60, 61, 88-93, 105-106, 121, 146, 230, 266, 284
raster, 238
refresh rate, 109, 176, 234, 237-239, 243
remarking, 281
replace, 17, 27, 36, 60, 64-65, 69, 75, 77, 98, 102, 106-108, 135, 155, 173, 188, 205-208, 219, 244, 276
resolution, 47, 49, 92, 104, 105, 108, 109, 113, 168-169, 174, 178, 193-194, 214, 218, 227-229, 231, 234, 237-239, 240, 242-244, 248, 259, 275
RFI, 263-267
Ricoh, 173, 218
RJ-45, 215
RLL, 122

sags, 262-267
sampling rate, 141, 144
satellite, 52, 161, 251
scanners, 17, 19, 54, 110, 126, 141, 143, 162, 165-169, 175, 189, 203, 217, 218, 242, 277
SCSI, 17, 19, 39, 78, 91, 110, 111-112, 120, 122, 124-127, 130-134, 167, 179, 256
SDRAM, 44, 45, 75, 92, 104
Seagate, 122, 127, 274
sequencer, 155
serial port, 53, 77, 179, 257, 265
shared slot, 44, 77
Sharp, 99, 100, 216, 217
Sharptooth, 69
shopping strategies, 2, 8
SIMM, 76
SiS, 15, 231
Sony, 47, 136, 139, 173, 234, 241, 247
Sound Blaster, 50-51, 142, 146-149, 154-155, 275
SparQ, 134, 189
spikes, 128, 263, 266-277
standards, 44, 49, 51, 52, 73, 111, 123-125, 135, 145, 150, 155-156, 164, 165, 228, 235, 240, 249, 252
stereo, 149, 156
surges, 128, 263, 265-267, 277
SVGA, 22, 47-49, 60, 228, 239, 246-250, 252
SyQuest, 131, 134
System Optimization, 10

Tanner, 25, 65, 66
tape backup, 24
TCP/IP, 215
Teac, 139
technical support, 111, 158, 206
Tektronix, 186, 209, 214
television, 246, 248
ter, 158
thermal bubble, 190
throughput, 46, 80, 123-127, 131, 134, 218
too much memory, 45, 90

Toronto Computes!, 9
Toronto Star, 9, 287
Toshiba, 45, 46, 103, 105-110, 113, 114, 134, 139, 217, 267, 280
tower, 12, 19, 22, 54, 255
trackball, 111, 259, 276
transfer rate, 46, 50, 123-127, 138
trap, 268
Trident, 232
True Type, 208
Turtle Beach, 92, 146, 149
TWAIN, 162, 163-165, 168-169, 175, 177, 218, 221, 252

UDMA (Ultra DMA), 16, 17, 45, 46, 80, 123, 124, 127
unscrupulous, 281
upgrade, 2, 26, 28-29, 52, 54, 64-65, 69, 73-79, 89, 92, 97, 98, 158, 195, 229, 256, 274, 276
UPS, 261, 262, 267, 268
USB, 19, 26, 53, 54, 77, 105-106, 108, 112, 124, 126, 131, 134, 154, 156, 167, 179, 191, 195, 226, 233, 250, 257, 260, 263

vertical refresh rate, 47, 234, 239-240, 248, 275
VESA, 26
VGA, 47, 228, 239, 240, 252
VIA, 15, 42
Apollo, 41, 45-46, 67, 74
volt/amps, 268, 269
volts, 77, 268

Wacom, 258
warehouse, 36
Warnock, 164
warranty, 22, 35, 37, 55, 101, 112, 114, 185, 191, 195, 203, 205, 206, 219, 244, 273, 277, 284-285
Watts, 55, 256, 268, 269
WAV, 160, 161
wave table synthesis, 146
We Compute, 9, 134, 227, 287
Western Digital, 122
Winbench, 42, 284
Windows Magazine, 9, 175, 284
Windows NT, 27, 45, 104, 112, 153, 185, 194, 206
Windows Sound System, 150
Winstone, 284
WinTune, 284
World Wide Web, 2, 4, 10, 37, 41, 43, 68, 73, 105, 140-141, 164-165, 169, 174, 176, 184, 201, 206, 215, 249-250, 251, 258, 276

X3T10, 125
Xeon, 16, 25, 39, 45, 49, 57, 65, 74, 78-91
Xerox, 163, 188, 201, 209, 214-218, 221, 257
XT, 27, 63

Yamaha, 132, 145

Zip drive, 54, 130, 131, 135
Zoom Video, 111